Perspectives on European Film and History

Leen Engelen and Roel Vande Winkel (eds)

Perspectives on European Film and History

ACADEMIA
PRESS

Website: http://www.wgfilmtv.ugent.be/wgfilm&tvEN/Bookseries.php

Other titles in the Film & TV Studies Series:
Bewegend geheugen (2004), edited by Daniel Biltereyst and Roel Vande Winkel
Film/TV/Genre (2004), edited by Daniel Biltereyst and Philippe Meers
Publieke televisie in Vlaanderen (2007), edited by Alexander Dhoest and Hilde Van Den Bulck

© Academia Press
  Eekhout 2
  9000 Gent
  Tel. 09/233 80 88   Fax 09/233 14 09
  Info@academiapress.be   www.academiapress.be

The publications of Academia Press are distributed by:

J. Story-Scientia bvba Wetenschappelijke Boekhandel
Sint-Kwintensberg 87
B-9000 Gent
Tel. 09/225 57 57   Fax 09/233 14 09
Info@story.be   www.story.be

Ef & Ef
Eind 36
NL-6017 BH Thorn
Tel. 0475 561501   Fax 0475 561660

Lay-out: Press Point, Merelbeke

Editor: Daniel Biltereyst (Ghent University, Belgium)
Co-editor: Philippe Meers (University of Antwerp, Belgium)
Editorial board: Willem Hesling (Catholic University of Leuven, Belgium), Bert Hogenkamp (University of Utrecht, the Netherlands), Ernest Mathijs (University of Aberystwyth, Wales), William Uricchio (MIT, USA – University of Utrecht, the Netherlands), Roel Vande Winkel (Ghent University – Sint-Lukas Brussel, Belgium), Liesbet Van Zoonen (University of Amsterdam, the Netherlands)

Perspectives on European Film and History
Leen Engelen and Roel Vande Winkel (eds)
Gent, Academia Press, 2007, VI +294 p

ISBN 978 90 382 1082 7
U 1035
D/2007/4804/167
NUR1 670

Jacket picture: Bruno Ganz as Adolf Hitler in Der Untergang (Downfall, 2004)
© Constantin Film GmbH

Picture on final page: Bruno Ganz © Ullstein-Bild

Contents

Preface

The *Film & TV Studies Series* presents state-of-the-art research in the field of film and television studies. Its focus is on critical academic work on cinema, television and other dimensions of screen culture, both historical and contemporary. The series is constantly on the lookout for important issues, engaging with new trends in the international research field and translating them into scholarly but accessible texts. This book is the fourth in the multilingual series, and the first fully English-language collection.

This volume grew out of the perception that academic literature on historical movies focuses upon a rather limited sample of pictures, often Hollywood and some rare European art movies. In this volume, key questions of how historical movies shape the past are treated from a wider choice of European pictures. The scholars contributing to this volume have in common that they are all dealing with historical representation and the moving image. The result of their efforts is a series of essays that demonstrate the many challenging ways in which historical films can be studied, thus satisfying the professional standards set by both historians and film scholars.

The core part of the book consists of a series of ten case studies. Each chapter then deals with one or more European films representing structures and events of European history, great men and valiant women, facts and figures. The essays figure in historical chronology, starting in the fourteenth century with the life and times of the Russian icon painter, Andrei Rublev, and ending in the mid-twentieth century with the story of the British 'angel maker' Vera Drake. The case-studies are preceded by an essay offering a theoretical and methodological exploration of the field, by Bruno De Wever, and are followed by Robert Rosenstone's conclusions.

Daniel Biltereyst and Philippe Meers

Series Editors *Film & TV Studies*

Acknowledgements

We would like to thank a number of people and institutions for making the publication of this book possible. We are indebted to Professor Bruno De Wever, Professor Daniel Biltereyst and Professor Willem Hesling for organising the initiative that inspired this volume and for their continuous encouragement. We are especially grateful for Professor Robert Rosenstone's contribution to and enthusiasm for this book. Our chief thanks, of course, go to all the contributors and we thank them for their excellent essays, their quick response to our requests and their patience.

Financially and logistically the publication of this volume was made possible by the financial support of the Working Group Film & TV Studies, Department of Communication Studies, Ghent University; the Department of Contemporary History, Ghent University, and the Centre for Media Culture and Communication Technology, University of Leuven. We also would like to express our thanks to our English-language editor, Cleveland Moffett, a film buff who did much more than just correct linguistic mistakes.

Finally, we would like to thank all copyright holders for granting us permission to reproduce stills of their films. Rainer Rother (Filmmuseum Berlin), Wolfgang Gogolin (Bundesarchiv-Filmarchiv) and Jean-Paul Dorchain (Royal Film Archive Brussels) were most helpful in providing several of these photographs. Special thanks to Constantin Film and to Kevin Brownlow.

Leen Engelen and Roel Vande Winkel

Editors

Prologue: Historical Film as Palimpsest

Bruno De Wever

In the 1980s, Robert Rosenstone and, in his wake, some fellow historians and film scholars endowed the research on historical film with two crucial insights which, by now, may be considered common knowledge. First, they called our attention to the importance of the historical film as a field of research since historical films, both documentary and fiction, are increasingly and undeniably an important source of historical knowledge for the general public. Second, they demonstrated the need to conduct this research with respect to both the conventions and idiosyncrasies of the film medium and for the rules of engagement at stake in academic historiography.

Over the years, scholars have been thinking about questions surrounding historical film with increasing academic *sérieux*, as is testified by the numerous articles, conferences and journals dealing with the topic. Yet, some stubborn grey clouds still linger over the field. Too often, the discussion is monopolised by 'traditional' historians and angry critics who reduce the debate to the normative question of the historical accuracy of movies set in the past. Consequently, the discussion is often stranded in a deadlocked situation. Moreover, epistemological concerns about the nature and possibility of 'historical truth', an issue at the centre of current debates on historiography and the postmodern, are ignored by some critical opponents of historical films.

Among scholars making the effort to look beyond this impasse, another problem arises. Research seems to focus upon an interesting but rather limited sample of historical films. Consequently, the question of how cinema represents history is often reduced to a simplistic dichotomy between the mode of representation of Hollywood blockbusters and the very different ways in which art-house movies embody the past. Moreover, most of the films referred to tell famous stories of American or world history, thus leaving the slightly more 'marginal' films and histories out of consideration.

The above perceptions have inspired the editors of this book to focus on European films – both mainstream and art-house productions – that represent aspects of European history. Through a series of specific case studies, key questions of how historical movies shape the past are treated from a wide choice of European pictures, ranging from Herbert Wilcox' *Dawn* (1928) and Karl Grune's *Waterloo* (1928) to Oliver Hirschbiegel's *Der Untergang* (*Downfall*, 2004) and Mike Leigh's *Vera Drake* (2004). The films are looked at from a broad variety of disciplines and angles: history, film theory, literary studies, art history, visual studies, film analysis.... The approaches are interconnected by a few general underlying assumptions as to the social, cultural and political functions of historical films.

The essays in this volume mainly situate the films within the locus of the nation state. Although this means that certain relevant questions on the functioning of historical films within newly delineated international, transnational and interregional frameworks are left for future research, we claim that looking into the way historical feature films form a part of nationalist identity and national rhetoric is still relevant in an era when more people die in armed conflicts between nations than ever before. Films from Europe in particular – the scene of two World Wars and home to two of the most violent dictatorships in history – deserve research from that perspective.

British sociologist Anthony Smith, a leading figure in research on nationalism, showed that national identities are shaped through what he called a *mythomoteur*. The *mythomoteur* or 'myth-engine' offers a 'useable past'. It is a complex network of histories, myths and symbols that are instrumental in (re-)inventing, justifying or otherwise reinforcing a nation's self-image. As such, the *mythomoteur*, making claims about a nation's origins and lines of descent, is composed of mythical representations regarding an 'ethno-history', the 'ancestral homeland' and the 'ethnic election'.

In the nineteenth century, literature and art were the primary vehicles of the *mythomoteur* of nationalism because they conveyed national myths that appealed to the popular imagination. There is an inseparable connection between the building of national identities and the use of, as well as the need for, an illustrious national past. While the nineteenth century marked the heyday of historical painting, traditionally evoking great feats of arms from the national past, the twentieth century heralds the historical film as a powerful linchpin of the national *mythomoteur*. James Chapman demonstrates in this book that historical films that don't contribute to this usually have a hard time at the box office. Although praised by historians, the British productions *Winstanley* (1975) and *To Kill a King* (2003), both dealing with the revolutionary period in mid-seventeenth century Great Britain, were commercial flops for that very reason. In his article on *The Messenger* (1999), Brett Bowles shows that nearly all of the over 30 films made about Joan of Arc portrayed her as a patriot, thus contributing to the national heroine-martyr legend that is challenged by various historians. In this respect, the embedding of films into national traditions is important in order to uncover the meanings hidden below the surface.

That historical films often adopt and reinforce national myths is a hypothesis that can easily be accepted. It is interesting that such myth-reinforcing pictures are not always welcomed by contemporary leaders, who are more concerned with the present than with the past. This is demonstrated by Liesbet Depauw's account of the difficulties Herbert Wilcox encountered when filming *Dawn* (1928), an evocation of the 1915 trial and execution of British nurse Edith Cavell by the German military. Some ten years earlier, when the war was still on, the British government would have applauded Wilcox's film. In 1928, when European reconciliation and German reintegration ranked high on the international agenda, the British Minister of Foreign Affairs discarded the film as 'repugnant'. To avoid such controversies and offer more 'convenient' histories, historical films were sometimes altered before being exported; in other words, adapted to the expectations of particular foreign audiences. This is demonstrated by Uli Jung, who describes how Karl Grune's film *Waterloo* (1928) – which mainly centred on the German national hero, Marshall Blücher – was tailored to French audiences by changing its ending, making the film into a celebration of Napoleon.

There is a double dynamic that needs to be taken into account. Despite the importance of historical films in the national context, the hunt for large audiences and the globalisation of the film industry give way to the emergence of supranational themes and stories that result in the erosion of national myths. On the other hand, certain versions of national myths are sustained when put onto film by large production companies and distributed to global audiences. With film distribution and consumption increasingly taking on global dimensions, and in light of the production logic that successful films lead to more films about the same subjects, historical films contribute to the emergence of a global cinematic version of history, affecting the historical knowledge of audiences all over the world.

Since cinematic (hi)stories play a major role in identity-shaping, they have an ideological and political potential. More often than not they tell histories of great men and great deeds, of conquerors and victors, of survivors and heroes. Ordinary men and women, losers and strugglers, the working class and social and political movements are seldom to be seen on the screens of our multiplexes. (Mike Leigh's *Vera Drake*, in this volume analysed by Amy Sargeant, forms an exception to this rule.) On the political level, history on film is being used to defend certain interests. For example, the way in which the commercial film industry has turned the history of the Holocaust into a Western story has implications for both the international and domestic policy of the United States. American historian Peter Novick argues that the Six-Day War of 1967 provoked a shift in American consciousness regarding the Holocaust and that this was a direct result of the political needs of the American government in mobilising support for Israel, its prime client state in the Middle East. The television series, *Holocaust*, was a first attempt to integrate the Holocaust into popular memory.[2] Steven Spielberg's *Schindler's List* links the Holocaust with the foundation of Israel in a final scene symbolising Israel as the only safe haven for the European Jews. The film has been seen by a quarter of the population in Great Britain, nearly a third of the population in Germany, and had a profound effect on global historical consciousness.[3] At a different level it is apparent that the Holocaust theme is slowly but surely disconnecting from its purely historical content and is being transformed into an archetypical meta-story about good and evil and the human condition. The cinematic representation of the Holocaust is well on its way to creating a modern 'myth', a cinematic version of the past, comparable to the Shakespearian representation of the Wars of the Roses.

Yet, much in the same way as Shakespeare reflected the interests of Queen Elisabeth's reign, the cinematic construction of modern myths can tell us something about the paradigms dominating contemporary society. They are situated not only at the concrete political level, but also at a more abstract meta-level. One example is the Western liberal-capitalist paradigm of the responsible individual capable of intervening in reality and determining his own fate through well-directed action. This *Leitmotiv* is reflected in the narrative conventions of mainstream historical films: individual characters and their personal *peripeteia* represent larger historical issues, and historical development coincides with the solutions the characters find for their problems. This individualised and closed historical narrative supports the liberal-capitalist ideology and also fits in with the logic of the commercial enterprises that produce films.[4]

As I have said, the need to imagine and shape history predates cinema. Nineteenth century historical paintings featuring such 'characters' as Emperor Charles V fashioned history mostly to endorse the morality and ideology of bourgeois society. Painters preferred specific scenes (e.g. accession to the throne), which were often depicted, using the same composition diagrams, movements and props, in such a cliché manner that the protagonists seemed interchangeable.[5] The parallels with historical mainstream films are notable.

With their vast amounts of period detail, historical films cater for the need to make visual representations of past reality. In this regard, the 'visual turn' coined by cultural studies and by now adopted within most humanities, establishes the visual as a legitimate research subject and may finally reconcile film scholars and historians on the issue of historical films. William Mitchell shows that in post-industrial society cultural identity is increasingly shaped by images functioning as the source of information for reality.[6] In this way, the 'imagined' reality becomes an essential part of identity-shaping. This is also true of past reality, which is also a point of orientation in building personal and collective identities. The imagined, cinematic past will therefore become an ever-growing part of cultural identities.

Films work in symbolic ways and scenes of historical films are often not only interpreted as reconstructions or interpretations of single events, but as symbolic representations of wider historical views and discourses. In his analysis of *Downfall*, Roel Vande Winkel argues that for this very reason, historical films can sometimes do historical 'reality' more justice by slightly altering historical 'facts' than by trying to recreate them 'as they really happened'. Nevertheless, in order to understand and interpret historical films, thorough knowledge of the historical 'facts' is often indispensable, as is illustrated by Pascal Vandelanoitte's contribution on Andrei Tarkovsky's rather hermetic historical allegory *Andrei Rublev* (1966). In addition, Jasmijn Van Gorp describes how Alexei German was convinced that straight historical knowledge was not enough to understand his film *My Friend Ivan Lapshin* (1983-1985), but that audiences needed to have lived through the Stalinist era.

Makers of historical films rely on a wide variety of sources, historical and others. As a result, historical films often have a complex intertextual structure. This makes every historical film – and for that matter historiography itself – a palimpsest of mounted meanings, facts, images, experiences, memories, records, fantasies, structures, traditions, ideologies and stories. Yet, in order for a historical film to be credible, it needs to structure its multiple 'origins', contexts and intertexts and aim for symbolic coherence and significance. To reveal and unravel that structure, to unveil the past of the perpetually changing present, is the task that confronts the researcher of film and history. In this respect, the intertextual model Leen Engelen proposes in this book, constitutes a viable research avenue, as is demonstrated by Willem Hesling's dissection of the authorised and more unorthodox sources that Alexander Korda and his collaborators used to create the artist biopic *Rembrandt* (1936).

Notes

1   Smith, A. (1998) *Nationalism and Modernism. A Critical Survey of Recent Theories of Nations and Nationalism.* London/New York: Routledge, pp. 170-198.

2   Novick, P. (2000) *The Holocaust in American Life.* Boston: Houghton Mifflin. See also Roel Vande Winkel's chapter on *Downfall* (2004).

3   Gold, T. (2005) An overview of Hollywood cinema's treatment of the Holocaust, pp. 193-197 in T. Haggith and J. Newman, *Holocaust and the Moving Image. Representations in Film and Television since 1933.* London/New York: Wallflower Press.

4   Despite the obvious links with literary studies, reference is rarely made to the extensive research into the genre of the historical novel. Within the context of the 19ᵗʰ century nation state, the authors endowed the nations with fabulous historical stories in which a suitable past could be constructed. The literary procedures adopted in these historical novels fit in closely with the narrative strategies of mainstream historical films. The second half of the twentieth century saw the development of the post-modern historical novel, which, due to the 'crossing of boundaries and the blurring of genre distinctions, opened up new possibilities for representing the past'. The repertoire includes fragmentation, discontinuity, indeterminacy, plurality, meta-fictionality, heterogeneity, inter-textuality, decentring, dislocation, ludism, reflexivity. These are some of the buzzwords in the analyses of post-modern historical films. (Heirbrant, S. (1995) *Componenten en compositie van de historische roman. Een comparatistische en genologische benadering.* Leuven/Apeldoorn: Garant, pages 17-32; Nünning, A. (1997) Crossing Borders and Blurring Genres: Towards a Typology and Poetics of Postmodernist Historical Fiction in England since the 1960s, pp. 217-238 in *European Journal of English Studies,* 1 (2); Rosenstone, R. (1995) *Visions of the Past. The Challenge of Film to our Idea of History.* Cambridge: Harvard U.P., pp.198-225).

5   Gobyn, R. et.al. (1999) Proloog, pp. 11-13 in Hoozee, R., J. Tollebeek, and T. Verschaffel (eds) *Mise-en-scène. Keizer Karel en de verbeelding van de negentiende eeuw.* Gent: Mercatorfonds/Museum voor Schone Kunsten.

6   Mitchell, W. (1994) *Picture Theory: Essays on Verbal and Visual Representation.* Chicago: University of Chicago Press.

Reconstructing history: filming *Cromwell* (directed by Ken Hughes, 1970) © Columbia Pictures

No Way to do History?
Towards an Intertextual Model
for the Analysis of Historical Films

Leen Engelen

Introduction

From its very beginning in the late nineteenth century to today, fiction film has displayed a great fascination with historical topics. Throughout the years, many scholars have taken an interest in these historical films. As a field of research, historical film is in danger of coming down between two stools: film studies and historiography. Conflicting basic assumptions, diverging research questions and a different professional ethos have long caused Babylonian misunderstandings. A long-lasting and tiring debate between both disciplines seems to have hijacked methodological and conceptual progress in the field.

In this article I want to (re)consider the categories scholars from both sides have used so far to think about cinematic history. First, the merits and limitations of a generic approach to historical fiction films, as practiced by many of the scholars in the field, are taken under scrutiny. Subsequently, I try to explain and overcome the limitations by introducing an intertextual approach to historical film. This intertextual model of film analysis enables scholars of different professional affiliation to answer a manifold of research questions. By proposing this intertextual model, I hope to formulate important challenges to the theory and practice of film and history in the future.

The debate

In 1926, the Belgian weekly film journal *L'Écran et la Scène* launched a competition among its readers to point out factual mistakes made in films. In the first article, the journalist started off with some examples of flagrant blunders. *Robin Hood* – the 1922 version written and starred by Douglas Fairbanks – is cited as a case in point. The story of the Earl of Huntingdon and King Richard I the Lion-Hearted is set in the early thirteenth century. Disguised as Robin Hood, the Earl goes from castle to castle to recruit men for his knighthood, leaving behind printed invitations with instructions for those interested. The collaborator of *L'Écran et la Scène* mockingly remarks that Robin Hood must have been some kind of a prophet then, since Gutenberg didn't invent the art of printing before the 1450s.[1]

On a well-known academic mailing list on First World War studies, the news about the making of a film on the German air ace, Manfred von Richthofen, alias *The Red Baron*, was greeted with great scepticism. One member of the list wrote the following reaction:

> 'Oh boy this can't be good news. We all know what happens when the movie makers start getting involved in history right? They'll end up causing more confusion about the actual events. If one were to go by "Gone with the Wind" you'll be under the impression that all black people were just happy to be slaves. Just like if you go by "Rosewood" you'll get a completely misconstrued version of events that the survivors of the tragedy said was total crap. Richtofen [sic] is an example of one of those things that many people heard of but not many people really know in depth. A movie misrepresenting him, like Rosewood, could lead to very bad consequences.'[2]

As these anecdotes illustrate, nothing much seems to have changed since the 1920s. Audiences and critics still use historical facts and historiography as points of reference and as evaluation standards for historical films. Yet, up until the 1970s, historians hardly showed any interest in these films, discarding them as mere entertainment without any value as history. While in the last four decades the prominence and importance of historical films has steadily grown, 'traditional' historians still air great scepticism about the histories represented in historical films.[3] Historical accuracy, verifiable by means of footnotes, references and explicit self-reflexivity, and a constantly critical attitude vis-à-vis the historical sources and narratives are at the centre of the academic historical profession. History is conceived of as a debate about what exactly happened, why it happened and what would be an adequate account of its significance.[4] In this debate however, only trained historians seem to be allowed to participate. Certainly, it is hard to reconcile the rules of the historical profession with what happens in mainstream historical films. In the latter, seamless stories seduce the audience into believing what it sees. The suspension of disbelief, the difficulty of systematically verifying a film's historical accuracy and the closed, progressive narrative of most films makes the gap between historical film and traditional historiography for many scholars almost unbridgeable. Save some exceptions like Ian Jarvie and David Herlihy, historians have not taken part in the debate on historical film because they didn't feel historical film was a subject they should be interested in as historians. Only in the 1970s some French historians from the *Annales* school became interested in (historical) film. From a neo-Marxist perspective and influenced by the *nouvelle histoire*, they looked at film as a new type historical source for research on the era in which the film was made. They claimed historical films shed a light on contemporary interpretations of the past. Moreover, film could enlighten 'l'envers d'une société' (the backside of a society) and could help historians to make a counter-analysis of historical structures and events to counterbalance the existing historiography.[5] In the late 1980s, the discussion was carried on in a special issue of the *American Historical Review*. Robert Rosenstone's contribution created a lively polemic. He stated that historical films are a legitimate and complementary way to do history.[6] Historical films don't only speak to us about their time of production, but also about the historical past itself. Although many scholars protested against his point of view[7], Rosenstone managed to put historical film on the agenda of many historians worldwide.[8] Film scholars have often approached the debate from a different angle. They usually don't consider historiography the main point of reference for understanding historical films. Above all, they look at historical film as film, not as an alternative form of historiography. For long historians and film scholars have fundamentally disagreed on the importance and centrality of the concept of historical accuracy in the study of historical film. Although their opinions on the subject of cinematic history still diverge, as John E. O'Connor and more recently Robert B. Toplin and Robert Rosenstone[9] correctly state, I do believe the gap is narrowing. The increasing understanding of the rules of engagement of each other's profession is slowly beginning to bear fruit.[10]

It seems to me that today it is no longer fruitful to continue defending historical fiction films against the criticism of zealous historians of the old stamp who are relentlessly trying to unmask fiction films as incomplete and historically inaccurate versions of history. Films can, and do represent history. Cinematic history is legitimate as cinema and history alike. It has its own merits and its own contributions to make. It is not solely a complement of written history, it is a full-fledged supplementary way to interpret and give meaning to the past. Alike written history, cinematic history has idiosyncratic limitations: for instance, not all historical subjects are easily adapted for the screen (e.g. the emergence of the (idea of) the nation state in Europe) and some historical insights might be difficult to integrate in a traditional narrative. It is clear that cinematic history has its own idiom in which it favours a poetic-symbolic instead of historiography's rational-scientific encounter with the past.[11] Let's take this as a starting point and try to take the debate and the research a step further.

Genre: Differences and similarities

Comprehension of the structures at work in cinematic history is a *sine qua non* for the understanding of historical fiction films. The lion's share of theoretical writing on film and history is either dedicated to identifying the specific structures, codes, conventions, and formulas films use to put history onto screen, or advocates that other scholars should identify these.[12] To define the conventions of cinematic history, scholars often introduce the concept of genre. The notion of genre is in itself problematic. Depending on the field of research (e.g. nineteenth century literature or Hollywood film) and on the historical and theoretical context, the term is understood differently. Going into this fascinating discussion would lead me too far now, but I will refer to different genre theories throughout the text.[13] Here, I should like to take a pragmatic approach and look at the concept as it has been used in the scholarly writing on film and history.

Over the years, both film scholars and historians have participated in the debate on the description of the generic features of historical films. Robert A. Rosenstone[14] and Robert B. Toplin[15] have continuously participated in the Anglo-American debate. Their work, together with the research performed by Pierre Sorlin and Marc Ferro in France, has inspired the issues raised in the first part of this paragraph. In a second section I look at the way film scholars have dealt with historical film as a genre.

Historiography: historical film as a way to 'do history'

Most historians writing on film and history use pragmatic (and often simplistic) *ad hoc* definitions of genre, cut to the size of the historical films dealt with in their work. For example, in his book dealing with historical Hollywood films, Toplin explicitly defines genre as the skilful retelling of an archetypical narrative that has always exerted a powerful grip on our collective imaginations.[16] To this definition he adds that genres are never static and that they are used over and over again because of their approved commercial success. This ritualistic definition fits the Hollywood blockbusters addressed in his book, but may prove problematic for more marginal cinemas.

Rosenstone's thinking about the historical film is permeated by the idea of the historical film as a genre. In a recent article in *Cineaste*, he plainly states that like historiography, historical film is also a genre with conventions.[17] Simply understanding genre as a set of conventions, he tries to avoid the complex problem of its definition. This traces back to his training as a historian. In the introduction of *Visions of the Past* (1995), in which he elaborates on his initiation as a historian to history on the big screen, he first introduces 'history on film' as way of doing history, instead of a (generic) way of 'doing film'. He herewith acknowledges Sorlin stating that 'the peculiarity of historical films is that they are defined according to a discipline [history] that is completely outside the cinema' and that there is no special term to refer to historical films. '[W]hen we speak of them', Sorlin continues, 'we refer both to the cinema and to history'. Yet Sorlin as well as Rosenstone seem to look at historical film as a group of films with (at least a few) common features. Sorlin states that historical films, although different from traditional 'cinematic types' (he cites classic genres like the western and the musical) contain signs by which audiences can recognise them as such.[18]

A question that immediately comes to mind is whether even mainstream historical films can *überhaupt* be considered as a group. The great diversity of historical films in terms of subject matter, settings, plots, characters and types of story situations makes the recognition of historical film as a genre or a group highly problematic. Even in regard to a relatively clear-cut series of films, like for example the Hollywood historical film, the genre would include a plethora of very different films dealing with different historical eras. Ridley Scott's *Gladiator* (2000) seems to have very little in common with John Huston's *Moulin Rouge* (1952) or King Vidor's *Billy the Kid* (1930), except that they all deal with the past. For Pierre Sorlin, this is the main feature that discriminates historical films from other genres. Whether an audience reads a film as being set in the past, depends on its knowledge and understanding of its own history. Sorlin refers to this knowledge as to the 'historical capital' of a group or individual.[19] Rosenstone as well as Toplin is convinced that all mainstream historical films together do incorporate a shared set of strategies, icons, and characterizations.[20]

In several books and articles, Robert Rosenstone systematically explores the general characteristics of mainstream historical films. He states history in film is presented as a closed, progressive story in which a limited number of individuals play a central role. Films usually stress the emotional and visual aspects of history. Better than traditional historiography, historical films are able to present integrated historical processes. On this feature historical films and historiography definitely differ the most. In film economic, political, social and aesthetic statements can be made simultaneously through the different layers. While in historiography all elements have to be explained one after the other, in one scene or even shot many different assumptions about the past can be made at once. Although based on a fictive story, Peter Webber's *The Girl with a Pearl Earring* (2003) for example, gives us at once clues about daily life (public markets, dress code, poverty…) in seventeenth-century Amsterdam, the life of the famous painter Johannes Vermeer, the seventeenth-century role models for husbands and wives and members of the upper class and the lower class, common economic and social activities in Holland's golden age, etc.[21] This example plainly illustrates that historical films, even if based on a largely fictional story, have a great potential for the presentation of history. At the same time it is clear that in their selection and presentation of history filmmakers make an interpretation of past events or characters. Next to fictional modifications for dramatic purposes, filmmakers also have to 'fill in' visual and aural elements for which simply no historical evidence exists. E.g. there's no historical evidence for what clothes Vermeer wore while he was working on his *Girl with a Pearl Earring*, nor for the timbre of his voice or the way he moved. While filmmakers have to find a creative solution for missing historical data, historians writing monographs on Vermeer are usually not confronted with the necessity to provide this kind of detailed visual information. Historical films that present the past according to the conventions cited above, present the past in a symbolic way.

Robert B. Toplin defines nine major components of Hollywood mainstream cinematic history.[22] For the larger part, the rules he lists equal Rosenstone's findings. For Toplin, the reasoning behind these conventions is mainly economic: the audience at the box-office punishes filmmakers that don't obey to these conventions. He thus downplays the contentious and coercive aspects of the Hollywood industry and its genres.[23] Most of the 'rules' cited above have to do with the selection and organisation of historical data. In the selection phase, complex historical processes are simplified, details are omitted and from a wide range of historical characters, protagonists are chosen. Subsequently the selected information is organised in a logical and causal narrative structure. In doing so, characters are juxtaposed (e.g. the good vs. the bad; the male protagonist vs. the female protagonist) and fictive elements and storylines (e.g. a romantic storyline) are added. The historical and fictional elements are located in all 'layers' of the film: the story, the mise-en-scène, the camera movement and position, the editing and the soundtrack.[24]

The existing body of theory and case studies on cinematic history has brought us some general categories and conventions applicable in the study of historical films. Most scholarship has approached this quest for common ground in a deductive way, using the analysis of specific films to deduce general characteristics.[25] Although there might not readily be an alternative, this method causes an important bias in the 'abstract' rules deduced from the series of films under scrutiny. The films dealt with in past and current scholarship on film and history all belong to a few specific categories. The rules that are identified in these monographs or edited collections usually fit best with the cinematic canon addressed in the volume. For example, a large amount of scholarship is dedicated to Hollywood and other mainstream cinemas. The rules of historical engagement of box office successes like *Schindler's List* (1993), *Bonnie and Clyde* (1967) and *Apocalypse Now* (1979) do not necessarily hold firm ground for films produced outside a strong Hollywood tailored studio system or in other parts of the world.[26] My own work on a very marginal cycle of films produced in a non-organised production context, i.c. Belgian patriotic dramas from the 1920s, made it clear to me that the existing categories, although applicable at first sight, in the end fall short of the mark.[27] Indeed, in the films complex historical processes like e.g. the run-up to and the outbreak of the war are simplified and many historical actors are omitted. Yet, this assessment doesn't inform us about the meaning of the actual representations of the events taking place in the summer of 1914. Alike literary adaptations, adaptations of history generally obey to certain 'rules'. Looking at films through the raster proposed by Rosenstone and Toplin definitely uncovers the structures used to adapt the stories of history/historiography to film, yet the mere presence of these conventions doesn't enlighten the underlying meaning of the historical representations in the films under scrutiny. Therefore, the generic approach of the authors mentioned above leaves many questions we consider important unanswered. In my opinion, their understanding of genre as a series of conventions is so static that it leaves little space for the dynamic relations between genre and society. As Rosenstone clearly indicates in his article *Confessions of a (Postmodern?) Historian*, this can be explained by their professional training and affiliation. In the first instance Rosenstone is a historian looking for new ways to do history; ways that will enable him to link specific events with the underlying structures and to present history in a lively way.[28] In this respect, historical film offers many possibilities. When studying historical film, historians are looking for new ways to do history. Film scholars on the other hand ask different questions: when they study historical films the meaning of the historical representations is questioned. Therefore, more specific idiosyncratic categories are needed for a profound understanding of the representation of history in a designated (body of) film(s). We will now look at how the historical film as a genre has been dealt with by film scholars.

Film Studies: historical film as cinema

Most film scholars don't consider historical film a genre as such. At least it is not dealt with as a separate category in most genre readers.[29] Most monographs focus on narrower sub-categories as the heritage film, the war film (with subdivisions like the combat film, the Vietnam War film and the Civil War film) or the biblical epic or see to films set in the past from another generic perspective, e.g. as a film noir or western. As already said, especially in regard to the historical film a lot of generic cross-breeding is going on. In her book on British film genres, Marcia Landy distinguished the historical film from other 'historical genres' like the costume drama or the war film, and chiefly British genres like the 'films of empire'.[30] As the generic features of the historical film she cites the following: history is at the very heart of the story and functions as a catalyser (1) and the overall dynamic of the film originates in the tensions between the public and the private sphere (2). How this historical dynamic and these tensions are to be examined, the author leaves an open question. She puts the reader (and the researcher looking for a way to analyse and understand historical film) off with some sketchy examples. In this reader on British genres, the author takes a neo-Marxist approach. She describes genre as a coherent, value-laden system of conventions that stems from complex interactions between the narrative, the author, the industry and the audience.[31] She also stresses the subversive potential of genres, meaning that although repetitive, variation within genres can shed light on contemporary cultural conflicts. Consequently it is not surprising that Landy locates the meaning of a historical film mainly in its commenting on the present through a depiction of the past.[32] For the study of historical films as a representation of past as well Landy's approach is too limited.

Film scholar Leger Grindon amends some of these shortcomings in his book *Shadows on the Past. Studies in the Historical Fiction Film* (1994). Alike Landy, he takes a ritual approach to genre, ascribing the latter a socio-cultural function. Not only do genres affirm existing interests and attitudes, through their variation they also resolve tensions, conflicts and ambiguities within society. Central to his analysis of the historical genre is the structural relation between the individual and society in the film. This comes down to what Landy coined the dynamic between the public and the private. The (often causal) dynamic between personal (private) and extrapersonal (public) forces is considered the driving force behind the film's narrative as well as history itself. In refining the categories used to analyse the tension between these two spheres and in situating this dynamic in all layers of the film (the story, the mise-en-scene, the editing and camera movements and the soundtrack), Grindon comes closer to an analysis of the actual representation of the past, without losing sight of the messages conveyed about the present.[33] Grindon formalised this dynamic through the use of two central generic elements figuring in every historical film: respectively romance and spectacle. An archetypical relation between a 'leader' and a 'romantic couple' structures the romantic component; spectacle is structured by the dynamic relation between 'mass conflicts' on the one hand and 'ceremonies' on the other hand.[34] Taking the film itself and the many complex relations between the generic elements as the starting point of his analysis, Grindon convincingly demonstrates that the complexity of the text refers to the complexity of the contemporary and historical context.

Yet Grindon's model still falls short of the mark in the formalisation of the relations between the generic film text and its socio-cultural context. The analysis of the context is presented as something that has to be done next to the analysis of the text. Moreover, Grindon's conception of context seems to be mainly limited to the contexts of production and reception. It is however safe to assume that the meaning of historical representations in historical films are related to a much greater diversity of contexts.

As far as I'm concerned, the generic approach to historical film has too many limitations; in the study of historical film, the genre-concept used is still too much of a Procrustes' bed.

I thus suggest to drop the concept of genre as (implicitly or explicitly) understood by the authors mentioned above and to alternatively adopt more pragmatic and less theory-laden concepts like a 'film cycle', a productions cylce[35] (e.g. the Merchant Ivory costume dramas) or a 'school' (e.g. the Iranian Makhmalbaf school) to designate a more or less coherent corpus of historical films. Herewith, the question whether the historical film can or should be considered as one genre partially lapses. Yet, there's no need to discard a generic approach to historical film altogether. I would like to plea for a repositioning of the concept of genre in the model of analysis. I will look at this in depth in the next paragraph.

Intertextuality

The concept of genre, as used above, establishes links between film texts. The relations between text and context lack formalising. In his work on television, media scholar John Fiske integrates the concept of genre in an intertextual framework aimed at the understanding of the meaning of specific media contents. He therefore suggests a socio-cultural approach to genre with ritual as well as ideological spearpoints.[36] This means genres are conceived of as systems of orientations, expectations and conventions that circulate between industry, text and audience.[37] The cultural practices of producers and audiences are identified as the most influential structuring elements of genre. The social, economic, and cultural contexts in which these practices take place are in their turn of crucial importance. These cultural practices result in texts belonging to the same genre (primary texts), in reviews and advertisements (secondary texts) and in readings of the audience, e.g. letters to the editor (tertiary texts). The intertextual relations between all those texts are structured by Fiske's concept of genre. Genre is thus seen as the intermediary element through which different contexts are at work. In adopting this structure Fiske formalises the relations between media texts and their context in an intertextual model.

I agree with Fiske that intertextuality is central to the understanding of the meaning of media contents. Every text, whether a television program or a historical film, must be read in relation to a variety of others texts, this is in relation to an intertextual network. Yet, in my opinion Fiske's genre-centered intertextual analysis of television texts falls short of mark in quest for a way to understand and research the meaning of historical fiction films. First, although his approach may be useful for studying traditional media genres in a capitalist, economy-driven system, it does not seem to rise to the demands of studying marginal media, produced outside an organised studio system. When studying for example postcolonial films from the African diaspora dealing with African history, Fiske's approach won't shed sufficient light on the films' meanings. Second, Fiske's selection of contexts/intertexts is still too limited. In looking at historical film, more and different intertextual relations have to be taken into account.

Moving from the more classical aesthetic genre theories towards a more flexible genre approach may be helpful. In his standard work *Film/Genre* (1999), Rick Altman identifies the major problems of the classical genre-theory.[38] Some of the aspects he refers to are of great importance when looking at historical film. Altman states genres are no steady unchangeable categories. On the contrary, they transform (in a non-teleological way) over time and with changing circumstances. Keeping this in mind, it is preferable to think of genres not as fixed categories but as open and intermittent systems. Moreover, more than often films are an implicit or explicit mix of genres.[39] Hybridity is in fact very often a feature of historical films. Arthur Penn's *Bonnie and Clyde* (1967) for example is not only a historical film, but also a gangster film and a biopic; a more recent example, Oliver Stone's *Nixon* (1995) can be labelled a historical film, but also a thriller; and not just any thriller, but a political thriller. Consequently, films do not only have multiple relational possibilities with films belonging to the same generic category, but with films belonging to other generic classifications as well. A shared subject matter, common objects or settings or similar types of story situations can activate these generic and cross-generic relations.[40] This understanding of genre hints at a whole 'new' field of intertextual relations that was not taken into account by Fiske. In what follows we will draw the lines of an intertextual model that will be useful for the study of the meaning of concrete historical representations in historical film.

Developing an intertextual model – building blocks

What is needed in the first place is a broader understanding of the notion of context. This can't be limited to an aggregate of the (cross-)generic contexts and the contexts of production and reception. In literary studies context is described as the sum of the universe to which the text refers and the universe surrounding the film text as far as it is part of the text's frame of reference and contributes to its meaning.[41] Following Graham Allen, the structures, codes and traditions of these contextual elements can be conceived of as separate but interconnected 'texts' or discourses contributing to the meaning(s) of a (film) text at a specific moment in time.[42] Consequently, the relations between text and context can be understood as interactions of 'texts'.[43] The way to an understanding of a film's meaning is thus intertextual. As a concept, intertextuality has been used for many years in literary studies. Based on the concept of 'dialogism' as understood by the Russian literary scholar Mikhail Bakhtin, it has been introduced to European (and hence American) literary studies by French poststructuralists in the late 1970s. Since then it has been employed in many different forms in structuralist, feminist, post-colonial and postmodernist studies. If understood in a non-theoretical way, the concept is, according to Mary Orr, also applicable to any electronic medium conceived after the closed form of print text, including film.[44]

This broader understanding of the concepts of context and intertextuality has as a consequence that genre can no longer be the central structuring element of the relations between text and context. Generic affiliations between texts are now seen as only one of the possible intertextual relations. Moreover, while generic intertextuality is in the first place based on similarities between texts, the intertextual approach has great critical potential.[45] It is clear that texts also obtain meaning from resistance, conflict and contrast with certain intertexts.

Thus, next to genre there are many more separate intertextual relations that link a text to its intertexts and consequently link a text to its context. First, what Fiske calls secondary and tertiary texts, e.g. reviews, posters, commercials or popular reception texts, are in my approach considered independent intertexts that 'directly', without necessarily being mediated through genre, contribute to the meaning of a film text. These kinds of intertexts are common to the intertextual networks of as good as all media texts, they are not specific for historical films. In contrast to Fiske's point of view, in my approach primary texts (films that belong to the same genre) do not have a priority over secondary or tertiary texts. While some scholars see a film's historical reception as a crucial key to a film's meaning, I suggest this is only one of the intertexts defining meaning.[46] Second, certain characters, actors or events can be the linking pin between texts and thus structure the intertextual relations. An example can clarify this. A historical fiction film on the sinking of the American hospital ship *Lusitania* in 1917 is intertextually related to a wide range of primary and secondary historical sources on this event (newsreels, newspaper articles, pictures, historical studies) as well as to fictional accounts (films, poems or novels) of this same event. Often, historical films refer more to other films on the same era or historical event, than they refer to the past itself. This results, as Willem Hesling rightly indicates, in a filmic-historical reality that is almost solely intertextual and that is characterised by a poetic-symbolic idiom. This idiom differs significantly from, for example, the rational-scientific vernacular of traditional historiography. Of course, the intertextual network of historical films extends to a wide variety of texts and their intertextual networks.[47]

More often than not, meaningful contexts are less straightforward than the possibilities cited above. The intertextual relations between a film text and e.g. ongoing political debates, social policies, fashion trends or diplomatic tendencies, to name only a few, are much less structured. Only a thorough analysis will transcend the relation between these contextual elements and the film or films under scrutiny.

Intertextual relations

I propose a rather radical interpretation of intertextuality, which casts its net wider than the in literary studies traditional investigation of sources and influences and includes a wide variety of intertexts. Each relation between two (or more) texts is possibly bi-directional. Moreover, every relation between a film text and an intertext opens up a new intertextual network of which the initial intertext is the centre. The intertextual network thus expands continuously what leads to the ultimate entanglement of all intertextual networks into what Roland Barthes calls 'the book of culture' from which all texts cite. This rampant rhizomic network has no longer a fixed or referential centrepiece. As Graham Allen suggests, intertextuality reminds us that all texts are potentially plural, reversible, open to the reader's own presuppositions, lacking in clear and defined boundaries, and always involved in the expression or repression of the dialogic 'voices' which exist within society.[48]

The intertextual network of a specific film or set of films is not unlimited. Intertextual relations that don't contribute to the film's meaning are excluded. It is clear that the boundaries of intertextual networks are diffuse and change over space and time. The meaning of a film can change because a different audience, e.g. a younger generation or an audience from a different geographic region looks at the film. Evolutions in film history or historiography can also bring about changes in the initial intertextual network of a historical film. An intertextual analysis is thus always historical. It does not allow us to define the one and only fixed meaning of a historical film. It is important to stress that in our intertextual model all intertexts that contribute to the film's meaning participate to the intertextual network on a potentially equal basis. Still, it is undesirable, and above all impossible, to take into account all meaningful intertexts. Consequently, the researcher has to make a choice. This choice is not arbitrary but depends on the specific research questions formulated. For example, looking at 1990s Polish heritage epics as narratives of national identity, Dina Iordanova does not deal with certain intertexts, considered irrelevant for her research question, like, to name but one, the use of computer generated synthetic images in Western heritage epics of the same era, an intertext of crucial importance when researching, for example, the influence of modern technology on the depiction of crowd scenes in historical films.[49]

Within the framework set by the research questions, relevant intertexts are suggested by the film text itself. Contrary to literary texts, where the use of 'intertextual rituals' or an intertextual pragmatic, like references, quotes and footnotes is very common, historical films don't always use formal 'markers' to indicate intertextual quotations. References, located in the film's narrative, mise-en-scène, camera-use, editing or music, are complex and difficult to formalise. Only, what Robert Stam calls explicit or strong reflexive intertextuality will be explicitly indicated in the film text. He distinguishes three kinds of explicit reflexive intertextuality: playful references, aggressive or subversive/reactionary references and educational references.[50] Yet, the specific formal features of this intertextual pragmatic seem to have to be identified *ad hoc*. Danish media scholar Helle Kannik Haastrup draws the contours of a formal quotation system or intertextual pragmatic used to indicate specific (explicit) intertextuality in film.[51] A first variable is the element of the film form where the quotation is situated (e.g. in the dialogue or in the mise-en-scène). Second, she distinguishes between literal quotations and reinterpretations, and between marked (the beginning and ending of the quote are clearly indicated) and unmarked quotations. She also looks at patterns, repetitions and uniqueness of the quotation. Finally she takes into account whether a whole text is quoted, or only one element of it.[52] Next to these formal devices for making quotes, she distinguishes four kinds of specific intertextuality on the basis of the wider discursive field of the quote: *(media) cultural references* (references to elements from culture and media), *'inside' references* (e.g. references in the clothing or name of a character), *direct clip/inserts* and *genre-in-dialogue* (explicit references to the film's genre).[53]

Yet, more often than not, intertextual relations are not formally indicated in the film text at all because references are implicit, unconscious or indirect. Awareness of this kind of intertextuality requires a powerful and continuous self-reflexivity of the researcher. In any case, the researcher (as well as the audience) has to recognise intertextual references through a familiarity with a wide variety of possible intertexts.

Historiography as intertext

It is clear that when researching historical films historiography will often be a privileged intertext. Yet different importance will be given to the historiographic intertext in the case of a research project on Merchant Ivory costume drama's like *Sense and Sensibility* (1995) or historical films like *Der Untergang* (*Downfall*, 2004). The relation between a historical film and historiography can become very complex. Griffith based his *The Birth of a Nation* (1915) on both contemporary historical sources (e.g. Woodrow Wilson's *History of the American People*, 1902) and Thomas Dixon's popular, but virulently racist, novel, *The Clansman* (1905), thus dramatizing then prevailing views about the race, slavery and the Civil War. Due to scholarly reassessments of the Reconstruction and the American Civil War, the film is nowadays seen as a flagrant misrepresentation of history.[54] In the intertextual model proposed in this essay, historiography looses its privilege as central point of reference for studying historical film. The fact that history looses its prime position has indirectly been one of the key issues in the epistemological upheaval postmodernism caused in both upper (ideological) and lower case (academic) history. With its incredulity towards meta-narratives – as Jean-François Lyotard has put it – postmodernism has dethroned empiricist and objectivist historiography and denounced it as being just another (next to upper case History) species of historiography inspired by bourgeois ideology. Postmodern approaches to historiography created a rapprochement between (postmodernist) history and film studies. Scholars often lean on Hayden White's theory of historical relativism to defend cinematic history against historical criticism. They denounce the truth-claim of traditional historiography and assert that both historiography and cinematic history are discursive constructions.[55] As Frederic Weinstein puts it 'interpretation always involves an 'imaginative leap' from social relationships or events to mind or mentality, a leap that is rarely confirmed or, under current conditions, confirmable by evidence.'[56] In cinematic history, this 'leap' is prominent because of the necessity for cinematic data. The filmmaker has to find a solution for numerous visual and aural details he needs to fill in but he hasn't got any historical evidence for.

This brings us back to the first part of this essay where we concluded that film scholars ask different questions to historical film than historians do. The quest for understanding specific historical representations in film does not end with the assessment of historical accuracy; this is with the investigation of the intertextual relations between a film text and historiography. Therefore the intertextual model offers a possibility to take many other contexts into account.

Notes

1   Erdé (1926). Les enquêtes de "L'écran et la Scène". Les erreurs dans les film, p. 13 in *L'Écran et la Scène. Informations,* 4 (50).

2   Message posted by brainiac1082 on the WWI-list hosted by the University of Kansas (wwi-l@listproc.cc.ku.edu) on September 30, 2004. Subject: [WWI-L:50994] Re: Now it's Red Baron - the movie.

3   When we use the predicate 'traditional' or 'progressive' in this matter, we only do this in relations to the group's position in the debate on film and history. On no account we want to make general statements about the groups mentioned.

4   Jarvie, I. (1978) Seeing through Movies, pp. 374-397 in *Philosophy of Social Sciences,* 8 (4).

5   Ferro, M. (1973) Le film, une contra-analyse de la society, in *Annales,* 44 (1).

6   Rosenstone, (1988) History in Words / History in Images: Reflections on the Possibility of really putting History onto Film, pp. 1173-1185 in *American Historical Review,* 93 (5).

7   Herlihy, D. (1988) 'Am I a Camera?' Other Reflections on Film and History, pp. 1186-1192 in *American Historical Review,* 93 (5).

8   See e.g. Toplin, R.B. (1999) Needed: An Interdisciplinary Dialogue, in *Perspectives,* November 1999 [http://www.historians.org/perspectives/issues/1999/9911/9911fil2.cfm].

9   O'Connor, J.E. (ed.) (1990). *Image as Artifact. The Historical Analysis of Film and Television.* Malabar: Robert E. Krieger Publishing Company, pp. ix-x; Toplin, R.B. (2002) *Reel History. In Defense of Hollywood.* Kansas: University of Kansas Press, pp. 160-162; Rosenstone, R. (2004) Inventing Historical Truth on the Silver Screen, pp. 29-33 in: *Cineaste,* 29 (2).

10 Toplin, R.B. (1999) 'Needed: An Interdisciplinary Dialogue', in: *Perspectives,* November 1999 [http://www.historians.org/perspectives/issues/1999/9911/9911fil2.cfm].

11 Hesling, W. (2000) Het verleden als verhaal. De narratieve structuur van historische films, pp. 8-15 in *Communicatie,* 29 (1).

12 Harlan, D. (2003). Ken Burns and the Coming Crisis of Academic History, pp. 186-192 in *Rethinking History,* 7 (2).

13 For an interesting alternative discussion of genre: Altman, R. (1999) *Film/Genre.* London: BFI and Altman, R. (2004) 95 Theses about film genre. On the generic implications of studio publicity, pp. 31-87 in Biltereyst, D. & Ph. Meers *Film/TV/Genre.* Gent: Academia Press.

14 E.g. Rosenstone, R. A. (ed.) (1995a). *Revisioning History. Film and the Construction of a New Past.* Princeton: Princeton University Press; Rosenstone (1995b). *Visions of the Past. The Challenge of Film to our Idea of History.* Cambridge: Harvard University Press.

15 Toplin, R.B. (1996) *History by Hollywood: the Use and Abuse of the American Past.* Urbana: University of Illinois Press; Toplin, R.B. (2002). *Reel History. In Defense of Hollywood.* Kansas: University Press of Kansas.

16 Toplin (2002), p. 10. Toplin's definition is based on the definition of Schecter en Semeiks as used in: H. Schecter & J.G. Semeiks (1993) Leatherstocking in 'Nam: Rambo, Platoon and the American Frontier, p. 116 in: Combs, J.E. (ed.) *Movies and Politics: The Dynamic Relationship.* Hamden: Garland.

17 Rosenstone (2004), p. 30.

18 Sorlin, P. (1980). *The Film in History. Restaging the Past.* Oxford: Basil Blackwell, pp. 19-22

19 Sorlin calls this an audiences 'historical capital'. (Sorlin (1980), p. 20)

20 We must keep in mind that Toplin only deals with historical Hollywood films and that the set of rules he proposes only applies to contemporary Hollywood film, a subgroup of historical film.

21 *Girl with a Pearl Earring* is adapted from a novel by author Tracy Chevalier. It tells a story about the events surrounding the creation of Vermeer's famous painting *Girl With A Pearl Earring.* In fact, very little is known about the girl in the painting, it is speculated that she was a maid who lived in the house of the painter along with his family and other servants, though there is no historical evidence. The film attempts to recreate the unknown girl's life.

22 Toplin (2002), pp. 17-53.

23 Neale, Steve (2000) *Genre and Hollywood.* London & New York: Routledge, pp. 226-227.

24 Rosenstone (1995b), pp. 68-69.

25 Toplin (2002), p. 91.

26 Toplin (2002); Rollins, P.C. (1997) *Hollywood's World War I Motion Picture Images.* Ohio: Bowling Green; Rollins, P.C. (1983) *Hollywood as Historian. American Film in Cultural Context.* Kentucky: University of Kentucky Press; O'Connor, J.E. & M.A. Jackson (1979) *American History/American Film. Interpreting the Hollywood Image.* New York: Ungar Publishing Co.

27 See for instance, Engelen, L. (2005) *De verbeelding van de Eerste Wereldoorlog in de Belgische speelfilm, 1913-1939.* Leuven, unpublished Ph.D. thesis.

28 Rosenstone (2004), pp. 149-166.

29 See for example Altman (1999); Neale (2000).

30 Landy, M. (1991) *British Film Genres. Cinema and Society, 1930-1960.* Princeton: Princeton University Press.

31 Landy (1991), p. 10.

32 Landy (1991) , pp. 54-55.

33 Grindon, L. (1994) *Shadows on the Past. Studies in the Historical Fiction Film.* Philadelphia: Temple University Press.

34 Grindon (1994) , pp. 6-14.

35 According to Steve Neale the term 'cycle' is usually used to refer to groups of films made within a specific and limited time-span, and founded, for the most part, on the characteristics of individual commercial successes. As an example, Neale cites the adventure films made in the wake of *Treasure Island* (1934) en *The Count of Monte Christo* (1934). Neale (2000), p. 9.

36 Fiske, J. (1992). *Television Culture.* London: Routledge: 108-127.

37 Steve Neale, cited in Fiske (1992), p. 111.

38 A good overview of the classical genre theory is offered by Thomas Schatz: Schatz, T. (1981) *Hollywood Genres: Formulas, Filmmaking and the Studio System.* New York: Random House. For a critique on his theory: Neale, S. (2000) *Genre and Hollywood.* London: Routledge, pp. 207-214.

39 Altman (1999), pp. 204-214.

40 Bordwell, D. & K. Thompson (1986), p. 97, cited in Neale (2000), pp. 219-220.

41 Van Gorp, H., R. Ghesquière et al. (1991) *Lexicon van literaire termen.* Leuven: Wolters, pp. 85-86.

42 Allen, G. (2003) *Intertextuality.* London: Routledge, pp. 1-2.

43 Orr, M. (2003) *Intertextuality. Debates and Contexts.* Cambridge: Polity Press, p. 20.

44 Orr (2003), p. 20.

45 In contemporary genre theory meaning is ascribed to variety and discontinuity within genres. In production as well as reception, there is space for oppositional meanings and readings (see e.g.: Altman, R. (1999)).

46 Staiger, J. (1992) *Interpreting Film. Studies in the Historical Reception of American Cinema.* Princeton: Princeton University Press.

47 Hesling (2000), pp. 8-15.

48 Allen (2003), p. 209.

49 Iordanova, D. (2003) *Cinema of the Other Europe. The Industry and Artistry of East Central European Film.* London: Wallflower Press, pp. 47-53.

50 Stam, R. (1992) *Reflexivity in Film and Literature.* New York: Columbia University Press, pp. 8-9.

51 Haastrup understands specific intertextuality as intertextual relations that are expicitly articulated in the film text (Haastrup, H.K. (1999) Scream. An Intertextual Tale, p. 145 in Bondebjerg, I. & H.K. Haastrup (eds) *Intertextuality and Visual Media.* Copenhagen: University of Copenhagen/ Department of Film & Media Studies).

52 Haastrup (1999), pp. 166-167; This model is elaborated on in Haastrup, H.K. (2004) *Beyond the Quote - Cinematic Intertextuality in the 1990s.* Unpublished PhD thesis: University of Copenhagen

53 Haastrup (1999), pp. 145-148.

54 For a concise assessment of the *Birth of a Nation* case, see: Browne, A.R. & L.A. Kreiser (2003) The Civil War and Reconstruction, pp. 58-60 in Rollins, P.C. (ed.) *The Columbia Companion to American History on Film.* New York: Columbia University Press.

55 White, H. (1988) Historiography and Historiophoty, pp. 1193-1199 in *American Historical Review*, 93 (5).

56 Weinstein, F. (1990) *History and Theory after the Fall.* Chicago: University of Chicago Press: 31, quoted in Rosenstone (1995), p. 6.

Publicity shot of Andrei Rublev (Anatolii Solonitsyn) © Mosfilm

An Icon of Change: *Andrei Rublev* (1966) as a Historical Film about the Birth of Russia

Pascal Vandelanoitte

This essay focuses on Tarkovsky's *Andrei Rublev* as a historical movie. More specifically, I look at the historical context in which the story of *Andrei Rublev* unfolds, and reconsider the overall meaning of the film against the background of this historical context. By connecting Rublev's psychological quest with the facts of his life, and placing this in the broader context of his time, I argue that Rublev's catharsis can be read as an allegory of the broader social changes in Russia around 1400-1430.

Andrei Rublev: a man, a movie

The historical person Andrei Rublev was born between 1360 and 1370. He entered the monastery of the Holy Trinity in Sagorsk where he received his education as an icon painter and was instructed in the art by Sergei Radonezjki. Later on, he stayed in the monastery of Andronikov in Moscow. The earliest icons attributed to Rublev are part of the frescos in the church of the Assumption in Zvenigorod (1399). Rublev's first major commission was the decoration of the iconostasis for the church of the Annunciation in the Kremlin (1405), which he did together with Theophanes the Greek, an icon painter from Byzantium who after arriving in Novgorod around 1370 became widely recognised as one of the best Russian icon painters.[1] In 1408, Rublev decorated the cathedral of the Dormition in Vladimir with his friend Daniel Tcherny. Less is known about the period between 1410 and 1420, but it is generally accepted that he created his finest paintings, including several icons at Zvenigorod, in this period. Of his later work, only two major assignments, both from the late 1420s, seem to have survived, both in cathedrals belonging to the monasteries where he resided: the church of the Holy Trinity in the monastery of Sergei in Sagorsk (here he created his most famous icon, the Holy Trinity) and the cathedral of the Andronikov monastery in Moscow, where he died on the 29 January 1430.[2]

The movie *Andrei Rublev* (1966) is the second feature film by Andrei Tarkovsky, and his most complex one. Tarkovsky's movies are known for their poetic character and manifold layers of meaning, and *Andrei Rublev* is no exception. As Tarkovsky's only historical film, it focuses on the crisis of an individual rather than evoking a particular historical period. The initial viewing opens up many questions that often remain unanswered and even after subsequent viewings the movie continues to be enigmatic and fascinating.

The film begins with an untitled and undated prologue, followed by eight dated and titled episodes, all shot in black and white, and concludes with an untitled and undated epilogue in colour.[3] Throughout the different episodes (dated from 1400 to 1423), the film presents several stages in Rublev's life, like leaving the monastery with his companions Daniel and Kyrill and working with Theophanes the Greek, historically true facts that are combined with some fictive or subjective elements as for instance Rublev's doubt or his vow of silence. These episodes also confront the viewer with some broader historical facts: the Tatar domination in Russia and its slow decline; the Tatars' assault on the city of Vladimir in 1408; the rivalry between the small principalities in the region, etc. This episodic structure makes *Andrei Rublev* a difficult movie to watch. The dates of the episodes immediately show that there are several gaps in the time continuum.[4] Through the different episodes, Rublev is absent in many scenes and the attention is dispersed over several persons and actions.

Furthermore, there is no unity of action throughout the film. Kovàcs classifies the actions, which for the most part coincide with the episodes, in two groups: on the one hand, those that play a direct role in the life of Rublev, as the invitation of Theophanes in the second episode or the melting of the bell in the last episode; on the other hand, those that play an indirect role, such as the scene of the juggler in the first episode or the pagan festivity in the fourth.[5] While in the latter actions Rublev's inner struggle predominates, the previous actions provide the structure of the narrative. Equally important is the fact that Rublev is not so much the active agent of the story, but rather a passive observer meditating upon what happens. If he *is* involved in the action, it is only in a secondary way since his purpose in the film is something else, namely trying to deal with existential questions about his faith and his function as an icon painter in society.[6] In addition to this passivity of the protagonist, it is not until halfway into the movie that the dramatic key question is formulated: 'Will Rublev paint again or not?'[7]

This ambiguity is further reinforced in the mise-en-scène: first, the figure of Rublev is quite anonymous and distant; physically, too, he often seems anonymous. Rublev and his companion Kyrill resemble each other so much that they are easily mistaken for one another, both by the viewer as well as by some of the characters in the film. Second, the stage setting is timeless. Tarkovsky is very much aware that even a historically faithful representation of Rublev's time would be a twentieth-century view of the fifteenth century. Hence his deliberate choice of creating a timeless past through such simple objects as a log fire or sheepskin coats, etc., rather than using museological artefacts.[8] Unlike most other historical films that painstakingly try to evoke the past through locations, costumes and faithful replicas of historical objects, Tarkovsky purposely refuses to recreate the early fifteenth century, but rather creates a timeless setting somewhere in the past.[9] It is this choice of mise-en-scène that gives the film a universal quality; images and objects are set outside of time and space to add to a more idiosyncratic, more personal whole. The staging is unique and inseparably linked to the film *Andrei Rublev*. As a result, *Andrei Rublev* is more than only an object-film that tells more about the period in which it was conceived than about the past it represented, as Marc Ferro has labelled it: 'Let's reconsider *Alexander Nevski* or *Rublev*, these masterworks. The reproduction of the past is exemplary; is it still possible to understand medieval Russia without building on the compulsive images of these reconstitutions?'[10]

The inner conflict and the historical figure of Rublev

Since neither the historical basis nor background of the events are emphasised or explained in the film, the historical significance will be confusing or absent for those unfamiliar with Russian history. For Russian viewers, the period described belongs to the national cultural and historical heritage of familiar dates, events and characters, making it easier for them to interpret *Andrei Rublev* as a historical film.[11] On the contrary, Western audiences lacking prior knowledge of the historical context will fail to appreciate the strands of history that are woven throughout the film. Since the setting stresses the universality of the story, and the episodic structure does not allow for a coherent presentation of historical developments, Tarkovsky does not present an unambiguous image of history, but simply offers us a huge puzzle leaving it up to the viewer to fill in the blanks. As a result, non-Russian literature concerning *Andrei Rublev* generally stresses that it is not a historical film and that Tarkovsky only used the character of Rublev as the starting point to tell the story of an artist's existential crisis (of faith) or his artistic self-doubt. Youngblood even states that every interpretation will always be a personal one made in ambiguous or conditional terms.[12] I believe that the existential crisis of Rublev is an important part of the picture, but it should be borne in mind that the historical context is seamlessly integrated: the inner conflict of Rublev reveals much of both the actual life of the painter and his paintings, and the historical era in which he lived. Historical facts are used as structuring elements and the psychological quest is reinforced by the historical facts. In the making of the film, Tarkovsky did pay attention to its historical context:

> 'Of course we collected material, read source material and the historical and historiographical works, based ourselves on chronicles, on the studies of art historians dedicated to Rublev and his contemporaries, and on everything that we could find to read about the epoch.'[13]

Sufficient reason to look at the way the film deals with both the historical figure of Rublev and the context of his lifetime. Rather than to consider them separately or to focus only on the psychological or theological questions, as most critics have tended to do, it seems a more fruitful approach to handle the personal story of Rublev's catharsis and the historical facts as one.[14]

This part of our essay focuses on the relation and interaction between the life and paintings of the historical figure of Rublev and the inner conflict in the movie; further on, the relation with broader social and historical changes will be examined. Rublev's inner conflict is shown most clearly in the discussion with the icon painter Theophanes, then in a conversation with his companion Daniel, and again in his relation with Boriska, the bell-maker. In the second episode, a conversation between Theophanes and Kyrill helps to clarify certain things about Rublev. When Kyrill meets Theophanes, who hears that Kyrill comes from the Andronikov monastery, the words, 'Then you must be Andrei Rublev, everyone talks about him' haunt Kyrill so much that he immediately tries to disparage Rublev's reputation: 'Rublev indeed has some talent, but he is far from your perfection. He lacks the dread, the belief that comes from the deepest part of the soul, and the simplicity.' Kyrill here manoeuvres around Theophanes' request to decorate the church of the Annunciation in the Kremlin together, and forces Theophanes to ask him in front of the entire monastery communion, especially in the presence of Rublev. But it is Rublev who is asked to join Theophanes, and together with Prochor of Gorodec, he indeed accompanied Theophanes to decorate the church of the Annunciation in the Kremlin (1405). Nothing has been preserved of this decoration.[15] What is already apparent in this episode is that the most radical events in Rublev's life have external causes and are not rooted in his own ambitions. The film thus breaks with the conventions of the traditional biopic, in which all events are centred round the actions of one hero. It is external reality that determines Rublev's deeds, not the other way round.[16] This external world is represented as merciless and cruel: arrogance, treason and torture infiltrate the everyday-life.

As Rublev identifies belief as well as art with purity, this becomes the pivot of the film. Rublev cannot accept that the clergy stays enclosed in its shell and justifies and sentences, blesses and curses, beatifies and dooms from an isolated position outside reality. This is particularly clear in his conversations with Daniel and Theophanes. The discussion with Theophanes takes place in the third episode. This is the essential part of the dialogue:

> Theophanes: 'Tell me honestly, are the people ignorant or not?'
> Rublev: 'Yes, but who's to blame?'
> Theophanes: 'The people are ignorant because they are stupid. Soon the Last Judgment will come, and everyone will try to pass the buck to another.'
> Rublev: 'Do these thoughts not prevent you from painting?'
> Theophanes: 'I am in the service of God, not of the people.'

Theophanes has no faith in human beings, only in a distant God who has no faith in human beings either. Rublev on the other hand, believes that God's son has come as a savior and wishes to convince people that good exists. He believes that there are earthly things beyond the immediate realm of the senses, such as beauty, goodness, love and order, the basic virtues that were central to the teachings of his spiritual guide in the monastery of the Holy Trinity (Sagorsk), Sergei Radonezjki. Here Tarkovsky stresses the inner freedom of belief: Theophanes, a profane painter, escapes into the transcendence of faith, while Rublev believes that humanity can be saved. Theophanes gets his strength from the idea that he serves God and not mankind. Rublev reverses this attitude: he wants to serve mankind by bringing men closer to God. Hence it is impossible for him to paint as long as he cannot accept the presence of evil in the world. In the discussion with Daniel in the fifth episode Rublev takes a similar position. The men are appointed to paint the Last Judgment in the cathedral of Vladimir[17], but Rublev cannot accept the terrifying visions of a hell filled with monsters and boiling pitch:

Rublev: 'I can't paint these things. I disgust it. Do you understand? I do not want to frighten the people.'
Daniel: 'But that is the Last Judgment, you know! I didn't invent anything.'
Rublev: 'I can't, Daniel.'

In the film, the audience first gets the impression that Rublev won't paint this Last Judgment, but in the end of the episode, a feeble-minded woman enters the church while Daniel is reading a passage from one of the epistles of Saint Paul[18] which discusses the relation between man and woman and the reasons why a woman must not pray bareheaded. They jeer at the bareheaded 'idiot girl' as a sinner, but Rublev defends her by saying that entering a church without a headscarf cannot be a sin. Here, Rublev's faith in human goodness wins over Daniel's literal fidelity to the Holy Scripture. Even when the episode ends here and it is not shown whether Rublev will or will not paint the Last Judgment there is a suggestion that the meeting with the 'idiot girl' is a turning point for him. Later, in the penultimate episode, it becomes clear that Rublev has taken the girl to the monastery where she can be looked after. Moreover, in the original script of the film a scene was planned where Rublev and the 'idiot girl' would have been seen working on the Last Judgment. The dialogue between Theophanes and Rublev after the attack of the Mongols also refers to Rublev's icons (cf. infra). And even if the infernal part of this Last Judgment is not saved, it is clear that Rublev has not created classical visions of hellfire in Vladimir: 'We do not know what *The Last Judgment* would make if the infernal torturing scenes had been preserved. I imagine that the design must have been different from the Byzantine canon. In Byzantium, the idea of chastisement and revenge were very present. In the frescos of the Dormition cathedral, it is the human spirit that triumphs, and it is this idea that brings together the two masters, Danil en Andreï, even if they have different temperaments. There is nothing grim about the angels, the apostles, the righteous men and women and the saints; they are all shown as eager to come to the aid of their neighbour. The painters of the Dormition cathedral have succeeded in retaining an atmosphere of serenity, even in the scene of *The Last Judgment*.'[19] Here, Tarkovsky not only uses a historical order as pivotal event for the gradual progress of Rublev's doubts, but even manages to fit the spirit of the frescos perfectly into the narrative.

Although a fictional element, Rublev's 'vow of silence' is also linked to the historical facts. The issue is not whether the historical Rublev actually witnessed the attack on Vladimir as shown in the sixth episode, but that this historical event is used as a motive of change for the persona of Rublev and his wider aspirations towards freedom. Rublev witnesses how the brother of the grand prince of Moscow, allied with the Tatars, takes advantage of the grand prince's absence to conquer Vladimir and seize the throne. In this cruel assault even the people who flee into the church are butchered pitilessly. It is in the devastated church that Rublev tells Theophanes in a hallucination that he cannot continue to paint:

> Rublev: 'I will never paint again.'
> Theophanes: 'Why?'
> Rublev: 'It serves no purpose.'
> Theophanes: 'Because your icons are burned?' [The earlier mentioned *The Last Judgment*]
> Rublev: 'I haven't said the most important thing. I have killed a man. A Russian... When I saw he wanted to take her [the 'idiot girl']... Look at her, look!'
> Theophanes: 'Our sins give human shape to cruelty; by attacking evil, you attack the human...'
> Rublev: 'I decided to devote my silence to God. I have nothing more to say to my equals.'

Here also, Tarkovsky connects historical facts with personal interpretation that exceeds the total sum of what we know. The Tatars attacked Vladimir in 1408 and Rublev's frescos were severely damaged when the cathedral was burned. When Rublev murders the Russian soldier who tries to rape the 'idiot girl', his doubts are settled. Even if the act is justifiable and, within his faith, forgivable, Rublev is conscious of the fact that evil not only dwells in other people, but even in himself, and that the line between good and evil is often fragile, that even the strongest principles can be broken under certain conditions.

These examples not only demonstrate how Tarkovsky integrates facts and fiction, but also show that Tarkovsky's approach in creating a historical movie is particular. Historical references and Rublev's personal religious quest are intertwined and continuously reinforce one another. And it is only with reliable knowledge of Russian history that the viewer can interpret some of the actions as described above. Herlihy describes the experience of watching a historical film as a passive experience, enjoying the illusion of directly observing historic happenings, but there's much more at stake here.[20] *Andrei Rublev* is a

Publicity shot: Andrei Rublev takes a vow of silence and resumes icon-painting. © Mosfilm

movie that asks the viewer to fit together the parts of a puzzle, with or without knowledge of the factual background. In any case, we always watch the past through modern eyes and have to accept that, in whatever way we watch the past, we will always have a partial view; there will always be gaps that need to be filled in.[21] In *Andrei Rublev* this imaginative responsibility of the audience is crucial to an understanding of the film – just as it is in Tarkovsky's other movies such as *Solaris* (1972) or *Zerkalo* (*The Mirror*, 1975) – as emblematic puzzle. It is the viewer who has to link different parts and pieces together, and the more historic notions he has when watching *Andrei Rublev*, the more complete the picture will be.

Andrei Rublev is remarkable on a biographical level as well. Most artist biopics, such as *Love is the Devil – Study for a Portrait of Francis Bacon* (1998), directed by John Maybury; Milos Forman's *Amadeus* (1984), or Ken Russell's kitchy biopics of composers (like *Mahler* (1974) or *Lisztomania* (1975)), genuinely stereotype the artist's life without much retrospect of the historical or artistic context. In *Andrei Rublev*, nothing is dramatised, Rublev is not presented as a tormented artist but as a character with strengths and weaknesses that turns inward when he feels he can no longer answer his nagging doubts. He is more of a passive spectator than an active visionary. Here the artist is not the vehicle for dramatic action. His life is not represented as a subject of scandal or fierce controversy or even heroic deeds, but simply as a way of recounting certain aspects of the past and at the same time a reflection on the universal human condition, where doubt becomes a motive for individual, social and political change.

Robert Rosenstone makes a distinction between the traditional historical drama that tends to highlight individuals rather than movements or impersonal forces and the films that avoid glorifying the individual and present the group as protagonist (such as *Battleship Potemkin* (1925) or *October* (1927) by Sergei Eisenstein).[22] *Andrei Rublev* fills the gap between these two approaches by not letting the individual take over the historical process, but limiting him to the role of a passer-by who is nevertheless aware of historical changes taking place. Here, the individual is not history, but becomes history. As a result, his actions, that are not crucial for the historical march of events, do fit into this and make the figure of Rublev a sort of mediator for the course of events.

The brother of the grand prince of Moscow (Iurii Nazarov), allied with the Tatar Khan (B. Beishenaliev), takes advantage of the grand prince's absence to conquer Vladimir and seize the throne. © Mosfilm

Doubt as a symbol of historical change

As said before, *Andrei Rublev* can also be read on a level of social and historical evolutions. Rublev's time was one of great changes. By the end of the fourteenth century, after nearly two centuries of Tatar domination, the tide was slowly turning. The defeat of the Tatars near Kulikivo (1380) signalled the starting point of the gradual decline of their rule.[23] Even if the struggle was not over yet (the Mongols did not leave Russia definitively until 1480), the Mongols lost their reputation for invincibility.[24] There were also parts of Russia in which the Tatar armies never penetrated, like the ancient city-states of Novgorod and Pskov.[25] But these areas were divided under many local princes, so that unity was far in the future. It is clear that in the film Rublev's doubt cannot be isolated from the historical events of his time, it can even be seen as an 'icon' of that turbulent period.

In this ambiguous period of violence and uncertainty, the first renaissance of the Russian national dream came about. The Tatars felt their empire was vacillating and lashed out even more against the cities, as in the crushing assault on Moscow in 1382 – that came as revenge for the defeat in Kulikovo – or the attack on Vladimir (1408) that is shown in the sixth episode of the film. Faith was the linchpin holding this slow process of unification together. In those days, there was no unity of language and culture in Russia. The cultural patrimony mainly consisted of the Church's Slavonic language, its script and its religious texts.[26] What united the Eastern Slavs and differentiated them from the 'barbarians' was their Orthodox faith that provided them with a common enemy against whom they could unite and thus rediscover a sense of common purpose.[27]

Right from the start of the Mongol invasion, the Russian Church became the driving force in the pursuit of a national identity. While before the invasion, the Church concentrated on the higher classes; it now focused on the populace.[28] In addition, the Mongols' tolerance of the Orthodox Church allowed it to steadily gain influence.[29] The art of icon painting that had evolved greatly in the thirteenth and fourteenth century played a major role in this, not only because icons could be 'read' by everyone, literate or not, but also because they conferred a sense of glory to the dream of unity: 'The omnipresent holy pictures provided an image of higher authority that helped compensate for the diminished stature of temporal princes.'[30]

The Russian-Orthodox Church even formed a political unity in a country that in the course of the thirteenth, fourteenth and beginning of the fifteenth century became more and more disintegrated under the appanage system, by which the right of succession to the principalities remained with the members of the ruling dynasties. This means that each principality was frequently divided among the heirs and each created its own dynasty. Moreover, they rivalled each other continuously for the title of grand prince, who had the first position over the princes that descended from the same dynast. The outcome was continuous enmity and mutual destruction.

Tarkovsky was fully aware of this political rivalry and resulting cruelty. In a sequence in the fifth episode, the grand prince of Moscow blinds the artists that have just finished the decoration of his palace in Vladimir and were on their way to Zvenigorod to decorate the palace of his rival brother. In his writings *The Sealed Time* Tarkovsky wrote:

> 'It is easy to see how ill-equipped Andrey was for this confrontation with life, after being protected from it within the rarefied precincts of the monastery, from which he had a distorted view of the life which stretched out far beyond it. ... And only after going through the circles of suffering, at one with the fate of his people, and losing his faith in any idea of good that could not be reconciled with reality, does Andrey come back to the point from which he started: to the idea of love, goodness, brotherhood. But now he has experienced for himself the great, sublime truth of that idea as a statement of the aspirations of his tormented people.'[31]

This focus on rivalry and suffering as incentive is the reason why *Andrei Rublev* stayed in the vaults for five years before finally being distributed in the Soviet Union in 1971.[32] During preproduction, there had already been numerous discussions about the movie, the script was published in an important magazine, and expectations had grown that *Andrei Rublev* would become an epical movie about the rise of Russia. The debate on *Andrei Rublev* in the Soviet Union focussed firstly on its socio-political and historical content and only secondarily on its broader artistic concerns: Rublev was seen as the incarnation of the humanistic and nationalistic yearnings of the Russian culture.[33] Since the 1930s, Rublev's glorious icons created in the early unification period, were identified with Russia's spiritual unity and became a symbol of national solidarity.[34] Furthermore, this process of rehabilitation of Rublev's icons reached its zenith in the decade in which Tarkovsky shot *Andrei Rublev*, 1960 being the start of an extensive celebration of the 600th anniversary of Andrei Rublev's birth. Rublev was turned into a key figure in an era of the Russian history (the late fourteenth, early fifteenth centuries) that represented a 'progressive' step towards Russian national independence and unification along the path to Russia's ultimate destination as realized under Soviet communism. He and his icons seemed to embody that 'poetic' dream of a happy, beautiful, new person on a beautiful earth.[35]

What went against the grain of the Soviet authorities was the film's existentialist point of view and mood of continuous despair, instead of a glorious biography of one of Russia's central figures. The mise-en-scène itself was another cause of official discontent. *Andrei Rublev* is far removed from the Socialist Realist credo that guided and determined cultural production in those days. Officially the movie was criticised and classified because of its extreme length (195 minutes) and the scenes of excessive violence. That the Russian princes are not always depicted as amiable, and the whole movie seems to be immersed in one vast quagmire, also contributed to its fate. 'Vaunted Russian nature, prized and celebrated in the work of beloved 'realists' like Turgenev or Tolstoi, here appears squalid, muddy, and uncomfortable...'[36]

Tarkovsky never meant to emphasize the splendour of the early unification of Russia or the superiority of Rublev as an icon painter. On the contrary, he wanted to stress the conflict between the objective world and the subjective perception of the environment; in the film, Rublev recognizes this battle and tries to reach beyond it: 'He [Rublev] looks for an ideal moral that he carries inside himself and in this way even expresses the hope of the people, their aspirations that come out of their life circumstances, the attraction towards union, fraternity, love – all that the people lack and that Roublev feels to be indispensable for the people around him [....] That's the genius of Roublev [...] He expresses the hope and the ideal moral of a whole people and not only subjective reactions of an artist towards the world that surrounds him.'[37]

The catharsis as a new start

The question as to whether Rublev will succeed in reconciling the conflict between external reality and his inner spirituality becomes the key question in the film. The last episode, 'The bell (spring-summer-fall-winter-spring 1423-1424)' forms the final piece and the keystone of the film as a puzzle, and is a fine example of the interaction between the personal story of Rublev and the historical lines of change in early fifteenth-century Russia. The central character here is the (fictional) young boy Boriska who claims to be the only one who knows the 'secret of the bell-casters' and thereby gets the commission to cast a new bell for the grand prince in Vladimir. By means of Boriska's energy – who, even if he doesn't know the secret of the bell-casters, succeeds in casting the bell – this creative act is presented as a metaphor of the art of painting of the re-born Rublev.

All of Tarkovsky's films oppose the practical world, the world of action, to a more spiritual and inner-directed world. For Rublev, there are two possibilities: either he accepts that the world is not completely evil, which means that the presence of the good guarantees the possibility of the good conquering evil; or he leaves the ethical question to one side so that he can serve the virtual good with his art. By letting Rublev choose the first solution, Tarkovsky stresses individual choice and the possibility of change, and makes Rublev the force harmonising the practical and spiritual world. With this leap forward by Rublev, Tarkovsky represents a leap at the individual as well as the social level: Rublev will not simply paint and submit to the laws of the community; he wants to paint in his own way, and as a starting-point the took that mankind deserves to be included in a world of beauty: 'It is a totally individualist conception of creation: Rublev wants to be the master of his own creative force and rejects the sovereignty of the community. He insists on the right to paint as if mankind deserved to be represented in the form of a beautiful being. Cyrille says, 'It is a crime to put out the divine spark'. But his phrase does not move Rublev who thinks that mastery over his creativity is part of his personal integrity. He does not have to render account to anyone. This attitude of Rublev is opposed to the tradition.'[38]

It is once again no isolated fact that Rublev wants to paint in his own way as an artist and as an individual outside of the monastic community, and will not let his personal vision be determined by Christian doctrine and tradition. Russia was clearly a country that had gone through many critical changes, and the church played an important role in this process. I would suggest that Rublev's existential crisis that is followed by a catharsis can be seen as the externalisation of feelings secretly brooding in society, a slow growth towards national consciousness that in the following decades will lead to the tentative creation of Russian unity. This change is even stylistically visible in the film:

the viewer's attention is continuously drawn to the vastness of the world; the whole screen is alive and moving, from the foreground to the most distant corner. Not only Rublev but many other characters can be seen moving and stirring. By means of this extremely vivid mise-en-scène, the eye of the camera becomes the eye of the beholder. The camera often does not select what is the most important in these rich *tableaux*, but leaves it up to the viewer to interpret the many moves and characters. The events not only form the motivation for Rublev's inner struggle, but serve as challenges to which everyone, the viewer included, brings a possible answer. There is also a parallel to be drawn with Rublev's icons: in Russian iconography, the saint is not the central feature, but is presented within a whole, in a unity, and draws its power there from. Icons in an Orthodox church are often elements of an iconostasis with internal thematic complexities that have to be contemplated to provide a full image and interpretation of the icon screen. Once again, it is the sum of all parts, screened from a distance, that provides a bigger unity and reveals a complete portrait, a universal meaning, and in the end an appealing clarity.

The casting of a bell as catalyst of the turning point is not chosen loosely. A bell used to mark the distinction between the city and the country, and was used, as were the icons, to praise God. The casting and ringing of bells was a sacramental act in Moscow. It is estimated that in the sixteenth century, the four hundred churches of Moscow had a total of 5.000 bells. The development of the elaborate and many-tiered Russian bell tower – with its profusion of bells and onion-shaped gables – parallels in many ways that of the iconostasis. The rich 'mauve' ringing of bells so that 'people cannot hear one another in conversation' became the inevitable accompaniment of icon-bearing processions on special feast days. There were almost as many bells and ways to ring them as icons and ways to display them.[39]

Even the effigy of Saint Gregorius on the outside of the bell that Boriska casts exemplifies the link between the catharsis story and the greater historical context (and their mutual reinforcement). The best-known version of the Gregorius legend tells how a dragon that guards the spring in a certain pagan city demands a daily human sacrifice in exchange for supplying the city with water. Every day a youth is chosen at random to be sacrificed. But one day, when that fate threatens to befall the king's daughter he pleads in vain for the princess's life. Just at that moment, Gregorius, a Christian pilgrim, passes by and slays the dragon, thus saving the princess. His act inspires the town's inhabitants to convert to Christianity. For that reason, Saint Gregorius is always represented slaying the dragon to which the children had been sacrificed. In Russia, Saint Gregorius is the symbol of justice and civilization and of the country's unification.[40] It takes but little imagination to see the dragon as Tatar domination and its death as the liberation of the oppressed people from the tyranny of the princes. So the celebration of the people at the first tolling of the new bell can be seen as a confirmation of the changes at hand. This is underlined by Tarkovsky's masterful use of the camera: slow tracking shots link the joyful crowd with the workers and the bell, a final symbolic touch that gives them all one and the same voice. The former contrasts between the internal and external world are erased: everything happens outside and the people mingle together with the clergy as they anxiously watch the bell being hauled up and tolled. While the clergy and the people are united in their newly found happiness, the rulers – the prince and his entourage – remain distant and aloof. Their arrogant attitude clearly shows there is little love lost between the rulers and the people. Or perhaps in this way Tarkovsky wants to show that the princes are aware of the evolution that Russia is undergoing and that the unity of the Church and the people will spell the doom of their little individual fiefdoms.[41]

Andrei Rublev concludes with images of Rublev's rediscovered belief in himself and in his craft.[42] The harmony and vivid colours of his icons mark a triumph over the disharmony of life and offer a moment of reflection for the viewer who is free to crystallise the impressions into a significant whole, tie together the different events and episodes of the film, in the same way that the camera first focuses on details of Rublev's icons and subsequently provides a partial overview of the Trinity icon. The Trinity icon that forms the final fragment of this last sequence, focuses on the values of fraternity, love and faith, the components of Rublev's faith that supply a key to his sense of the absolute. Apart from the stunning rhythm of colours perhaps the most remarkable characteristic of the icon is the unity-in-diversity[43] that brings the different parts of the whole together. Tarkovsky's purpose is to demonstrate the necessity of fraternity, love and faith, and to affirm that the quest for the ultimately unknowable is crucial to the survival of humanity.[44]

Conclusion

In the case of *Andrei Rublev*, knowledge of the historical facts clearly adds an extra dimension to the understanding of the film. The meticulous intertwining and reinforcing of the story lines of Rublev's personal catharsis with the historic events carries a valuable layer of meaning for the viewer. Only then can the film constitute a well-rounded unity with all the pieces of the puzzle joining together in a radiant whole.

And yet, this further dimension is not indispensable for the enjoyment of the film. Many articles and meticulous analyses have been written about *Andrei Rublev* without examining the historical basis of the film. Most critics focus on the story of Rublev's catharsis, which is of course at the heart of the film. My research into the historical basis of the film, however, has taught me that it is only through an understanding of the time frame in which the icon painter lived and worked that *Andrei Rublev* discloses its real secrets.

Notes

1   Felicetti-Liebenfels, W. (1972) *Geschichte der Russischen Ikonenmalerei*. Graz: Akademische Druck-und Verlagsanstalt, pp. 29-30.

2   Milner-Gulland, R. (1980) Art and Architecture of Old Russia, pp. 39-42 in Auty, R. and D. Obolesnky (eds) *An Introduction to Russian Art and Architecture*. Cambridge: Cambridge University Press.

3   For an extensive synopsis of the film, see Johnson, V. and G. Petrie (1994) *The Films of Andrei Tarkovsky: a visual fugue*. Bloomington: Indiana University Press, pp. 265-272.

4   The widest gap is between episode 7 (1412) and episode 8 (1423).

5   Kovàcs, B. and A. Szilàgyi (1987) *Les mondes d'Andreï Tarkovski*. Lausanne: L'Age d'homme, p. 62.

6   Turowskaya, M. (1989) *Tarkovsky: Cinema as Poetry*. London: Faber and Faber, p. 37.

7   Johnson and Petrie (1994), pp. 191-192.

8   Turowskaya (1989), p. 88.

9   Tarkovsky, A. (1986) *Sculpting in Time*. London: The Bodley Head, pp. 78-79.

10 Ferro, M. (1984) *Cinéma et Histoire*. Paris: Gallimard, p. 74. (My translation). Later on, Marc Ferro proposes to consider *Andrei Rublev* as a global interpretation of history that, far more than being a reconstruction, casts light on past events, or their relation to the present. (Ferro (1984), p. 223.)

11 Sorlin, P. (2001) How to Look at an 'Historical Film', p. 37 in Landy M. (ed.) *The Historical Film, History and Memory in Media*. New Jersey: Rutgers University Press.

12 Youngblood, D. (1996) Andrei Rublev, the medieval epic as post-utopian history, p. 130 in Sobchack, V. (ed.) *The Persistence of History*. London: Routledge.

13 Andrei Tarkovsky in an unpublished interview with Aleksandr Lipkov, translated by Robert Bird. [http://www.acs.ucalgary.ca/~tstronds/nostalghia.com/TheTopics/PassionacctoAndrei.html], 30 August 2004.

14 Le Fanu devotes three paragraphs to the historical context in which the movie unfolds; Turowskaya only tells us that 'Rublyov's time was also a time of internecine struggle, of suffering beneath the Tartar yoke, and of many lesser sorrows and troubles.'; Johnson and Petrie place little historical information in the footnotes or appendices; Kovàcs and Szilàgyi explicitly state that history is absent from the film; Youngblood begins her article with twenty lines of historical contextualisation to sum up quickly in a retelling of the story of the film, only to return to the topic of *Andrei Rublev* as 'post-utopian history' in the last pages. An exception is Robert Bird who, in his recent monograph *Andrei Rublev*, devotes the first chapter to the historical context of the figure of Rublev. (Le Fanu, M. (1987) The Cinema of Andrei Tarkovsky. London: British Film Institute, p. 36-37; Turowskaya (1989), p. 37; Johnson and Petrie (1994), p. 312, footnote 9; Kovàcs and Szilàgyi (1987), p. 66; Youngblood, D. (1996) p. 128-129. Bird, R. (2004), Andrei Rublev. London: British Film Institute).

15 Lazarev, V. (2000) *Mosaïques et fresques de l'ancienne Russie*. Paris: Les Editions de l'Amateur, p. 226.

16 Kovàcs and Szilàgyi (1987), p. 62.

17 Rublev and Daniel worked together on the frescos in the church of the Assumption in Vladimir in 1408 by order of the Grand Prince of Moscow. The frescos are only partially preserved, but these fragments contain scenes of a monumental last judgment. (Lazarev (2000), pp. 228-232).

18 The first epistle of Saint Paul to the Corinthians, I, 11, 4-16.

19 Lazarev (2000), p. 235. (My translation).

20 Herlihy, D. (1988) Am I a Camera? Other Reflections on Films and History, pp. 1186-1192 in *American Historical Review*, 93 (5).

21 Austin, G. (2002) Were the peasants really so clean? The Middle Ages in Film, pp. 138-140 in Film History, 14 (2).

22 Rosenstone, R. (1988) History in Images / History in Words: Reflections on the Possibility of Really Putting History onto Film, p. 1178 in American Historical Review 93 (5).

23 The Tatars, allied with the Lithuanians, wanted to fight the Russians, but before they could join the Lithuanians, the Tatars were defeated on 18 September 1380.

24 Andreyev, N. (1976) Appanage and Muscovite Russian, pp.86-87 in Auty R. and D. Obolensky (eds) *An Introduction to Russian History*. Cambridge: Cambridge University Press.

25 Milner-Gulland (1980), p. 28.

26 Bird (2004), p. 13.

27 Billington, J. (1970) *The Icon and the Axe - An Interpretive Study of Russian Culture*. New York: Vintage, p. 14.

28   Andreyev (1976), p. 81.

29   Andreyev (1976), pp. 86-87.

30   Billington (1970), p. 31.

31   Tarkovsky (1986), pp. 89-90.

32   For an extensive overview of production and distribution difficulties, see Johnson and Petrie (1994), pp. 79-85.

33   Johnson and Petrie (1994), p. 79.

34   Figes, O. (2002) *Natasha's Dance - A Cultural History of Russia.* London: Allen Lane, p. 300.

35   Hughes, L. (2003) Inventing Andrei: Soviet and Post-Soviet Views of Andrei Rublev and his Trinity Icon, p. 87 in *Slavonica,* 9 (2).

36   Youngblood (1996) p. 132.

37   Ciment, M. (1969) L'artiste dans l'ancienne Russie et dans l'URSS nouvelle, p. 8 in *Positif,* 18 (8). (My translation).

38   Kovàcs and Szilàgyi (1987), p. 91. (My translation).

39   Billington (1970) pp. 37-39.

40   Alpatov, M. (1975) *Histoire de l'art Russe des origines à la fin du XVIIième siècle.* Paris: Flammarion, p. 121.

41   The whole film can also be read as an allegory of the role of the artist in a totalitarian society, more specifically as a reference to the modus vivendi of Tarkovsky himself and the 1960 Soviet State. Despite the troubles with the authorities the director went through with every movie he made (one reason why he stayed in Italy in the 1980s), he managed to make strong personal films under the totalitarian regime, much alike Rublev himself, who, despite the oppressive social darkness that surrounds him, is able to create light and colour. On this level, Andrei Rublev becomes a plea for artistic freedom, for art in the service of the people, a homage to the imagination against the rules and proscriptions of society, repressive or not. And it is not faith but belief in life and in mankind that makes this possible for Rublev and Boriska just as it does for Tarkovsky.

42   de Baecque, A. (1989) *Andrei Tarkovski.* Paris: Editions de l'Etoile, pp. 100-101.

43   Milner-Gulland (1980) pp. 42-43.

44   Youngblood (1996) p. 141.

Milla Jovovich as Joan of Arc in Luc Besson's *The Messenger* (1999) © Europa Corp. – Gaumont – Columbia

Luc Besson's *The Messenger* (1999): Remaking Joan of Arc for the New Millennium

Brett Bowles

The history of representations surrounding Joan of Arc is extraordinarily rich and varied, spanning 500 years and virtually every conceivable genre.[1] Since the late nineteenth century cinema has played a statistically small but disproportionately influential role in shaping her legend.[2] The Maid of Orléans was one of the first historical subjects seized upon by the so-called seventh art in France, first appearing on the silver screen in an 1898 film directed by Georges Hatot and distributed by Pathé.[3] Although only a 30-second segment of this short survives today (the original version probably lasted no more than a minute or two), it established the dramatic tone for Joan's cinematic career by showing the protagonist on her knees pleading for her life before a clergyman, being tied to the stake by a hooded executioner, and disappearing in a cloud of black smoke. Since then she has inspired more than 30 feature films from some of cinema's most influential directors, including Georges Méliès (*Jeanne d'Arc – Joan of Arc*, 1900), Cecil B. DeMille (*Joan the Woman*, 1916), Carl Theodor Dreyer (*La Passion de Jeanne d'Arc – The Passion of Joan of Arc*, 1928), Marco de Gastyne (*La merveilleuse vie de Jeanne d'Arc – The Marvellous Life of Joan of Arc*, 1929), Victor Fleming (*Joan of Arc*, 1948), Roberto Rossellini (*Giovanna d'Arco al rogo – Joan of Arc at the Stake*, 1954), Otto Preminger (*Saint Joan*, 1957), Robert Bresson (*Le Procès de Jeanne d'Arc – The Trial of Joan of Arc*, 1962), and Jacques Rivette (*Jeanne la Pucelle – Joan the Maid*, 1994). Her exploits have been recounted using a wide range of aesthetic and narrative approaches, including historical realism (Gastyne, Rivette), psychoanalytical expressionism (Dreyer), epic melodrama (De Mille, Fleming), and theological meditation (Bresson, Rossellini).

Despite variations in style and emphasis, none of these films has seriously contested the canonical account of Joan's piety, patriotism, and selflessness.[4] This implicit inviolability is understandable in light of her story's exceptional power and versatility as an ideological tool. Over the years movies about Joan have promoted a kaleidoscope of divergent, often directly antagonistic agendas: exhorting the United States to join the First World War (DeMille); glorifying Hitler as a human instrument of divine will (*Das Mädchen Joanna – Joan the Girl*, Gustav Ucicky, 1935); celebrating the role of women in the French Resistance during the Second World War (*Joan of Paris*, Robert Stevenson, 1942), and urging American vigilance against Communism during the early days of the Cold War (*Joan of Arc*, Victor Fleming, 1948), to name only a few.

Challenges to Joan's legend have long attracted controversy and public protest, from the licentious, biographical parody that Voltaire published in 1755 under the title *La Pucelle d'Orléans* (*The Maid of Orléans*) to the infamous 'Thalamas Affair' of 1904. Voltaire's irreverence prompted public burning of the book in Paris and Geneva, a nine-year prison sentence for its French printer, and widespread calls for the philosopher's extradition from Switzerland to stand trial. Amédée Thalamas, a staunchly secular history professor at the prestigious Lycée Condorcet, met a similar fate when he failed a student who wrote that Joan was 'a religious glory who came to bring France back to Christ.' After a high-profile public hearing that sparked a flurry of violent street demonstrations pitting Socialist militants against Catholic members of the *Action Française*, the Municipal Council of Paris rejected Thalamas's defence that Joan was simply 'a courageous peasant who had auditory hallucinations which she claimed to be of divine origin' and reprimanded him for an act of *lèse-patrie*. The judgement was all the more telling given the French government's firm commitment to the official secularisation of the Third Republic, which would take place the following year.[5]

Building on Voltaire and Thalamas, Luc Besson's *Jeanne d'Arc* (*The Messenger*, 1999) achieved a provocative new level of revisionism by presenting Joan not as an enlightened martyr or a precocious patriot, but as a vengeful schizophrenic whose all-consuming desire to crush the English stemmed from their brutal rape and murder of her sister during the Hundred Years War. Besson forces the heroine (Milla Jovovich) to face the fallacy of her own myth through an enigmatic monk (Dustin Hoffman) who appears while she awaits trial. The Hoffman character, named in the credits as The Conscience, can also be seen as the voice of historical scepticism about Joan's legend and of the belief that waging war in the name of a religious or nationalistic cause is never fully altruistic. Though critics lambasted *The Messenger* as bad history and formulaic cinema – pointing to factual inaccuracies, Besson's Hollywood production values, and his portrayal of Joan as an eroticised action hero – the film clearly made an impact on the French public, selling almost 3.000.000 tickets and ranking among the year's biggest hits.

This chapter reevaluates *The Messenger* by situating it in a long line of films about Joan and by comparing its representation of history with two classic nineteenth-century texts that first made her a national hero and a popular-culture icon. I would like to suggest that while *The Messenger* may qualify as mediocre cinema, its attempt to rewrite a revered representational tradition provides valuable insight into the impact of mass-media historiography on French identity and raises key questions about the evolution of nationalist discourse in twenty-first-century European culture.

Nineteenth-Century Joan: Michelet and Lavisse

As a basis for evaluating Besson's portrayal of Joan, it is worthwhile recalling the circumstances in which she was rediscovered in the nineteenth century after largely disappearing from view from the Renaissance through the Enlightenment. The modern image of Joan as patriotic martyr resulted from a convergence of factors: her appropriation for political purposes by Napoleon, who reinstituted and financed the annual series of Johannic festivals commemorating her life and exploits; her celebration in Romantic literature by authors such as Chateaubriand; perhaps most important, the emergence of France as a nation-state and of history as distinct academic discipline dedicated to forging a sense of shared patrimony and identity.[6]

Among the first historians to rescue Joan from oblivion was Jules Michelet, who devoted a chapter to her in volume five of his monumental *Histoire de France* (1841). Michelet's innovation – a distinct departure from previous histories – was to base his narrative not on popular legend, but an extensive corpus of fifteenth-century primary sources compiled by Jules Quicherat, his junior colleague at the *Société d'Histoire de France*.[7] Michelet drew extensively on the transcripts of Joan's 1431 trial at Rouen and the subsequent rehabilitation hearing initiated by her mother in 1455, integrating Joan's responses to her judges with testimony from contemporary witnesses and his own characteristic brand of patriotic lyricism. 'Yes, Joan of Arc was a saint in both religious and patriotic terms,' he exclaims in his conclusion.

'What legend could be more lovely than this true story? But one must take care not to make it into a legend; one must scrupulously preserve all its pieces, even the most pathetic, and acknowledge its touching and terrible reality. [...] The Saviour of France was destined to be a woman. France was herself a woman. From the beginning she had a woman's capriciousness, but also her endearing tenderness, natural compassion, and excellence.'[8]

By using primary sources to craft a reverently patriotic interpretation of Joan, Michelet established the narrative conventions that would dominate her historical, literary, and cinematic representations until the mid-twentieth century. The prolonged success of this model lay not only in its obvious ideological appeal for a developing nation-state, but also in its immense commercial value. Shortly after its publication in 1841, the volume of *Histoire de France* containing the chapter on Joan became the best selling in the series. By 1853 popular demand was such that the chapter was reissued separately in Hachette's *Bibliothèque des chemins de fer*, a low-priced collection of paperbacks sold at train stations and newspaper kiosks. This edition became one of the most popular books in France between 1850 and 1900, reprinted eleven times during that period.[9]

Beginning in 1884, Michelet's history of Joan was supplemented, and gradually supplanted, by Ernest Lavisse's *Histoire de France, cours moyen*, the renowned textbook that definitively imprinted the modern image of Joan onto French consciousness via the recently founded public school system.[10] An integral component of the national renewal campaign prompted by France's humiliating defeat at the hands of Prussia and the loss of Alsace-Lorraine, Lavisse's text quickly became the standard bearer of a *histoire providentielle* whose guiding themes were France's divine mission, cultural grandeur, and above all, unity through the ages. Lavisse's originality lay in his account of Joan's divine voices, which replaced the classic declarative formula used by Michelet and previous textbook authors, 'Joan heard voices,' with 'Joan thought she heard voices,' an intentionally equivocal turn of phrase designed to satisfy believers and non-believers alike. In a further revision of Michelet, Lavisse also refrained from attributing the voices specifically to Saints Michael, Catherine, and Margaret, as well as from quoting their conversations with Joan.[11]

To console Catholics for Joan's apparent loss of conviction and Bishop Cauchon's role in her execution (a point Michelet also stressed), Lavisse emphasised Cauchon's loyalty to the English and the benevolence of a Dominican monk named Jean Massieu who comforted Joan during her execution by holding aloft a cross.[12] Otherwise, however, Lavisse followed Michelet closely, making 'Jésus' the heroine's dying word and concluding with an italicised paragraph that combines the secular and the religious, using the ideologically neutral theme of patriotic martyrdom: 'In no other country does one find a story as beautiful as Joan's. All Frenchmen must love and honour the memory of this young girl who loved France so much and who died for us.'[13]

Pre-War Joan: Dreyer and Gastyne

Although Lavisse's attempt at reconciliation did not quell the growing ideological battle over Joan, there was little controversy surrounding her on-screen portrayal between the end of the nineteenth century and the Second World War. All the films released during this first phase of Joan's cinematic history adhere closely to the narrative conventions established by Michelet and Lavisse. Three works stand out: Méliès's *Joan of Arc* (1900), Dreyer's *The Passion of Joan of Arc* (1928) and Gastyne's *The Marvellous Life of Joan of Arc* (1929). In addition to using highly didactic inter-titles to explain and contextualise the action taking place on screen, in some cases quoting the historians directly, Méliès and Gastyne base the visual composition of many shots on nineteenth-century iconography.[14] The result is a cinematic history lesson that transposes the classic episodes viewers had learned in school: Joan's celestial visions, her pilgrimage to Chinon, the liberation of Orléans, the coronation of Charles VII at Reims, Joan's capture at Compiègne, her imprisonment and trial, and her death at the stake in Rouen. These films gave the story a new emotional depth by allowing the first generation of movie-goers to experience Joan's patriotic martyrdom visually, and thereby to identify with her more closely than ever.

Méliès used innovative special effects to depict Joan's visions of Saints Margaret and Catherine, but financial and technological limitations prevented him from making a realistic, full-length rendering of Joan's life. Gastyne completed the task twenty-five years later in a big-budget production featuring lavish sets (the reconstructed marketplace at Rouen is especially impressive), extensive on-location shooting (at Reims cathedral and in the Tarn department, where the well-preserved fortress of Carcassonne stood in for medieval Orléans), high-quality replica costumes and accessories (including swords, armour, crossbows, trebuchets), and non-professional extras. The battle scenes at Orléans display a savage intensity unmatched in French silent cinema, thanks to sweeping cavalry charges and gory hand-to-hand combat captured in a frenetically paced montage and dizzying variety of camera angles. Gastyne gave the battle an epic scale by using a newly developed anamorphic camera lens called Hypergonar (the predecessor of modern CinemaScope) which maximised frame width and depth of field. Despite critical acclaim and a strong performance by Simone Genevois in the title role, the film was overshadowed commercially because its premier in late 1929 coincided with the arrival of the first talking pictures in Europe.

Dreyer's *The Passion of Joan of Arc*, released a year earlier, contrasts with the work of Gastyne and Méliès because of its narrow synchronic focus, expressionist aesthetic, and emphasis on the Church's persecution of non-conformist individual faith.[15] Often characterised as 'Protestant' in tone, *The Passion* is by far the most critically engaged of the early films about Joan. Not coincidentally, it was also a thoroughly international production that teamed the Danish director with French actors, a pan-European crew, and German distributor Tobis. Rather than telling Joan's entire life story, Dreyer limits himself to the trial and execution, using sparse inter-titles composed primarily of her own words from the trial transcripts. In the interest of historical authenticity, Dreyer also hired noted medievalist Pierre Champion, who had several years earlier published an authoritative two-volume study of the trial, to supervise the writing of the screenplay and the mise-en-scène.[16] Dreyer's cinematography was exceptional in its use of extreme, seemingly inexorable close-ups to create a detailed psychoanalytical profile of Joan (played by the incomparable Renée Falconetti) and her judges at Rouen. Whereas she appears by turns humble, proud, confused, terrified, and courageous, they are condescending, manipulative, ruthless, and sadistic.

The film made a deep impression precisely because, as one contemporary reviewer put it, 'one does not find the images of French history that school textbooks have engraved in our memory.'[17] Other critics described the film as 'an anguish-laden tragedy that practically tortures the spectator at the same time as the Maid'[18] and 'an experience too cruel for sensitive souls.'[19] By shocking the expectations of spectators accustomed to non-threatening stock images, Dreyer effectively tested the narrative limits of the classic Third-Republic account of Joan and pushed her image as patriotic martyr to the breaking point.

Post-War Joan: Rossellini and Bresson

After *The Passion of Joan of Arc* there was little more that cinema could do with the canonical narrative established by Michelet and Lavisse, which perhaps explains why only one full-length feature about Joan was made in Europe over the next twenty-five years.[20] Roberto Rossellini broke the long silence in 1954 with *Joan of Arc at the Stake*, a filmed version of his stage production based on a 1938 oratorio by Paul Claudel (words) and Arthur Honegger (music).[21] In 1962 Robert Bresson followed with *The Trial of Joan of Arc*, a 'Jansenist' interpretation that serves as a counterpoint to Dreyer. Together these films make up the second phase in Joan's cinematic history, preserving the traditional image of Joan as a martyr to political and religious corruption while minimising the patriotic dimension of her sacrifice and suspending her agency as a national saviour. Their emphasis, at once simpler and more profound, falls on individual spirituality: Joan struggles to make sense of her life and her faith, thereby inviting spectators to do the same.

Joan of Arc at the Stake, which features Rossellini's then-wife Ingrid Bergman in the lead, fragments the linear narrative presentation of previous accounts by telling Joan's story though non-sequential flashbacks, beginning with her death. Rossellini rejects neo-realism in favour of a medieval aesthetic that combines allegory (the Rouen judges appear disguised as pigs and goats) with minimalism (simple painted backdrops are the only scenery used and Bergman wears throughout the burlap smock of a condemned heretic). Caught in a liminal space between heaven and earth, Joan reflects on the major episodes of her life as they are re-enacted before her. Her self-evaluation takes the form of a dialogue with an enigmatic Dominican monk (identified as 'Brother Dominic' in the credits) who acts as a serene devil's advocate to test her capacity to forgive injustice and to repent for her own misdeeds.

After supporting the ecclesiastical court's accusations of heresy and citing Joan's violations of Catholic dogma (wearing men's clothes, fighting battles on feast days, disobeying her parents' order not to leave home, etc.), Dominic urges her not to pardon the Church for condemning her, then criticises her pride in having resisted the inquisitors. Though she wavers at times, Joan manages to resist these inflammatory tactics, free herself from all ties to the Church, and accept her martyrdom as part of a cosmic cycle in which life and death nourish each other eternally, a realisation expressed metaphorically near the end of the film when she recalls the annual withering and rebirth of a favourite tree near Domrémy (the so-called 'Fairies' Tree' mentioned in the trial transcripts). In the final scene, Dominic disappears and Joan stands alone on an empty set, bathed in celestial light, having finally attained a state of divine grace.

Bresson's *The Trial of Joan of Arc* also focuses on spirituality, but expresses a profound scepticism about the accuracy of retrospective representation and the possibility of understanding Joan. Whereas Gastyne begins his film with a quotation from Michelet ('Let us always remember that our motherland was born from the heart of a woman, from her tenderness, and from the tears of blood she shed for us'), Bresson opens with an on-screen text stating that we possess no reliable physical portrait of Joan and no identifiable gravesite, only the transcripts of her trial at Rouen and of the rehabilitation hearing initiated by her mother twenty-five years later. To drive home the point, he later inserts a close-up of the court scribe's hand that stops writing at a signal from Bishop Cauchon. The image is particularly emphatic since the film is composed primarily of static, medium-range shots which, in sharp contrast to Dreyer, intentionally maintain a spatial and emotional distance between Joan and the spectator.

By repeatedly filming Joan through the keyhole of her cell, Bresson piques a desire for intimacy that he leaves tantalizingly unfulfilled and forces viewers to share the frustrated voyeurism of the English guards who spy on and speculate crudely about their captive. Joan's inscrutability and our frustration are further exacerbated by the rapid, uninflected tone in which the actors deliver their lines and by their expressionless faces. The judges exhibit none of the sadistic glee or condescension so prominent in *The Passion*, while Joan (played by Florence Carrez) shows only two brief moments of emotion: tearful despair in her cell when she believes her celestial voices have abandoned her, and panic after she is condemned to death.

Though this approach impoverishes the film affectively and historiographically, it successfully frames Joan's trial as a Jansenist parable in which the attainment of grace requires overcoming belief in salvation based on good deeds and without suffering. Until the end of *The Trial* Joan clings to the conviction that God will spare her life in recognition of her divine mission. Citing as proof the fact that she did not die after jumping from the tower of Beaurevoir prison while attempting to escape, she insists that her 'martyrdom is the pain [she] suffer[s] in prison' and that she 'will be delivered by a great victory during the proceedings.' She recognises her fateful error only after confessing to heresy in order to avoid execution and her voices condemn her for interfering with God's plan. In the end, Jansenist Joan can achieve spiritual purity only by recanting her confession and freely welcoming death by fire. As Bresson explained in an interview shortly after the film's release: 'Joan wills herself to accept God's grace even though doing so precipitates the end of her earthly life and the beginning of a purely spiritual existence. All the schemes of the ecclesiastical court to condemn Joan served only to fulfil the promise of her faith. [...] In this film I tried to find an ahistorical truth with historical words, but without recourse to theatricality or masquerade.'[22]

Fin-de-Siècle Joan: Rivette and Besson

Following *The Trial of Joan of Arc* Joan disappeared from European cinema for thirty years, eventually resurfacing in Jacques Rivette's two-part *Jeanne la Pucelle* (*Joan the Maid*, 1994), then in Besson's *The Messenger* (1999). As the third and final phase in Joan's cinematic history, these films continue the process of distancing begun at mid-century by demystifying Joan completely, stripping away her roles as precocious patriot and enlightened martyr in favour of a more earthly, realistic persona. Rivette demonstrates a profound scepticism regarding the miraculous aspects of Joan's saga by refusing to represent her divine revelations, her vision of a sword bearing five crosses buried behind the church altar at Sainte-Catherine-de-Fierbois, or her sign from God at Chinon when meeting Charles VII. *Joan the Maid* places historical accuracy above all else, incorporating only those elements substantiated by primary sources from the period or by the research of recognised scholars in an attempt to rehumanise the legendary protagonist and render her more accessible to modern viewers.[23]

Rivette's Joan (interpreted by Sandrine Bonnaire) is a thoroughly unspectacular figure who sobs in pain when wounded, shivers from sleeping on the cold ground, displays adolescent impetuousness when her wishes are questioned, and purges her self-doubt through prayer and confession. Along the way, the audience is treated to a meticulous reconstruction of the Maid's daily existence which focuses on episodes overlooked in previous films: the misogyny she endured at all stages of her journey; her long wait at Vaucouleurs; the preliminary examination by an ecclesiastical jury at Poitiers; her military training at Chinon, and her relationship with Jeanne de Luxembourg while interned at Beaurevoir. More generally, Rivette's careful attention to ethnographic detail provides insight into the harsh material conditions of fifteenth-century life, simple peasant piety and the primitive state of medieval European medicine.

In conjunction with its documentary realism, the film offers an unprecedented richness of historical exposition that shows how Joan's contemporaries could believe in her divine mission (a folk prophecy that a virgin from Lorraine would save France); how her army was financed (taxes levied on besieged towns such as Orléans and loans from wealthy lords intent on usurping royal power such as Georges de La Trémoïlle), and why Jean de Luxembourg, a staunch Burgundian ally, hesitated four months before delivering her to the English (his aunt's moral objections). Most important, viewers see that it was for fear of rape by her guards at Rouen that Joan reverted to wearing men's clothes and broke her oath of abjuration, thereby condemning herself to the stake.

Yet this high level of intellectual sophistication ultimately causes the film to fail on a narrative and emotive level because its accumulation of detail is not balanced by the scenes of high drama that viewers have come to expect from Joan-of-Arc movies. Rivette spends thirty minutes on military preparations for the assault on Orléans, depicting the fabrication of assault ladders and debates over strategy, but devotes barely five minutes to the battle itself. Like the rest of the action, it is rendered in a static, homogeneous series of medium-range shots without accompanying music. Formally speaking, the sequence is decidedly unimpressive by any standard, especially when compared to Gastyne's fast-paced montage of close-ups and wide-angle panoramic views sixty-five years earlier. Joan's subsequent attack on Paris is equally banal, appearing little more than a half-hearted skirmish undermined by low troop morale and the taboo of fighting on a feast day.

More surprising still, the film skips the trial at Rouen entirely and closes with a mundane rendering of Joan's execution. Lasting just under a minute and a half, the scene is a truncated collage of Bresson and Dreyer: after a metonymic close-up of Joan's feet walking toward the scaffold, she is chained to the stake, the fire is lit, and smoke rises around her as she repeats the word 'Jésus' three times in a rising tone of voice. Amidst flames building in the foreground and Jean Massieu holding up a cross for her to see, Joan's head disappears and the screen abruptly goes black. The shot is visually disappointing in its lack of originality and has the feel of an obligatory, anti-climactic afterthought.

Joan the Maid received generally positive reviews from critics, almost all of whom appreciated its historiographic value and its attempt to dispel the representational clichés surrounding Joan. *Les Echos* praised the film as 'slow and subtle magic full of rare authenticity'. *Cahiers du cinéma* added that it 'frees Joan's image from all political and aesthetic prejudices [...] while transforming her into a character incredibly close to us.'[24] Others, however, could not quite forgive the film's shortcomings as spectacle and entertainment. As the *Mensuel du cinéma* put it: 'Joan of Arc moves through this film as though absent from herself. Building a story around a hollow character can be very productive, but it is difficult to explain the terrible aphasia from which Rivette's film suffers. His overly scrupulous attempt to avoid all possible pitfalls has made Joan into an anaemic body that can be defined only by default.'[25] Commercially the film was a flop, selling a combined total of fewer than 144.000 tickets in France.[26]

Luc Besson's *The Messenger*, released in October 1999, offers the most radical departure to date from the classic image of Joan as patriotic martyr by using an eclectic style that draws on the entirety of Joan's cinematic history. The film opens with a motif present in virtually all the earlier films: a didactic printed text establishing the historical background of Joan's story and her importance as national hero. While blood spills over a parchment map of France to mark the territory conquered by the English between 1420 and 1429, viewers are reminded of the key events following the Treaty of Troyes and that 'France is going through the darkest period in its history. Only one thing can save it… A miracle.' Though the tone is superficially reminiscent of Lavisse and Michelet, Besson and co-writer Andrew Birkin (who also wrote *The Name of the Rose* screenplay) are in fact piquing the spectator's expectations as a prelude to dashing them later in the film.

The initial portrait of Joan as a thoroughly happy, devout child who confesses two or three times a day and frolics through fields of vibrant poppies quickly gives way to a defining psychological trauma: she witnesses an English mercenary brutally murder, then rape her older sister Catherine while pillaging Domrémy. Joan subsequently develops an intense complex of survivor's guilt and a desire for vengeance against the English. In addition to refusing to say 'Amen' at the dinner table, she tearfully berates her village priest, saying: 'Why did Catherine have to die instead of me? It was my fault, I was late; she gave me her hiding place. Why did God save me? I know Jesus says to love your enemies, but I can't. I just want the English to burn in Hell for ever and ever!' Her torment only intensifies her obsessive religious tendencies, prompting her to break into a church and gorge herself on communion wine although she is not yet of age. At first glance this revisionist version of events will strike even the most open-minded historian as tendentious and irresponsible. Although Joan's family did in fact flee Domrémy in mid-1428 for fear of attack by the English and she did have an older sister named Catherine who died in 1429, there is no evidence that Catherine was raped or killed by the English.[27] However, there is no proof to the contrary either, and the fabrication serves a legitimate historiographic purpose: to ask if there might not have been some traumatic worldly event that sparked Joan's purportedly divine, patriotic quest. Such a scenario is not outside the realm of possibility given the fragmentary information we have regarding Joan's childhood, most of which comes from the rehabilitation hearing of 1456. If she had been guided by some force other than the hand of God, witnesses would not have dared reveal it for fear of undermining her growing legend and Charles VII's ongoing efforts to legitimise his crown. In essence, Besson invites spectators to suspend disbelief in order to explore the possibility of a Joan driven by personal, less-than-noble motivations, and thus to rethink the significance of her story.

To this end, the film uses digital technology and special effects to represent Joan's visions as symptoms of mental illness rather than spiritual enlightenment. Whereas Dreyer, Bresson, and Rivette avoided the subject altogether, and Gastyne showed Joan conversing placidly with the ghostly apparitions of Saints Margaret and Catherine, Besson has Joan fall to the ground unconscious and experience an accelerated series of vivid, disjointed images that resemble LSD-induced (or in the medieval context, ergot-induced) hallucinations. As her eyes dart back and forth, she is transported to a forest clearing, deafened by ringing bells, swept up in a dizzying dance with an enigmatic Jesus-like figure who rises from a stone throne, and is presented with a sword that materialises beside her. A subsequent hallucination in which a stained-glass window of Saint Michael shatters and comes to life convinces Joan definitively that she is a divine messenger charged with saving France.

In a further departure from convention, the film embraces the generic devices of Hollywood westerns and action movies, transforming Joan from a pious, self-possessed peasant into an almost superhuman hit woman who will stop at nothing to exact justice. She thus adopts the persona of Besson's protagonists from *La Femme Nikita* (*Nikita*, 1990) and, with a change of gender, *Léon* (*The Professional*, 1994).[28] Her simmering personal vendetta becomes all too clear in the hyper-violent battle scenes at Orléans, where she hacks through enemy hordes on a white horse and removes with one hand the arrow shot into her shoulder. Though the cinematography has a contemporary feel thanks to swooping aerial views, the use of slow motion to highlight detail, and the rapid juxtaposition of wide-angle shots with evocative close-ups, the aesthetic of gory realism and psychological intensity owe just as much to *The Marvellous Life of Joan of Arc* as to *Braveheart* (1995). In fact, Besson's long-range shots of the French army scaling the fortress walls and dramatic focus on episodes of bloody single combat echo Gastyne directly, as does the later sequence depicting Joan's tearful remorse and horror at the carnage caused by the battle. In light of such parallels, Besson's claim to having systematically ignored previous films about Joan is difficult to accept.[29]

Whatever the case, *The Messenger* is indisputably modern in the eroticism it creates by casting Milla Jovovich in the lead role. Already internationally known as a L'Oréal cosmetics model, Jovovich had married Besson shortly after starring in his science-fiction blockbuster *The Fifth Element* (1997).

According to Besson, 'the role of Joan was made for her; both are ill at ease in their century, inspired, crazy, hypersensitive, and capable of anything.'[30] This personal infatuation is played out on screen in a quintessential male fantasy that mixes fetishistic sexual desire with misogyny: a beautiful young woman briefly usurps a phallic signifier of male power (whether Nikita's .44 Magnum or Joan's sword) and provocatively dominates the men who surround her, but in the end succumbs to hysteria and in so doing reaffirms traditional, gender-based power relations.

The sexual subtext surfaces explicitly on two occasions. The first, an elaborately staged, utterly ahistorical scene in which Joan's virginity is publicly confirmed by a group of nuns, features amplified sound effects and suggestive, voyeuristic camera work that stops just short of full visual disclosure. The second, a more gratuitous instance, occurs during Joan's third set of visions, in which Jovovich suddenly appears lying on her back while digitally enhanced grass covers her breasts and binds her wrists and feet. Here again Besson stops short of nudity in favour of titillation, but the effect is no less disturbing because of the parallel between this imaginary bondage and the ensuing prison scenes where Jovovich is shackled, beaten, and nearly raped by her guards.

The film's crudely adolescent psychology and violent eroticism cannot help but undermine its historiographic value, which thankfully re-emerges in the final half hour following the abrupt arrival of a cloaked figure in Joan's cell at Beaurevoir. Identified in the credits as 'The Conscience' and played by Dustin Hoffman, the character serves the same dramatic function as Brother Dominic in Rossellini's *Joan of Arc at the Stake* by forcing Joan to judge herself and her faith. Whereas Dominic tested Joan's power to forgive but acknowledged the nobility of her deeds, The Conscience summarily dismisses her divine mission as an exercise in arrogance. On his first appearance, he asks with Voltairean disdain: 'How can you possibly believe that God, the creator of Heaven and Earth, the source of all life, could need you? Don't you think He's big enough to deliver His own messages?' The Conscience visits Joan on three subsequent occasions after her transferral to Rouen, each time bringing her closer to admitting that her patriotic crusade was in fact a pretext for avenging her murdered sister. Part trial lawyer, part psychoanalyst, he systematically deconstructs Joan's supposed signs from God, in particular the sword she found in a field during a vision. After showing her several worldly means by which the weapon might have come to lie there, he shows her a sword descending from the heavens surrounded by a halo of ethereal light and concludes wryly: 'Yet from an infinite number of possibilities, you had to pick divine intervention. You didn't see what was, you saw what you wanted to see.'

After Joan agrees to the abjuration offered by the court in exchange for leniency, The Conscience informs her that she 'has just signed away God's existence' and that 'in the end it was [she] who abandoned Him.' This revelation, combined with the threat of rape by her guards, prompts her to recant. Sentenced to death, she requests a last confession and is refused, admitting instead to The Conscience that she fought to satiate her hatred for the English rather than to serve God: 'I saw so many signs, signs that I wanted to see. I fought out of revenge and despair. I was all the things people believe they're allowed to be when they're fighting for a cause. I was proud and stubborn ... and selfish ... and cruel.' As an oratorio performed by the London Session Orchestra and the Metro Voices slowly builds to a crescendo, The Conscience absolves Joan formally and the camera cuts to a Dreyeresque extreme close-up of her contorted face burning at the stake. The film ends with a rapid montage that juxtaposes medium-range shots of Joan's body being consumed by flames with close-ups of her feet and a cross held aloft amidst swirling smoke.

Impressive as it is cinematically, this final sequence is also ingenious in the way it adapts the historical record of Joan's trial. The ecclesiastical tribunal did in fact accuse her of obstinacy (for disobeying her parents' order not to leave home), cruelty (for hating the English and causing so much bloodshed), and selfishness (for accepting money, horses, and other material rewards from Charles VII for herself and her family), but she consistently asserted that any sins she had committed would be forgiven because she was doing God's will.[31] Indeed, Joan believed that her sole transgression of faith – having falsely abjured 'for fear of the fire'-would be absolved by her recantation and acceptance of death. She asked to confess and to receive communion one last time, which Cauchon surprisingly allowed.[32]

By having The Conscience voice the tribunal's accusations against Joan (significantly, it is he who first suggests that she was selfish and cruel), the film restores their legitimacy and saddles Joan with a complex of self-recrimination which by all evidence never existed. If on the surface this modification appears historiographically irresponsible and ethically questionable, it nevertheless articulates a legitimate critique of Joan's character based on a close reading of period documents. Historians such as Régine Pernoud and Marina Warner have long admired the impenetrable aplomb and wry irony with which Joan resisted the tribunal's obvious gender prejudices, venality, and narrowness of faith, but evidence of her own self-satisfied arrogance and ethical misconduct has escaped scrutiny.

These attitudes are reflected most clearly in Joan's testimony regarding Franquet d'Arras, a Burgundian mercenary captain who was taken prisoner for ransom at Orléans. Joan attempted to exchange him for a Parisian nobleman (known as the *Seigneur de l'Ours*) in English custody, but after learning that her hostage was already dead she handed Franquet over to a French secular court which tried and executed him for treason and murder. Such conduct directly violated the medieval code of war, but Joan felt no remorse in the matter, reporting simply that she told the presiding French magistrate 'since the man I wanted to get is dead, do with [Franquet] whatever justice requires.'[33] Joan's rather coldly utilitarian disregard for the lives of her enemies and haughty sense of moral superiority are expressed most clearly in her famous letter to the English demanding their withdrawal from Orléans, which reads in part: 'If you do not do so, wait for news of the Maid who will come and see you shortly to your great misfortune. [...] If your people do not obey, I will have them all killed. [...] And believe firmly that the King of Heaven will give the Maid more strength than you could muster against her and her good soldiers by any assault; and in the fray we shall see whom God in Heaven deems right.'[34]

Though in their original context the Manichean view of morality and self-righteous, politicised megalomania implicit in Joan's words were taken as signs of her divine agency, 500 years later they appear fundamentally irreconcilable with modern humanism and the lessons of twentieth-century history. Besson thus offers a Voltairean corrective to Joan's historical image, forcing her to admit her flaws in order to merit divine salvation. Despite the film's non-traditional aesthetic and revisionist portrayal of Joan's motivations, its ending actually reaffirms the theological message of Dreyer and Rossellini: institutionalised religion is a dangerous, corrupting force that masks the truth and perverts morality; divine grace must be individual and can come only through honest self-judgement. *The Messenger* goes a step further by levelling the same charge against nationalism, which is portrayed as a weapon used by political elites at the expense of common citizens. In both the film and in reality, Charles VII withdraws his support for Joan after being anointed at Reims to protect his newly acquired power and pursue negotiations with the Burgundians.

Unfortunately, the film's philosophical critique was lost on most French critics.[35] Writing in *L'Humanité*, Jean Roy called *The Messenger* a 'stew of wasted talents ... which avoids offering any reading of history, be it didactic, spiritual, psychoanalytic, or other. What is terrifying in this film is that after hours of contemplation one still can't understand why Besson made it, except perhaps to repudiate altogether what we call cinema.'[36] A still more scathing review of the film came from *Cinémathèque de Toulouse* co-director Michel Roca, who bluntly accused Besson of having produced 'a banal commodity tailored to the American market without any vision or conception of history. The last Joan of the century dishonours cinema's first hundred years. Perhaps it even constitutes one of the century's defining characteristics: a loss of values and referents, not to mention spirituality and order. Let us quickly re-release the other Joan films, those that still speak to our hearts, our souls, our sensitivity. It is wrong to offend Joan.'[37]

Though justified in historiographic and aesthetic terms, in reality such denunciations were motivated by the sentiment that Besson had committed a double act of national treason. In addition to discrediting France's most revered patriotic martyr as a vengeful schizophrenic, he had implicitly repudiated the French *cinéma de qualité* tradition by embracing Hollywood production values, casting non-French actors in key roles (Jovovich as Joan, Hoffman as The Conscience, John Malkovich as Charles VII, Faye Dunaway as Yolande de Sicile), and recording the dialogue in English to facilitate international distribution. Moreover, *The Messenger* also violated the long-standing principle of *exception culturelle*, which defines French cinema as an art that should remain untainted by commercial pressures. In order to preserve a director's creative independence and ensure the survival of high-quality, small-budget pictures unable to compete with the mass-market studio productions imported from the United States, the French government has long offered filmmakers a variety of subsidies through the Ministry of Culture and organisations such as the *Centre National de la Cinématographie*. Besson emphatically rejected this model, shooting the film on location in the Czech Republic and assembling the film's 59.000.000-Euro budget himself. In interviews he proudly noted his use of an entirely French crew, but made no apologies for targeting an international audience or for relying primarily on American and British actors, even claiming that they were superior to French talent.[38]

In the context of late 1999 *The Messenger* also served as a lightning rod for ongoing debates over the future of French cultural specificity in the face of the increasingly powerful European Union, the impending arrival of the Euro currency, and mass-media globalisation. Two weeks after the film's premier, Pierre Bourdieu delivered a provocative, highly publicised address to the multi-national administrative council of the *Musée de la Télévision et de la Radio* (MTR) in which he excoriated the 'eruption of commercial cinema and the attendant regression from a work of art to a product which uses technical resources, special effects, or stars to manipulate or to satisfy the base impulses of the spectator.' Bourdieu also endorsed the notion of cultural exception, but noted its potential to serve 'a form of nationalism linked to archaic means of preserving sovereignty.' The ultimate goal of organisations such as the MTR, he concluded, should be to cultivate 'cultural resistance against the expansion of private commercial interests and to defend universal works of art produced by the denationalised international union of creators.'[39]

In *Cahiers du cinéma*, film historian Thierry Jousse defended Besson in exactly those terms, crediting him with 'creating something unique in world cinema which is neither completely French nor completely Hollywoodian ... . He heads an imaginary kingdom whose equivalent, for better or for worse, one can find nowhere else and which is thus a cultural exception in the strictest sense of the term. For this boldness alone, even if it sometimes borders on naiveté, Besson deserves special consideration and his Joan of Arc deserves salvation.'[40] A vocal minority of critics concurred by showing appreciation for *The Messenger*'s irreverence towards the traditional image of the Maid. Jean-Michel Frodon wrote approvingly that 'Besson's Joan fights not to kick the English out of France, but to kick clichés out of the story,'[41] while an article in *Libération* aptly titled '*Jeanne dépucelée*' ('Joan deflowered') praised Besson for having 'updated the heroine haunted by voices and making a strangely perceptive film about the unfulfilment of desire in excess—his best work to date.'[42] Most important, Roca's virulent denunciation of Besson drew an equally polemic response that denounced the critic's 'self-satisfied devotion to a picturesque Joan steeped in stainless steel nationalism. Let us hope that in future we will be spared such fits of historical outrage and dusty-museum cinephilia, which are tantamount to rashly erected gallows or kangaroo courts.'[43]

The French public agreed with that sentiment, for *The Messenger* sold just under 3.000.000 tickets in three months, placing it ninth overall for the year but second only to *Astérix et Obélix contre César* (*Astérix and Obélix versus César*, 1999) among French productions.[44] The film also won numerous awards, including Césars for best sound and costumes and Lumières for best picture and best director. In so doing *The Messenger* renewed public debate over Joan's significance and sparked a flurry of new texts on the subject aimed at students. Numerous middle- and high-school history teachers took their classes to see the film, and thirty-eight local stations in the Radio France network ran daily features on Joan in the weeks following its release.[45]

Whether the film's popularity can reliably be interpreted as evidence of a growing popular dissatisfaction with nationalist discourses inherited from the nineteenth century is open to debate, yet that conclusion does find support if we take a broader look at the development of French historical cinema over the past decade. Together with sombre 'heritage films' memorialising traumatic aspects of the nation's recent past – the workers' movement in Claude Berri's *Germinal* (1993), the Great War in Bertrand Tavernier's *Le Capitaine Conan* (*Captain Conan*, 1996), the Occupation in Berri's *Lucie Aubrac* (1997) and *Laissez-Passer* (*Safe Conduct*, Tavernier, 2001) – there has emerged a highly successful sub-genre satirising events or issues that are no longer problematic for the French collective memory and identity – the inequalities of feudal society in Jean-Marie Poiré's *Les Visiteurs* (*The Visitors*, Jean-Marie Poiré, 1993) and the invasion of Gaul by the Romans in *Astérix and Obélix versus César*.[46] Besson's film falls somewhere between the two genres by blending serious historical questioning with mass-market entertainment. Though *The Messenger*'s historiographic and philosophical value has been obscured by its garish packaging, there is reason to believe that this latest cinematic reinvention of Joan marks a collective willingness, particularly among young people, to embrace the humanistic, internationalist spirit of twenty-first-century European culture.

Notes

1   The Centre Jeanne d'Arc in Orléans, founded in 1974 by Régine Pernoud with support from Minister of Culture André Malraux, holds over 8,500 individual volumes dedicated to Joan, in addition to thousands of printed and audio-visual iconographic documents. Two selective annotated bibliographies on the subject are Margolis, N. (1990) *Joan of Arc in History, Literature, and Film*. New York: Garland Press and Raknem, I. (1971) *Joan of Arc in History, Legend, and Literature*. Oslo: Universitetsforläget.

2   To date the most comprehensive analyses of Joan's cinematic history are Blaetz, R. (1989) *Strategies of Containment: Joan of Arc in Film*. New York University: unpublished PhD thesis and Blaetz, R. (2001) *Visions of the Maid: Joan of Arc in American Film and Culture*. Charlottesville: University of Virginia Press. Equally valuable are the articles collected in Estève, M. (ed.) (1962) Jeanne d'Arc à l'écran, special issue of *Etudes Cinématographiques* (18-19) and de la Brétèque, F. (ed.) (1985) Le Moyen Age au cinéma, special issue of *Cahiers de la Cinémathèque* (42-43). For a concise survey of the major feature films about Joan, see Harty, K. (1996) Jeanne au cinéma, pp. 237-264 in Wheeler, B. and C. Wood (eds) *Fresh Verdicts on Joan of Arc*. New York: Garland Publishing and de la Brétèque, F. (2004) *L'imaginaire médiéval dans le cinéma occidental*. Paris: Honoré Champion, pp. 777-833.

3   In 1948 Georges Méliès claimed to have made a film about Joan in 1897, though it was not released until 1900 in substantially expanded form, comprising twelve *tableaux* and running approximately fifteen minutes according to film catalog descriptions from the time. See Méliès, G. (13 July 1948) Le premier 'Jeanne d'Arc' fut tourné en 1897, pp. 3-14 in *L'Ecran Français*. The only known trace of this film is an eight-minute version housed at the Centre Jeanne d'Arc.

4   The first comprehensive critical assessment of Joan's life was Quicherat, J. (1850) *Aperçus nouveaux sur l'histoire de Jeanne d'Arc*. Paris: J. Renouard. The best modern histories include Warner, M. (1981) *Joan of Arc: The Image of Female Heroism*. New York: Knopf and three classic works by Régine Pernoud: (1953) *Vie et mort de Jeanne d'Arc: les témoignages du procès de réhabilitation, 1450-1456*. Paris: Hachette; (1962) *Jeanne d'Arc par elle-même et par ses témoins*. Paris: Seuil; and (1986) *Jeanne d'Arc*. Paris: Fayard, the latter written in collaboration with Marie-Véronique Clin.

5   Quotations in this paragraph cited by Ferro, M. (1983) *Comment on raconte l'histoire aux enfants*. Paris: Payot, pp. 137-138. This and all subsequent translations from the French are my own.

6   For details see Winock, M. (1997) Jeanne d'Arc, in Nora, P. (ed.) *Les Lieux de mémoire*. Paris: Gallimard, vol. 3, pp. 4427-4473 and Krumeich, G. (1993) *Jeanne d'Arc à travers l'histoire*. Paris: Albin Michel.

7   Quicherat, J. (ed.) (1841-1849) *Procès de condamnation et de réhabilitation de Jeanne d'Arc, dite la Pucelle*, 5 vols. Paris: J. Renouard.

8   Michelet, J. (1974) *Jeanne d'Arc et d'autres textes*. Paris: Gallimard, pp. 148 and 151.

9   Viallaneix, P. (1974) Histoire du texte, pp. 315-316 in Michelet (1974).

10   For in-depth analysis of the book's genesis, evolution, and impact, see Nora, P. (1997) Lavisse, instituteur national: Le 'Petit Lavisse,' évangile de la République, in Nora, P. (ed.) *Les Lieux de Mémoire*, vol. 1, pp. 239-275.

11   Lavisse, E. (1922) *Histoire de France, cours moyen*. Paris: Armand Colin, p. 49.

12   Lavisse (1922), pp. 52-53.

13   Lavisse (1922), p. 53.

14   Leprohon, P. (1962) Les premières images de Jeanne d'Arc à l'écran, pp. 32-37 in Estève (1962).

15   For details on the film's production, see Bordwell, D. (1973) *La Passion de Jeanne d'Arc*. Bloomington: Indiana University Press.

16   Champion, P. (ed.) (1920-1921) *Les Procès de condamnation*, 2 vols. Paris: Edouard Champion.

17   Achard, P. (27 October 1928) Falconetti, révélation du film, in *Paris-Midi*.

18   Fayard, J. (9 August 1928) La Passion de Jeanne d'Arc, in *Candide*.

19   Flamant, A. (15 November 1928) La Tragédie des grosses têtes, in *Revue de Paris*.

20   Gustav Ucicky's *Joan the Girl* (1935) attempted to justify Nazi foreign policy by comparing Hitler to Charles VII, who is presented as a misunderstood visionary dedicated to saving his nation from foreign aggression by all necessary means. Commissioned by Joseph Goebbels and financed by the Reich through UFA, the film flopped critically and at the box-office outside Germany. For details, see Steinberg, H. (1962) *Das Mädchen Johanna* de Gustav Ucicky, ou Jeanne et Goebbels, pp. 53-57 in Estève (1962).

21 Estève, M. (1962) Jeanne au bûcher de Rossellini: les séductions de l'oratorio filmé, ou le merveilleux contre le surnaturel, pp. 65-71 in Estève (1962). For many years only two copies of the film were known to exist, both in poor condition. However, in 1987 the Luce Institute and Cinecittà restored a print for a festival commemorating the tenth anniversary of Rossellini's death. For details, see Comuzio, E. (December 1987) Giovanna d'Arco al rogo: un Rossellini anticipatore, pp. 53-56 in *Cineforum*, 27 (10). Though the film has never been officially released on either VHS or DVD, it is currently available from Video Search of Miami [www.vsom.com].

22 Cameron, I. (1963) Entretien avec Robert Bresson, p. 29 in *Movie*, 7.

23 Frodon, J-M. (10 Februrary 1994) Jeanne la Pucelle de Jacques Rivette: rencontre avec le réalisateur, p. 12 in *Le Monde*; Strauss F. and V. Vatrican (February 1994) Entretien avec Sandrine Bonnaire, pp. 27-32 in *Cahiers du cinéma* (476). The film's closing credits specifically acknowledge Pernoud's *Jeanne d'Arc par elle-même et par ses témoins*, *La Libération d'Orléans*, and *Jeanne d'Arc*, as well as Duby, G. and A. (1973) *Les Procès de Jeanne d'Arc*. Paris: Gallimard.

24 Coppermann, A. (9 February 1994) Jeanne la Pucelle de Jacques Rivette: charnelle, vivante, humaine, p. 42 in *Les Echos*; Nevers, C. (February 1994) Rivette chez Jeanne d'Arc: l'avenir d'une illusion, p. 23 in *Cahiers du cinéma* (476).

25 Lalanne, J-M. (February 1994) Jeanne la pucelle: le cache faisant foi, pp. 30-31 in *Le Mensuel du cinéma*.

26 The official figure published by the Centre National de la Cinématographie was 143.445 tickets sold between the film's release in February 1994 and the end of the calendar year. Tabulated in Powrie, P. (ed.) (1999) *French Cinema in the 1990s*. Oxford: Oxford University Press, p. 261.

27 Pernoud and Clin (1986), pp. 221-222 & 266; Clin, M.-V. (9 November 1999) Quand Besson malmène Jeanne d'Arc, in *Le Figaro*.

28 Strauss, F. (December 1999) Une pensée pour Jeanne, pp. 74-75 in *Cahiers du cinéma* (541).

29 He told one interviewer: 'I do not make films in reference to other films, but based on my own experiences. I detest cinema that feeds off other cinema.' Frodon, J-M. (27 October 1999) Luc Besson, réalisateur, in *Le Monde*.

30 Frodon, J-M. (27 October 1999).

31 For the full text of the court's accusation against her, see Duby (1973), pp. 125-130.

32 Pernoud and Clin (1986), pp. 133-134; Duby (1973), pp. 140-41.

33 Quoted in Duby (1973), p. 85.

34 Quoted in Pernoud and Clin (1986), pp. 249-250.

35 See for example : anonymous (27 October 1999) Jeanne Speaks English, in *La Tribune*; anonymous (30 October 1999) La Pucelle sans mystère de Luc Besson, in *La Croix*; anonymous (30 October 1999) Jeanne d'Arc, ou l'apostasie du cinéma, in *Le Temps* ; anonymous (27 October 1999) Jeanne d'Arc: un échec, in *Le Soir*.

36 Roy, J. (27 October 1999) Jeanne la Jedi, in *L'Humanité*.

37 Roca, M. (7 December 1999) Il est mal d'offenser Jeanne, in *Le Monde*.

38 Frodon, J-M. (27 October 1999) Luc Besson, réalisateur, in *Le Monde*; Anonymous (29 October 1999) Luc Besson préfère les acteurs américains aux acteurs français, in *Agence France Presse*.

39 Bourdieu, P. (14 November 1999) Questions aux vrais maîtres du monde, in *Le Monde*. The original French quotation, 'l'internationale dénationalisée des créateurs,' has a decidedly Marxist flavour.

40 Jousse, T. (December 1999) Il faut sauver le soldat Jeanne d'Arc, p. 25 in *Cahiers du cinéma* (541).

41 Frodon, J-M. (27 October 1999) Sainte Jeanne, comédienne et martyre, in *Le Monde*.

42 Péron, D. (27 October 1999) Jeanne dépucelée, in *Libération*.

43 Roy, E. (18 December 1999) Cinécrophilie, in *Le Monde*.

44 The official figure published by the CNC was 2.936.612. For a complete list of the top-grossing films of 1999, see the CNC's on-line archive [www.cnc.fr].

45 Anonymous (25 October 1999) Jeanne d'Arc, in *Le Monde*; Anonymous (28 January 2000) La Pucelle et l'an 2000: une série d'ouvrages historiques pour les années collège, in *Le Monde*.

46 According to official CNC figures, *Germinal* and *Captain Conan* sold 6.1 and 1.2 million tickets, respectively, whereas *Les Visiteurs* sold 13.7 million and *Astérix and Obélix* 9.1 million.

Publicity shot of Rembrandt contemplating himself in the mirror for one of his last self-portraits.
© London Film Productions – United Artists

Artist Legends and the Historical Film. Alexander Korda's *Rembrandt* (1936)

Willem Hesling

As a rule feature films maintain a highly flexible relationship with reality. With historical films things are no different; witness their often complex mixture of fact and fiction. Within this 'genre' the professional historian's methodological precision may not be respected, but that should not imply complete arbitrariness, nor the impossibility of pronouncing a meaningful judgment on historical reality. Like most films, instead of aiming straight at an objective representation of reality, historical films strive for symbolic coherence and significance. In function of such an approach they borrow freely from both authorised as well as more unorthodox sources, ranging from scientific studies to unpretentious pulp. In the end what matters for a filmmaker is not so much the trustworthiness of a specific source as the symbolic way in which it can be made subservient to the entertaining, informative or persuasive intention of his film.

To get a better understanding of the nature and genesis of the heterogeneous intertextual structure of historical films I will address the so-called 'artist biopic'. Taking Alexander Korda's *Rembrandt* (1936) as an example I will examine the relationship within this historical sub-genre between the tradition of the legendary artist story and the official art-historical discourse. The intention is to retrace the path along which the British producer-director and his collaborators have borrowed elements from both fields in order to integrate them into their own symbolic representation of the artist and his world. Throughout my analysis I will pay particular attention to the way in which both genre conventions and extra-filmic socio-cultural factors have played their part within this intertextual dynamic.

Artist biopics and artist legends

There is no arguing that at first view artist biopics bear a much closer resemblance to the legendary than to the art-historical discourse. Instead of analysing the artist's oeuvre with academic precision, they generally focus on his character with all the necessary poetic license. Like the artist legends, these biopics make no effort to display art-historical expertise, but seek a symbolic representation of the creative individual and his mysterious powers. *Rembrandt* is not an art-historical discourse about the painter who actually lived, but a dramatised narrative about a character who happens to resemble the 'historical' Rembrandt in many ways. The literary roots of such a fictionalised view of art and its practitioners reach back to antiquity where early text fragments of Duris of Samos bear witness to an awakening interest in the mysterious, awe-inspiring figure of the artist. Of the many literary genres that have built on this fascination the nineteenth-century artist novel was destined to be one of the most popular. Under the influence of Romanticism, the protagonist in these novels no longer appeared as the classical heroic superman which more often than not was still the case in the Renaissance *vitae*. Rather the leading figure was often a tormented, misunderstood eccentric. Partly because, in the first half of the twentieth century, a number of these artist novels, like so much other nineteenth-century literature, would be adapted by filmmakers, it was this romantic vision of the artist that came to dominate the screen.

In the process of adaptation it seems to have escaped most filmmakers that the artist novels they recycled contained narrative elements that reached back to far more ancient sources. For in *Die Legende vom Künstler* (*Legend, Myth and Magic in the Image of the Artist*) Ernst Kris and Otto Kurz have convincingly demonstrated that the stories in which writers like Duris began to lift the artist out of anonymity contained stereotypical notions regarding his life and work that partly turned out to be derived from much older stories about such mythological figures as Daedalus, Pygmalion, Pandora and Prometheus.[1] Typical of these stories was the way they departed from a historical core only to thicken it later in a mythological way in order to claim a 'higher' truth than the merely factual one. The narrative formulas that were developed in function of that goal proved to be so enduring that for centuries they could easily be recognised in the work of such divergent authors as Pliny, Vasari, Zola and Balzac. Eventually those narrative patterns also turned out to have found their way into modern media like the cinema. In order now to reconstruct the path along which fragments from this literary heritage of artist myths, legends and novels have found their place in Korda's *Rembrandt* I will start from certain key moments in the production history of the film.

Korda, *Rembrandt* and the historical film

Ever since his highly successful *The Private Life of Henry VIII* (1933) Alexander Korda had been searching for a big new film hit for his star actor Charles Laughton. For more than a year both of them had toiled away at an adaptation of *Cyrano de Bergerac* before cancelling the project because of the insurmountable problems they had in dealing with Rostand's poetic dialogue. With this fiasco, however, Korda had not lost his belief in an international market for biopics based on great historical figures. In addition to his own *Henry VIII*, such films as *Cleopatra* (1934), *Clive of India* (1935) and *The Story of Louis Pasteur* (1936) had convinced him that they could work. At the same time, Korda was well aware that a biopic of Rembrandt van Rijn would break new and thus risky ground. After all, the box office success of historical films about famous leaders or well-known scientists were no guarantee for the same result for a biopic about an artist. One of the rare examples Korda could fall back on was *The Affairs of Cellini* (1934). But fitting in more closely with the frivolous, ironic tone of his own *The Private Life of Don Juan* (1934), this Hollywood-production on the adventures and love life of the sixteenth-century sculptor-goldsmith had little to do with the serious approach he had in mind for his Rembrandt film.[2]

Even without a clear example to steer by, Korda had reason to believe his project would succeed, if only because the life and career of the Dutch master seemed to contain all the dramatic highs and lows a filmmaker could wish for. And though Rembrandt's love life, as far as was known, was not nearly as spectacular as that of the Tudor-monarch, his relationships one after the other with Saskia, Geertje and Hendrickje must have strengthened Korda's conviction that here in any case was an excellent opportunity to follow up on the success of *Henry VIII*.

After a film career that brought him from Budapest to Vienna, Berlin, Hollywood and Paris, Korda finally established himself in Great Britain at the beginning of the 1930s with his own production company *London Film Productions*. He appointed his old-time collaborator Lajos Biró as script supervisor. Arthur Wimperis, who started his career as a newspaper illustrator and a librettist of musical comedies, was hired to write dialogue. As a team Biró and Wimperis got involved in a score of *London Film* productions, including *Rembrandt*. Because Korda, who in this phase of his career still got closely involved in developing the scenarios for his films, conferred on a daily basis with his collaborators on the progress of the Rembrandt script, the film became one of those *London Film* productions bearing the unmistakable stamp of the 'Korda-Biró-Wimperis machine'. Typical was the use, as in *Henry VIII* and *Don Juan*, of a then unusual, but for *London Film* characteristic narrative structure; instead of opting for a tightly organised plot linking events in a continuous, chronological way, Korda and his scenario-team employed a sequencing of loosely connected 'tableaux' by means of which fragments from the life of the protagonist were narrated through irregular leaps in time.

In many other respects as well the production philosophy of *London Film* turned out to be clearly recognisable in *Rembrandt*. Though Korda has often been labelled more of an instinctive than a cerebral filmmaker, in several interviews he has revealed quite a lot about his views on the historical films he produced.[3] For instance, he clearly stated that he wanted to make his historical films acceptable to the taste of an international audience. In order to reach such an audience, consisting as he saw it primarily of women, Korda insisted that his films meet a number of strict conditions. He wanted them to focus as much as possible on individual details, with special attention to all manner of amorous vicissitudes. We can easily recognise this in *Rembrandt* which, just as in *Henry VIII*, evokes the atmosphere of a domestic drama in which the personal relationships between the protagonists are put first with virtually no reference to a socio-political context. With this approach Korda intended to present the past not so much as a stage filled with exotic mystery and superhuman figures, but as an easily recognisable place, thus offering the audience a chance to draw parallels with the present and their own personal lives.

This 'keyhole-approach' largely explains why in *Rembrandt* Korda has hardly touched the illustrious past of the Dutch Republic, which in any case would have been unfamiliar to, and probably of little interest for, a wide audience. Perhaps the most striking aspect of Korda's production philosophy, however, was his ambition to extract international films from national subjects. He was convinced that historical films had to be firmly embedded in a national context in order to achieve international success. With this somewhat paradoxical belief he indicated that in their representation of the past his films should rest on qualities that were typical of the culture that the subject was related to, and yet at the same time, in light of the scant interest American audiences had in difficult European films, had to be immediately recognisable by foreigners.

Henry VIII, for example, was based on a typically British subject, but with all the clichés duly respected (Henry's overstuffed appearance, his polygamy, his reputation as a glutton, etc.) and supposedly well-known to a general audience. The same applied to the narrative structure, which in the case of *Henry VIII* was based on the archetypal Bluebeard-story, albeit this time with Bluebeard as the victim of his six wives.[4] Furthermore, Korda was convinced that films on the history and the heroes of a specific nation had to be written and directed by foreigners, because such outsiders, not impeded by detailed, superfluous information, were in the best position to display national stereotypes internationally.[5] For his historical productions, Korda consistently collaborated with an international crew, always attempting to engage the big names (e.g. René Clair, Jacques Feyder, Robert Flaherty, Joseph von Sternberg) whenever he was unable to direct them himself.

Zuckmayer's role

Though *Rembrandt*, as I have indicated, displays quite a few characteristics of the traditional *London Film* production, there are some striking contrasts as well. Entirely different from the anecdotal-ironic approach so typical of Korda's earlier historic films, the tone in *Rembrandt* is deeply serious. Humorous moments are scarce, the character sketches remain introspective and there is a lot of room for intimate scenes. The story does not focus so much on the outward appearance of Rembrandt and his world as on his inner development. This more meditative approach can be at least partly attributed to Korda himself. Albeit a businessman through and through Korda longed to prove himself as a director and no doubt saw *Rembrandt* as a prestige project. Immediately after the premiere, when the critics were predicting that the film would never recover its expenses, Korda, according to his first biographer Paul Tabori, answered: 'I know but it is very beautiful'.[6] It is not inconceivable that Korda the art connoisseur whose house at Avenue Road was stuffed with paintings by Cézanne, Van Gogh, Renoir and many other masters, identified with Rembrandt. In spite of his humble origins Korda too had succeeded in reaching the top and considered himself a self-made artist who was not always willing to yield to the taste of his audience or patrons.[7]

As much as to Korda, however, the narrative structure of *Rembrandt* should be attributed to Carl Zuckmayer, the German playwright responsible for the original scenario. Zuckmayer, who in the 1920s had acquired a huge reputation in German theatre with plays like *Der fröhliche Weinberg* (*The Merry Vineyard*, 1925) and *Der Hauptmann von Köpenick* (*The Captain of Köpenick*, 1931) had taken refuge in the neighbourhood of Salzburg after his plays were banned by the Nazi-regime because of their anti-nationalistic and anti-militaristic character. There he was forced to supplement his income by writing screenplays. In this capacity between 1934 and 1939 he carried out a considerable amount of work for the British cinema.[8] When Zuckmayer started writing for *London Film Productions*, Korda was still searching for a new project for Laughton. Inspired by Frans Hals' painting of *The Laughing Cavalier*, Korda had once considered a film set in seventeenth-century Holland. Elaborating on this idea Zuckmayer came up with the figure of Rembrandt: 'I am convinced that Laughton could wonderfully play this sturdy potato-nosed, transparent, shaded, dim-witted, unsuspecting, knowing, extraordinary, lonely fellow who is constantly standing in the twilight of a heavenly-earthly sparkle.'[9] In a meeting that took place on 15 February 1935, only a few days after the decision to drop the Cyrano-project, Zuckmayer presented his Rembrandt treatment to Korda and Biró.[10] Their reaction was so positive that Laughton too was easily won over to the project. The scenario Zuckmayer subsequently wrote would become the basis for the film. Though Korda, Biró and Wimperis[11] later introduced changes in a number of places, they left Zuckmayer's initial version for the greater part intact as regards the narrative structure as well as the dialogue and character sketches.[12] Not coincidentally the latter, in his correspondence and in interviews, has always expressed a favourable opinion about the final result. All in all, therefore, Zuckmayer seems to be the obvious person to start from in analysing the way in which fragments from the legendary and the art-historical discourse have ended up in *Rembrandt*. To start with I will focus on his adaptation of what Seymour Slive calls the Ur-myth of Rembrandt.[13]

Rembrandt: the Ur-myth

According to this Ur-myth, at the beginning of his career, Rembrandt was an exceptionally successful painter who, first in Leiden and later in Amsterdam, acquired immense fame and fortune until in 1642, the year in which his wife Saskia died, he fell into disgrace with his group portrait of the civic guard of Captain Frans Banning Cocq. Shocked by the way he had pushed the Baroque style to the extreme, Rembrandt's patrons refused to pay for the sombre, chaotically organised and for the most part only half-finished figures in which they could barely recognise themselves. The painting that would go down in history as *De Nachtwacht* (*The Night Watch*), was cut up and put away in an anonymous place. Despite this disaster Rembrandt continued to paint in his idiosyncratic style, steadily drifting away from the Baroque without yielding an inch to the prevailing taste of his public that refused to go along with his artistic quest in which spiritual content increasingly prevailed over outward appearance. Because of this he received few if any new commissions and his life came to an end in poverty and solitude.

Emmens looks upon this myth as the climax of a gradual revaluation. Until the end of the eighteenth century, Rembrandt was considered a gifted colourist and draughtsman but in other respects a rather peculiar painter. Then under the influence of Romanticism he was transformed into a misunderstood genius of universal greatness.[14] According to Emmens it is chiefly the art historian Frederik Schmidt-Degener, director of the *Museum Boymans* and, later, of the *Rijksmuseum*, who is responsible for the popularisation of this myth. The initial impetus was given with his *Rembrandt. Een beschrijving van zijn leven en zijn werk* (*Rembrandt. A Description of His Life and Work*) published in 1906 and further developed in 'Het lot der Naetuereelste Beweeglijkheid' and 'Rembrandt en Vondel', published respectively in 1915 and 1916 in *De Gids*. In these texts Schmidt-Degener presented a Rembrandt who withdraws from the world beginning in 1642, while at the same time definitively turning away from the baroque style and thus from the taste of the public that no longer understood his quest for 'the inner self' and its artistic expression.

Schmidt-Degener took this image of a 'bipartite Rembrandt' from the famous Rembrandt biography by the German art historian Alfred Neumann. In 1905 this study, first published in 1902, came out in an expanded two-volume edition that dealt with the two periods Neumann distinguished in Rembrandt's career. For him the pivotal moment between the external ('objective') and internal ('subjective') period was represented by *The Night Watch*, without however accepting the late nineteenth-century myth of its seventeenth-century rejection, a view first put forward by Émile Michel in *Rembrandt. Sa vie, son oeuvre et son temps* (*Rembrandt. His Life, His Work and His Time*, 1893).

Art historians like Emmens are sceptical about the Ur-myth. They wonder whether, in view of the seventeenth-century conception of art, it is at all possible to paint a portrait of Rembrandt as a rebellious, misunderstood genius whose work distanced itself from that of his contemporaries by way of an increasingly intense pursuit of the representation of inner life. Instead, on the basis of a detailed comparison of pre-classicist and classicist conceptions of art Emmens is convinced that Rembrandt shared most of the pre-classicist art conceptions of his time and has provided plenty of evidence of them. In spite of this, the Ur-myth held up well into the 1960s, witness the Schmidt-Degener influenced monographs by Knuttel (1956), Benesch (1957) and Rosenberg (1964).[15] Typical is how in 1956, on the occasion of the retrospective organised to honour Rembrandt's 350th birthday, the designation 'heretic' was not considered a term of abuse, but a compliment. Already halfway through the 1930s Gerard Brom, in his essay *Rembrandt in de literatuur* (*Rembrandt in Literature*), grumbled that such exaggerated Romantic adoration of Rembrandt's misunderstood genius had the fatal consequence of letting the life overshadow the work to such an extent that, just as with Van Gogh, the paintings seemed to become almost superfluous.[16] In this respect Brom especially pointed the finger at what he regarded as the reprehensible genre of the *vie romancée*. Whereas Theun De Vries with his sensual, biographical novel could already hardly pass, he completely dismissed the pretentious Rembrandt novel of the 'Americanised Dutchman' Hendrik Willem van Loon as 'swollen and hollow'. In an even worse position, according to Brom, was the cinema, a medium he considered incapable of expressing anything worthwhile about Rembrandt: 'Nothing is further from the cinema, in which our generation is in danger of exhausting its aesthetic sense than his profound silence'.[17]

Rembrandt and the Ur-myth

Brom, whose essay on Rembrandt dates from the same year as Korda's film, must have had little difficulty in finding in *Rembrandt* an additional corroboration of his pessimistic view of the cinema. After all, a mere summary of the story makes clear the extent to which the Ur-myth has left its mark on the film. The viewer meets Rembrandt in the year 1642 when the painter is doing very well in his career. The sudden death of Saskia, however, comes as a heavy blow. To make matters worse, shortly thereafter, he starts losing credit with the Amsterdam elite because of his unorthodox group portrait of the civic guard of Captain Banning Cocq. Promising pupils like Govert Flinck see the storm gathering and take the opportunist decision to leave his studio. Geertje Dircks, the wetnurse who had taken care of young Titus after the death of Saskia, exploits Rembrandt's grief and confusion to take over as the new mistress of the house.

Ten years later, despite impending bankruptcy, Rembrandt stubbornly persists in his 'own way of painting', witness among other things his habit of paying beggars to pose for his biblical figures. Disillusioned and too proud to beg the Prince of Orange for new assignments, he decides to give up painting and return to his father's mill. There he quickly finds out that the only true place for him is in front of his easel back in the big city. Next, with Hendrickje Stoffels, the new maid, he regains the artistic inspiration he had lost with Saskia. In spite of Rembrandt's bankruptcy and Hendrickje's excommunication by a Church Council that doesn't approve of their sinful cohabitation the couple, together with Titus, lead an idyllic, bohemian existence. Hendrickje not only bears Rembrandt a daughter, but turns out to be a shrewd businesswoman. Her untimely death, even before Rembrandt has a chance to marry her, puts an end to this happy period. Rembrandt is condemned to spend his last years alone and in dire poverty. The only thing that keeps him going is his artistic drive. The last scene of the film shows him painting in his humble attic room, totally absorbed in the world of his imagination.

The fact that the film's narrative so clearly reflects the Ur-myth of the bipartite Rembrandt, not only has to do with its tenacious popularity in general, but also more specifically with the circles Zuckmayer was familiar with in his youth. He became aquainted with Rembrandt's life and work in his student days in Heidelberg, where at the end of the nineteenth century the first European chair for art history was established. During a half-hearted attempt to study natural science after the First World War, Zuckmayer had joined *Die Gemeinschaft*, a cultural community founded by Wilhelm Fraenger. This unorthodox art historian pressed Zuckmayer to write a doctoral dissertation on 'Rembrandt as director' under the supervision of Carl Neumann, with whom he himself had obtained a doctorate in medieval art. Though this project attracted the future playwright, he never managed to get around to it because, in his own words, of his 'lack of patience with working methodically'.[18] Nevertheless Zuckmayer must have been acquainted with Neumann's Rembrandt biography, published only a few years earlier, and the image presented therein of the 'bipartite Rembrandt'. It is highly unlikely that, in later years, he was not also well aware of the work of Schmidt-Degener whose Neumann-inspired portrayal of Rembrandt was presented to the German reading public in 1928 in the monograph *Rembrandt und der holländische Barock* (*Rembrandt and the Dutch Baroque*).

Except for the art-historical circles in which he moved, Zuckmayer's portrait of Rembrandt was also fed by the literary fiction of his time, with the most direct influence being Van Loon's *The Life and Times of Rembrandt van Rijn* (1930), the novel Brom had so heavily criticised. In 1938, during his study of the poet Carl Michael Bellman, Van Loon had come across Zuckmayer's work and written a letter to him in Switzerland after he had fled there from the Nazis in which he spontaneously offered to vouch for him whenever he decided to emigrate to the United States. When, on 6 June 1939, Zuckmayer arrived in New York on the *Zaandam*, it was Van Loon who stood waiting for him on Hoboken pier.

Born in the Netherlands, but emigrated to the States at an early age, Van Loon was the author of a great number of popular history books, among which *The Story of Mankind* (1921) and *The Story of the Bible* (1923). According to Zuckmayer the semi-fictionalised *Life and Times of Rembrandt van Rijn*, published in Germany as *Der Überwirkliche. Zeitbild um Rembrandt van Rijn* (1932), was the first Van Loon book he ever read. In this novel, in which the physician Joannis van Loon, an imaginary ancestor of the author, gives an account of the last years of Rembrandt's life and career, the Ur-myth is pointedly present. Van Loon, like Zuckmayer years later, begins the story at the moment that Saskia is dying. When Joannis is called to her sickbed, he meets Rembrandt, after which the two men maintain a close if irregular contact. When in October 1669, Rembrandt dies it is Joannis who sits by his side.

A year after the publication of Van Loon's novel, Theun de Vries' *Rembrandt* came out. Here once again, we not only encounter the classic image of the bipartite, misunderstood Rembrandt, but also a narrative structure in which events focus on the beginning of the second, less prosperous part of his life and career. Perhaps to avoid a too-close similarity with Van Loon's book, De Vries lets his story begin in 1650 when Rembrandt had plunged into a serious artistic crisis. De Vries' novel was translated into German by Franz Dülberg in 1934, which makes it likely that Zuckmayer was also inspired by this text.

1642: A dramatic turning point

The fact that the Ur-myth is so prominent in *Rembrandt* does not mean that the film is a slavish copy of it. Rather than a terminus, the myth forms a starting point for the development of the intertextual, symbolic structure of the film. To sketch this intertextual system in detail, I will concentrate on a small, but essential part of it, namely the so-called 'turning point' in Rembrandt's career.

In accordance with the Ur-myth, Korda and Zuckmayer pinpoint the year 1642 as the moment in which the successful and vigorous Rembrandt starts to change into the misunderstood, introverted loner. This metamorphosis is sketched in the light of the archetypal contradistinction between Life and Art. In his study of the image of the artist in literary fiction, Maurice Beebe speaks metaphorically of the antithesis between *sacred fount* and *ivory tower*.[19] Beebe finds that in many novels the artist is depicted as a fundamentally divided figure: on the one hand a normal human being of flesh and blood with everyday needs and desires, on the other a creative individual who lives for his artistic aspirations. This schizophrenia places the artist in a special relation to life. In many nineteenth-century novels it is thought that he has to live life with redoubled intensity and sensitivity in order to be able to transform it into art.[20] Within this *sacred fount* tradition the idea prevails that art is essentially a recreation of life experiences. But because life and art are so inextricably bound up together, they can also exhaust and finally even destroy each other. Typical are the artists who sacrifice their models to their artistic obsessions (cf. Edgar Allan Poe's *The Oval Portrait*) or who, the other way round, are themselves destroyed by life, usually a fatal love affair (cf. Gilbert Cannan's 'roman à clef' *Mendel* about the British painter Mark Gertler). The opposite image can be found within the *ivory tower* tradition. Here the artist can only fully develop by freeing himself from all domestic, social and religious ties and seeking compensation through his art for what he lacks in real life.[21] This image can, for example, be found in the work of Baudelaire, who in turn recognised it in Delacroix.

By having their protagonist cover the trajectory from *sacred fount* to *ivory tower* Korda and Zuckmayer are able to integrate both archetypal visions in *Rembrandt*. In the film we first meet Rembrandt on the day Saskia is to die. To increase the impact of the misfortune that lies in wait for him, the first scenes strongly emphasise Rembrandt's material well-being and great artistic success. The opening images show how he enters a painter's shop with zestful bravura. The respect with which the shop-workers treat him and the casual ease with which he buys his equipment (brushes, English etching needles, Flemish and French dyes) show that he is prospering, which is further emphasised by the presence of several merchants who easily succeed in selling him their goods: a florist is ordered to deliver his entire supply in the Breestraat and a jeweller manages to sell him a valuable necklace. Shortly thereafter we meet Rembrandt in a tavern where members of Frans Banning Cocq's civic guard, whose group portrait he has reluctantly promised to paint, propose a toast to him as the greatest painter of his age. On this occasion Rembrandt pays effusive homage to the vital artistic inspiration of his wife. Then suddenly Rembrandt's world is turned upside down when his master pupil Fabritius comes rushing in with the fatal message that Saskia's health is rapidly deteriorating. When he arrives in the Breestraat the doctors Menasseh and Tulp can only tell Rembrandt that his wife has just died. Life has dealt him a blow from which he will never recover. And thus the process is set in motion that sees Rembrandt start to turn away from the disillusioning, menacing outside world and begin to move in the direction of the ivory tower. The fact that the film, immediately after the opening sequence, should take this dramatic turn of events is quite surprising. After all, Korda and Zuckmayer had the opportunity and sufficient reason to concentrate on Rembrandt's most successful period. In this way, they could have remained within the conventional boundaries of the average biopic. Although an ending *en mineur* was not unheard of, especially when the historical facts were widely known (cf. *Abraham Lincoln*, 1930; *Mata Hari*, 1931) the genre generally opted for an approach bringing out the successes of the protagonist as clearly as possible. Often this was done by emphasising the most successful phase in the character's career (cf. *Disraeli*, 1929; *Voltaire*, 1933) or by providing a more positive twist to a tragic ending (cf. *Clive of India*, 1935).

In those days, in contrast to *Rembrandt*, the narrative route usually covered in biopics went from a troubled beginning towards a glorious finale (cf. *The Story of Louis Pasteur*, 1936; *The Story of Alexander Graham Bell*, 1939). By opting at least in the early part of their film for the more familiar trajectory, Korda and Zuckmayer would have supported the legendary image of the 'artist as heroic figure' as established by Duris and Pliny. This classic representation of the superhumanly gifted artist, expressing the idea that only superior individuals are capable of producing great art, would be reactivated in the sixteenth century by Vasari and others to be picked up again in the biographies of Victorian artists. By ignoring this tradition *Rembrandt*'s creators passed over a closely related stereotypical subplot in which the artist, after being discovered as a promising young talent, makes a quick and successful rise up through society.[22] With regard to Rembrandt abundant subject matter was available (whether or not of a legendary nature) to develop this formula in detail: his humble origin as a son of a miller from Leiden; his first success with a painting he sold for a hundred guilders to an art connoisseur in The Hague; Constantijn Huygens's high opinion of the young Rembrandt; his first students (among whom Gerard Dou); his successful entry into Amsterdam at the beginning of the 1630s; the promising commissions from the Amsterdam elite and the court at the Hague; his marriage in 1634 with the Frisian mayor's daughter Saskia Uylenburgh and, finally, the pinnacle of success with the purchase of a distinguished house in the Breestraat and the birth of his son Titus.

Virtually nothing of this material is brought out in the film. Instead of placing his golden years in the spotlight, Korda's film makes it clear that, on the contrary, in many ways Rembrandt did not correspond at all to the ideal image of the successful artist. For the most part this is done in a subtle way. When, for instance, on the occasion of Rembrandt's bankruptcy an inventory of his household goods is drawn up, the art dealer Ludwick[23], his former agent, draws the executors' attention to a sketch by Rubens which, as opposed to the barely appreciated work of the dealer's former client, represents a very high value on the art market. It is a scene where the film almost casually alludes to the traditional contrast between Rembrandt the boor and Rubens the aristocrat, between the bohemian who operates on the fringes of society and the gentleman-artist who has gained every kind of success. In some places the film even distances itself explicitly from the stereotypical image of the 'princely artist'. For example, the scene in which Govert Flinck leaves his master. Although Rembrandt agrees that it is better for his pupil to try his luck elsewhere, the film clearly casts Flinck's opportunistic striving for fame and wealth in a bad light and suggests that this decision will prove fatal to his artistic calling.

These critical asides have an important function within the film because they serve to represent Rembrandt's growing social exclusion as the price he must pay for producing truly great art. It is precisely because artistic achievement is a sublime gift that needs to be practised in seclusion from society that, according to Vasari, Michelangelo so often sought solitude.[24] In the same vein Korda's film presents Rembrandt as a symbol of the incompatibility between art and real life. Several scenes mark Rembrandt's increasing isolation and show how, step by step, he is losing his bearings in society: the studio with his pupils, the court at The Hague, the Amsterdam elite, the farmer's community of his birthplace, even his parental home. To emphasise this development a key scene is Rembrandt's affinity with the beggar he picks up in the street to pose for his portrait of Saul. Not only in the sense that Rembrandt too depends on charity from the upper classes, but more specifically because he is also someone who stands completely outside society. After Rembrandt has lost Hendrickje, his new muse, we see him in the very last scene of the film working in complete solitude in the ivory tower of his studio. After all the blows life has administered, it is only there, in the austerity of his working space that the painter is able to find the harmony he has striven for throughout the film, stating with Biblical resignation: 'Vanity of vanities. All is vanity'.

The death of Saskia

Within the Romantic imagination it is not unusual for a single dramatic event to cause a decisive turnabout in the life and career of an artist. Familiar causes are illness (Proust, Hölderlin, Goya, Beethoven), financial misfortune (Whistler, Degas) or a scandal (Wilde, Sargent). Besides the rejection of *The Night Watch* (cf. infra) Korda and Zuckmayer point to Saskia's death as the primary cause of Rembrandt's reversal of fortune. In the art-historical literature of Korda's days, her death was frequently regarded as a major factor in Rembrandt's life and in his way of painting. In 1932, on the occasion of the Rembrandt exhibition in the Rijksmuseum, Schmidt-Degener put this idea in words succinctly: 'Then, life breaks its bonds with the past, but at the same time it renews his development. Saskia dies'. With art historians indulging in psychological insights, it is hardly surprising that novelists too liked to project the tragic ending of Rembrandt's marriage on the further course of his career. Compared to the sentimentality of the fictional biographies by De Vries and Duchateau[25], Korda's film can be considered a paragon of restraint. In *Rembrandt* Saskia's face is not shown at all and Rembrandt's reaction to her death is kept extremely sober. After he receives the news from Menasseh and Tulp, we find him in the next scene working intently in his studio where he is calling upon Saskia's still fresh and tangible memory to finish his last portrait of her. The scene is typical of the film as a whole, not only because it refrains from easy melodrama, but because it focuses on a number of additional motifs derived from artist legends.

Sexual and artistic creation

Kris and Kurz indicate that in artist legends the mysterious process of artistic creation is often made comprehensible with the help of analogous life experiences.[26] In this respect the authors point to the tradition of picturing a work of art as the artist's 'child'. Typical is the anecdote from Macrobius' *Saturnalia* in which the Roman painter Lucius Malleus, in answer to the question why his own children are so ugly, but the ones he paints so beautiful, explains that this was because he had created his own at night but the others by day. Centuries later we find the same metaphor in Vasari where a priest who was a friend of Michelangelo said: 'It is a pity you never married, for you might have had many children, and would have left them all the profit and honour of your labours'. Whereupon Michelangelo answered: 'I have only too much of a wife in this art of mine. She has always kept me struggling on. My children will be the works I leave behind me'.

Within the tradition of the artist legend this supposed relationship between sexual and creative energy is encountered in many variations. The most succinct and, at the same time, most frank one is attributed to Renoir who, when asked by an admirer about his technique, is said to have answered: 'I paint with my penis'. In a more Romantic version, in the *sacred fount* tradition, it is said that the love for a woman guides the painter's brush. In this sense, it was said of Praxiteles, Van der Goes, Perugino, Bronzino and Goya that in their work they portrayed their loved ones. In the same vein Alpers points out that in the seventeenth-century Dutch Republic it was customary to compare the artist's commitment to his work with the love of a man for a woman.[27]

In *Rembrandt* this analogy between sexual and artistic creation is present from the moment Rembrandt, in the tavern scene, gives the company of Banning Cocq to understand that he will have no artistic problems as long as he is inspired by his love for Saskia. Later, the scene in which he tries to finish his last portrait of her shows how, even after her death, he draws strength from that love. Yet it is in vain because Rembrandt cannot paint without Saskia, as is symbolically emphasised after her funeral when he withdraws into her bedroom, only able to write her name in the dust that has gathered on her vanity table. The later scenes add to the impression that Rembrandt is about to go through a creative crisis. The noisy and meddlesome Geertje Dircks plays a crucial role in this. Instead of stimulating his artistic inspiration, she is only interested in the market value of Rembrandt's paintings and constantly nags him to ask the *Stadtholder* for new commissions. It is only after he meets Hendrickje that Rembrandt manages to overcome this crisis. Within minutes he has coaxed her along to his studio where a scene develops that clearly shows he has found his new muse: 'I'm not looking at you as a man looks. I'm a painter. Painters have a different way of looking at things'.

The words typify the ambiguous attitude that Korda's Rembrandt adopts towards both Saskia and Hendrickje. Although he is undoubtedly shaken by their deaths the film subtly leaves unspoken whether this stems from the loss of a loved one or from the loss of an ideal muse. It is striking that in the first scenes Rembrandt's interest in Saskia seems to be exclusively from a painter's point of view. When Ludwick urges him to start painting the militia of the Kloveniersdoelen, Rembrandt replies that he doesn't like their faces and, besides, he is busy painting his wife. To be sure, the flowers and jewels he has purchased are not presents for Saskia but the symbols and attributes for her portrait as Flora. The same ambiguity characterises the tavern scene in which Rembrandt, just when Saskia is dying, is being hailed by the officers of the civic guard as the greatest painter of his age. When the officers express amazement that after seven years of marriage he is not yet tired of painting his wife, Rembrandt explains what Saskia means to him:

> 'Throw a purple garment lightly over her shoulders and she becomes the Queen of Sheba. Lay your tousled head blindly upon her breast and she is a Delilah waiting to enthral you. Take her garments from her, strip the last veil from her body and she is a chaste Susanna covering her nakedness with fluttering hands. Gaze upon her as you would gaze upon a thousand strange women but never call her yours. For her secrets are inexhaustible, you never know them all. Call her by one name only. I call her Saskia.'

A declaration of love to Saskia? Perhaps, but certainly the profession of faith of an obsessed painter who sees his wife as a muse who endlessly stimulates his creative imagination.

Licentiousness and the bohemian artist

In the course of time the idea of the artist driven by the love for his model, initially meant to humanise the position of the artist vis-à-vis his work, would increasingly be associated with the sexual licence the artist was allowed, or allowed himself. While Pliny still expressed his indignation at the conduct of the painter Arellius who discredited his art by falling in love with every woman he met, sexual licence in the Romantic Age, under the influence of, e.g. Henri Murger's *Scènes de la vie de Bohème* (*Scenes of Bohemian Life*, 1851) and Giacomo Puccini's *La Bohème* (1896), became the prerogative of the artist. Wittkower and Wittkower notice that the beginning of this new attitude goes back to Renaissance Italy where, notwithstanding the fulminations of a Savonarola, licentious artists like Fra Filippo Lippi were not exactly thwarted. At the beginning of the seventeenth century, Agostino Tassi experienced little if any social opprobrium because of his involvement in the notorious 'Artemisia Gentileschi case'.[28]

In *Rembrandt* the image of the artist-bohemian who can allow himself more than average profligacy is clearly recognisable. Korda and Zuckmayer leave no doubt

Publicity shot of Rembrandt at the height of his career casually buying an expensive necklace for Saskia to wear while posing as Flora. © London Film Productions – United Artists

that Rembrandt has extra-marital affairs with both Geertje and Hendrickje. The candid way in which the film approaches this question and clearly takes sides when Hendrickje has to answer to the Church Council for her 'whoredom with Rembrandt the painter' (Korda portrays the Council as an extremely unpleasant assembly) contrasts sharply with the rather sanctimonious manner in which historians have kept Rembrandt's sexual relations with Geertje and Hendrickje outside their biographies well into the 1960s.[29] At the time that *Rembrandt* opened, Dutch novelists were not prepared to stain Rembrandt's carefully polished image with embarrassing details from his private life. De Vries almost completely circumvents the Geertje character. Without mentioning her name, she is briefly introduced as Rembrandt's former housekeeper, a crude woman who had stolen from her master and for this reason was carried away by the black men of the house of correction.[30] And as for Van Loon, Geertje fares even worse; he portrays her as a true harpy, constantly teetering on the edge of hysteria or insanity.[31] Her slanderous charges that Rembrandt had sex with her, borrowed money from her without repaying it and finally threw her out in spite of his promise to marry her are adduced as proofs of her insanity and justify her confinement in the madhouse in Gouda.

The extent to which novelists were prepared to tidy up Rembrandt's licentious lifestyle can be seen in Duchateau's novel where Geertje does not occur at all and where every suggestion of a sexual relation between Rembrandt and Hendrickje is painstakingly avoided. That Korda had fewer qualms in this respect can, of course, be explained by the fact that for him as an Englishman there was no reason to maintain the flawless image of a Dutch national hero. And yet with *Henry VIII* he had certainly shown that he was not afraid to attack one of the sacred historical icons of his adoptive fatherland. How much more decisive, then, must have been the commercial medium of film with its capacity to generate thrills and emotions. Nor was it easy to subdue the temptation to indulge in displays of eroticism. In the case of *Rembrandt*, the then prevailing film censorship notwithstanding, this freedom made it possible to create, at least in this respect, a more authentic historical representation than could be found in the novels or even in the historical studies of the day.

Living images: the artist as 'second God'

The scene in which Rembrandt is shown finishing Saskia's portrait after her death conjures up strong associations with Vasari's legend about Luca Signorelli painting the body of his recently dead son. A similar scene is portrayed in Léon Cogniet's well-known painting from 1843 in which we see Tintoretto sketching his deceased daughter. In both cases it is not so much a question of creating a commemorative picture, but of fabricating a substitute. The doggedness with which Rembrandt works at Saskia's last portrait suggests the same intention. Once again it is easy to draw a line back to Antiquity. The most striking example is the myth of Admetos, king of Pheres, who demanded a marble statue of his deceased wife Alkestis so he could embrace it as if it were alive. In such legends the theme of creating images coincides with that of the magical effect of images, e.g. with the belief that a person's soul or spirit is present in their effigy and that anyone in possession of it can exercise power over the portrayed person. Typical is the conviction that punishments executed in effigy will have the same effect on the person in question. And, the other way round, as in Wilde's *The Picture of Dorian Gray* (1891), the damage done to an individual will ultimately have the same effect on his portrait. In a broader sense the 'portrait scene' in *Rembrandt* also takes up the mythical idea of the artist who is capable of making images come 'alive'. This subject matter has its roots in the oldest artist legends, especially in the representation of the artist as a perfect imitator of nature. This theme is expressed in its simplest form in the countless anecdotes in which an unsuspecting observer is taken in by a lifelike image. According to Kris and Kurz such legends, initially intended to place the talents of the artist in an admirable light, are reinterpretations of a number of stories in which Daedalus, the mythical godfather of Greek art, is presented as the maker of statues that could not only move, but speak.[32] Thus for instance a statue of Aphrodite that he reputedly managed to set in motion by filling it with *argentum vivum* (mercury).

Such myths, and the artist legends derived from them, contrasted strongly with Platonic philosophy. According to this body of thought the plastic arts could never go beyond an imperfect imitation of a physical reality that in its turn merely reflected a higher world of ideas. This, in contrast to the divinely inspired poets and musicians who could transcend sensory reality in order to go straight to the true essence of things. Kris and Kurz, however, point out that even in

Plato's days the opposite conviction circulated that a work of art prevails over nature exactly because through his inner vision and imagination the artist is capable of surpassing its imperfections.[33] For centuries this image of the 'inspired' artist would lead a somewhat slumbering existence, before coming to full bloom in the *vitae* of the Renaissance artists. These masters were admired not so much for their ability to imitate reality as for their inventive, artistic imagination (*il furore dell'arte*).[34] Out of that developed the idea of the artist as *divino artista*, e.g., as someone who creates his work while being driven by an inner voice, an inner conception that makes him function as the pen of God.

Not coincidentally Dürer characterised artistic activity as 'creating the way God has done', while Alberti named the artist an *alter deus*.[35] Later we see how, as a late echo of this idea, under the influence of Romanticism in post-revolutionary bourgeois France of the first half of the nineteenth century, the status of the artist as *divino artista* becomes linked to, and partly replaced by, the cult of the artistic genius. Within the Romantic formation the *artiste* is presented as a superior, God-chosen individual who in his practise of the fine arts realises the human potential to its most complete and rewarding degree. With this the artist's social status took on a new aspect. After the collapse of the *ancien régime* the artist, chiefly tolerated until the French Revolution as someone who, usually originating in the Third Estate, depended completely on the Court or the aristocracy, grew to become a free social agent. Such a person was not likely to conform to the rules of a society which he deemed culturally and intellectually far beneath him.[36] Such feelings of superiority were also present on the side of the rising bourgeoisie in whose eyes art was not a form of labour and therefore in the end a rather useless activity. In *Rembrandt* the attitude of the Amsterdam elite, who dropped the painter entirely after the fiasco of his *The Night Watch*, seems to conform to this image. When after his bankruptcy, Rembrandt is forced to leave his house, he passes three money changers who, much like a Greek chorus, mercilessly draw up the balance of his new position: 'A man without money is a vagabond and a rogue'.

In Sénac de Meilhan's philosophical parable *Les deux cousins* (*The Two Cousins*, 1790) the genius of the artist is viewed as the main cause of his conflict with bourgeois society.[37] Genius is a deadly gift of God that offends and disgusts those who do not have it. The artist's genius condemns him at once to a brilliant isolation and to suffering; or, more precisely: it compels him to sublimate his agony into art. Along this way too the artist turned out to stand close to God. More than one would identify with Christ in agony and declare himself prepared to take up the cross on behalf of his art. In the same vein the late nineteenth-century image of the misunderstood Rembrandt showed a strong resemblance to that of the crucified Christ. Korda's film strongly emphasises the tragedy that plagues Rembrandt the genius. The screen text with which *Rembrandt* opens, announces the narrative trajectory of the misunderstood genius who is ahead of his time and therefore inevitably condemned to live and work in a society that cannot appreciate his talent:

> 'In the seventeenth century Holland was a world power, her ships carried treasure to Amsterdam from all parts of the earth. But her proudest glory was the son of a miller from Leyden, Rembrandt Van Rijn, the greatest painter that has ever lived. He died in obscurity, his belongings worth no more than a few shillings. Today no millionaire is worth the money the works of Rembrandt would realise, if ever offered for sale.'

Contrary to the Ur-myth, Korda's film does not locate the cause of Rembrandt's tragedy completely outside his own person. The question is expressly raised to what extent he is himself at least partly guilty of it. In this the cause of Saskia's death plays an important role. In the opening scene in the painter's shop, when Dr. Tulp asks after Saskia's health, Rembrandt answers that there is nothing wrong with it. When Tulp then warns him that, on the contrary, it is extremely delicate, Rembrandt, so obsessed by his work that he does not seem to understand that his wife is dying, replies that she has never felt better. And when Tulp insists once more that the artist must be more considerate of her weak condition, he indignantly informs him that this is precisely what he does: he doesn't ask Saskia to do anything more than rise from her sickbed and pose for him.

The way in which Saskia's life steadily ebbs away the closer her portrait nears completion recalls Poe's *The Oval Portrait* in which the character of the painter fails to notice that precisely by creating his work of art he is draining the life out of his wife: 'And he would not see that the tints which he spread upon the canvas were drawn from the cheeks of her who sat beside him'. The most macabre variation on this theme of 'the model painted to death by the artist' can be found in stories in which the artist thrives not on his love for his model, but on his hostility towards her. Kris and Kurz mention a number of anecdotes in which artists like Parrhasios, Michelangelo and Messerschmidt torture and ultimately kill their models so that they can portray their suffering and death in a manner as true to life as possible.[38] In *Rembrandt* Korda does not go this far, but it is revealing that the motif of 'modelling until death' is repeated with Hendrickje. She dies precisely at the moment when Rembrandt, well aware of her fragile health, is painting her portrait.

Saskia and Flora

In the representation of Saskia's death the intertextual complexity of *Rembrandt* once more reaches beyond the pure artist legend. Art historians have noted that in 1642, as Saskia was lingering near death, Rembrandt was completely absorbed by his work, witness his enormous production during that period.[39] Muller makes it clear that Rembrandt painted Saskia especially between 1632 and 1634; after that his interest in using her as a model appears to have lessened.[40] Significant is the fact that, while the Saskia portraits of 1633 show a couple in love, the later portraits come across as much more equivocal. For example, the well-known *Saskia and Rembrandt* (1635-1636) is a painting traditionally interpreted as an autobiographical work in which the artist has portrayed himself at the pinnacle of his success proudly raising his glass in the company of his wife. Schama finds it hard to believe that we have to do with a biographical painting because in that case, besides seeing Rembrandt as the Prodigal Son squandering his money in a place of ill repute, we would have to consider Saskia in the role of a courtesan or prostitute.[41] That Rembrandt, however, did not hesitate to portray his wife as a courtesan is clear from three paintings representing her as the goddess Flora.[42] It seems more than a coincidence that in *Rembrandt* Saskia is portrayed precisely in this capacity. After all, historically speaking another portrait that is at least as impressive should have qualified: *Saskia in a Red Hat*, started in 1633 or 1634, then reworked in 1642 during her fatal illness and perhaps even after her death and so in a sense Rembrandt's final portrait of her. Though in the film we never get to see the portrait Rembrandt is working on, there can be little doubt that he is painting her as Flora, since he says so explicitly in the opening scene in the painter's studio; the flowers delivered to the Breestraat address underscore his remark. The jewellery he purchases in the same scene makes it likely that it concerns the Flora of 1641, which also makes sense from a chronological point of view. The fact that of all the Saskia portraits Korda and Zuckmayer have chosen a Flora portrait ties in symbolically with the ambiguous relationship the film sketches between the painter and his wife.

The origin of the mythological Flora is the nymph Chloris, married to Zephyrus, the god of the west wind, who made her the goddess of flowers. Ovid tells in the *Fasti* (c. 8 AD) how Zephyrus conquers the fleeing Chloris by changing her into the goddess Flora, a transformation portrayed in Botticelli's *Primavera* (c. 1482). The Flora figure has been used many times as a model for women's portraits, usually in the form of a so-called *portrait historié* in which the sitter was shown dressed as Flora. In Venetian painting particularly, attractive courtesans were regularly portrayed in this way, which fits in with the equivocal function of Flora as the goddess of flowers and the spring, but also as the patroness of prostitutes.[43] Schwartz is convinced that Rembrandt's *Flora* of 1641 was strongly influenced by the one painted by Titian, greatly admired by Rembrandt, around 1515. This would imply that the way in which she offers her flower must be seen as a symbol of sensual pleasure. For Kelch, too, there is no doubt that Rembrandt was familiar with the ambivalent symbolism of the goddess as both *flora mater* and *flora meretrix*, which is further evidenced by his *Flora* of 1655.[44] Besides in the Flora portraits Rembrandt has also worked somewhat ambiguously in his other explorations of the 'Arcadian genre'. In his analysis of *De fluitspeler* (*The Flute Player*), an etching that for a long time was misleadingly known as *Tijl Uylenspiegel* (*Till Eulenspiegel*), Emmens points out that here Rembrandt has not painted an idyllic scene, but on the contrary, mocks in a rather vulgar way the idea of exalted poetic inspiration emanating from love. At the same time, he has underscored his belief that for an artist to surrender to a woman is tantamount to suicide.[45] For Emmens it is as instructive as it is distressing that Rembrandt made this etching in the very year Saskia died.

The rejection of *The Night Watch*

Following Saskia's death Korda and Zuckmayer show the rejection of *The Night Watch* as the next defining moment in Rembrandt's life and career. Here I will briefly describe how this incident is narrated. The scene opens with Captain Banning Cocq in the presence of the distinguished assembly that has gathered before the entrance of the 'Grote Sael' of the Kloveniersdoelen (the hall of the meeting place and shooting range of the militia). He is speaking of a memorable day in the history of the civil guard. In the name of the *kloveniers* he solemnly invites Mayor Adriaen Bickers[46] to unveil Rembrandt van Rijn's masterpiece. While the gathering enters the hall to the sound of trumpets, Rembrandt stays behind at the entrance waiting for the first reactions, which are not long in coming. Fabritius and Flinck have hardly removed the veil[47] or the applause that had expectantly set in, turns into a painful silence finally interrupted by the scornful laughter of the wives of the *kloveniers*. While their indignant husbands try to recognise themselves in vain in the figures in the painting, a confused Jan Six, one of Rembrandt's friends and patrons, lets the artist know that he too has a problem with the painting:

> 'I can't say. I don't understand it. I can't see anything in it … I can see nothing but shadows, darkness and confusion. You surely don't expect us to take this as serious art.'

Immediately thereupon an alarmed Ludwick announces that Rembrandt's civic guard patrons refuse to pay for the painting. He asks his client to speak to them in order to save the situation. After some hesitation Rembrandt consents and asks Banning Cocq straight if he has something to say. The latter reminds Rembrandt that at the time he accepted the assignment to paint his sixteen men for the price of 200 guilders each. However, only six of them are recognisable; he will certainly not expect the others to pay for portraits that weren't done? To make clear at once that he's not after their money, Rembrandt answers that those ten can keep their pennies in their pockets.[48] Asked if there's anything else that bothers him Banning Cocq answers:

> 'Yes, Rembrandt, there is something else. You undertook to paint a good, satisfactory picture for our messroom. But this … this thing, it's … it's a monstrosity. Look at it for yourself. Is that supposed to represent the officers of the noble civic guard, a collection of gentlemen? Do those look like gentlemen of rank and position?'

Banning Coq's criticism is deflected by Rembrandt with a biting counterattack:

> 'I wasn't trying to paint gentlemen of rank and position. I wanted to paint men … soldiers … a company marching out. (Laughing) Gentlemen of rank and position, indeed. (Waving with the hat he has torn off the head of one of the *kloveniers*) Here's your gentleman of rank and what's underneath it? (Pointing to their gaudy garments) And this, and this, and this? (Pointing to them one by one) Your nose is painted by bad liquor. Your mouth is reeking with bawdy kisses. Vanity and stupidity are written all over your faces. The only pretty thing about you are your ruffs and your breastplates. (Throwing the hat back to them) The only distinguished thing about you are your hats.'

At the end of this scene we return to Rembrandt's house in Breestraat where not a single guest has come to the reception that Geertje has prepared. Later that evening, Rembrandt, befuddled with gin, expresses his growing distance from the world around him: 'I live in a beautiful, blinding, swirling mist. The world can offer me nothing.'

When we review the reactions in Korda's film to *The Night Watch* the criticism comes down to three points: Jan Six indicates that the painting looks like a chaotic arrangement of shadows; Banning Cocq lets it be known that Rembrandt broke his engagement to paint a clearly recognisable portrait of all sixteen members of the civil guard, and finally there is the reproach that the characters as he has portrayed them are not distinguished enough. In short, in aesthetic, contractual and social respects Rembrandt has completely ignored the rules of the game.

The reception of *The Night Watch* in historical and legendary perspective

With their version of the rejection of *The Night Watch* Korda and Zuckmayer again lean heavily on the legendary Rembrandt discourse, especially on the myth of the misunderstood artist as it had sprung up from Romantic notions in the second half of the nineteenth century.[49] In order to make this 'Bohemian' Rembrandt conform to the then increasingly current status of the nonconformist artist an unbridgeable gap was assumed to exist between the respectable Amsterdam patrons and the painter who had dared to portray this distinguished company as a band of robbers.[50] In Baudelaire's eyes, for example, Rembrandt with his 'fantastic' style could only have disappointed his narrow-minded clients.[51] Art historians like Emile Michel were also of the opinion that Rembrandt's obstinate, 'fantastic' way of working with light simply could never have fitted in with the sober and rational mind of the seventeenth-century Dutch burgher.[52] Until well into the twentieth century quite a few of Michel's colleagues, including Schmidt-Degener, would persist in this Romantic vision of Rembrandt-as-Bohemian. For Schmidt-Degener the rejection of *The Night Watch* led directly to the transformation of Rembrandt the admired extrovert into Rembrandt the misunderstood introvert.[53] It is hardly surprising that the biographical novels of Rembrandt reflected this same persona of the solitary genius. In Van Loon, for example, we read how Rembrandt is convinced that he has painted a masterpiece, only later to discover much to his dismay that 'le tout Amsterdam' is laughing at him.[54] In Duchateau, opinions on the painting are more divided. Some speak in defense of it, but the ones who think they are not properly represented reject it out of hand.[55] In the end, Rembrandt is paid the pittance of 1600 guilders. To complete the humiliation the large canvas is cut to a smaller size right before his eyes, almost as soon as he finished it.

Art, commerce and 'vanitas'

In the scene of the rejection of *The Night Watch* Korda and Zuckmayer clearly exploit the classic antithesis between art and commerce. By means of this opposition the aspirations of the artist are explicitly set against the practical wishes of his patrons. As if this were not clear enough, halfway through the film Titus once more declares that his father only wishes to paint as he sees fit. This image of Rembrandt's intractability accords with the many anecdotes that he wanted his inspiration and freedom to prevail above all and that he had little or no interest in what his clients demanded. Korda's Rembrandt refuses to give in to the narrow taste of the Dutch 'bourgeoisie' and is stubborn enough to renounce assignments from Frederick Henry, the Prince of Orange. This legendary image of the autonomous Rembrandt, renouncing every commercial pressure stands out in stark contrast to the opinion of historians like Schwartz who think that, on the contrary, Rembrandt was completely dependent on his patrons. Not only did he frequently work on order, eg the important commissions he received from the Court at the Hague between 1627 and 1633, but, reportedly, was eager for payment to such an extent that he delivered some of his paintings while they were still half-wet.[56] One of Schwartz's most important conclusions with regard to Rembrandt's career is the noticeable way his productivity kept pace with the commissions. In this respect one can find that from the 1640s on – because of assignments failing to come through, especially civilian portraits – Rembrandt's output began to drop considerably.[57]

Another reason why Korda uses the image of the artistically autonomous Rembrandt is that it allows the director to touch upon the theme of vanity that as the plot unfolds takes up an increasingly central position. Rembrandt's trajectory from 'sacred fount' to 'ivory tower' encapsulates the demise of a vain

Publicity shot of Rembrandt in his studio entertaining little Titus after completion of 'The Night Watch'.
© London Film Productions – United Artists

individual who learns, painfully, to understand and accept the transience of life. Almost unnoticed, the trajectory appears in the symbolism of the empty picture frame that Rembrandt holds up during his visit to the paint shop. The symbolism of this frame works in two directions: from the spectator's point of view it gives the impression of one of Rembrandt's famous self-portraits; from the artist's view, however, it rather connotes the emptiness of his self-satisfied existence. In the first case ('sacred fount') there is the association with the cocky, successful Rembrandt that he painted in many a triumphant self-portrait. In the second instance (the 'ivory tower') there is the implicit reference to the genre of the *vanitas* painting with its traditional objects (skull, hourglass, timepiece, smouldering candle, toppled-over beaker, skeleton) that serve allegorically as reminders of the fleeting nature of earthly affairs and the inevitability of death. This moralising mentality, so characteristic of the seventeenth-century Dutch Republic, found a strong expression in the so-called *vanitas* still-life. Although Rembrandt did not seem to feel at home within this genre, Korda's film contains several segments in which the *vanitas* theme is further explored.

There are a number of scenes in which the notion of 'vanity' is employed in its modern, twentieth-century meaning, as in the scene where Rembrandt cuts the ostentatious officers down to size. With a touch of irony, however, the film suggests that the painter hardly seems to realise to what extent he himself displays a similar kind of conceit. The first scenes of the film show him as a socially successful, artistically self-confident painter willing to sacrifice everything for his art. The intertextual references by means of which this theme is further elaborated constitute a mixture of legend and historiography. In the classical legends several artists are attributed a certain amount of pride and arrogance in their contacts with princes and rulers. Duris, for instance, tells us how Apelles mercilessly laughs at Alexander the Great because of his nonsensical remarks on art. And about the Italian Renaissance artists countless stories circulated in which they haughtily approached their patrons as equals (cf. eg, Dürer and Maximilan, Titian and Charles V, Michelangelo and Clemens VII).[58] In Korda's film the proverbial arrogance of the artist-bohemian can be recognised in the indifference with which Rembrandt, concentrating intently on his portrait of Saskia, leaves the envoy from Frederick Henry waiting on the doorstep of his studio. This image of the haughty Rembrandt goes back to Arnold Houbraken, an author who because of his classicist prejudice is not widely regarded as a reliable source.[59] Well-known is his anecdote in which Rembrandt, in all his arrogance, abruptly stops work on a client's picture, then finishes it with a portrait of his recently deceased pet monkey. Most of these stories about Rembrandt's arrogance are now said to be apocryphal, but several facts make it hard to exonerate him completely in this or other similar incidents. Schwartz, for instance, does not hesitate to blame him for serious defects of character, among which a sometimes extremely arrogant behaviour.[60] The lowest point in this respect is his scandalous conduct towards the Sicilian art lover Antonio Ruffo, who was brushed of by Rembrandt with a clumsily patched up portrait of Alexander the Great. Other signs point in the same direction. More or less from the moment he settled in Amsterdam, for instance, Rembrandt signed his paintings almost exclusively 'Rembrantf' or 'Rembrantft' instead of 'RHL van Rijn' or 'RHL.' In this he was following the example of the Italians, of Titian, Raphael and Michelangelo, with whom he wished to be compared. His exceptional number of self-portraits, too, has frequently been cited as evidence of his vanity.[61] After being introduced to the circle of the municipal elite at the end of the 1630s he clearly had the intention of portraying himself in a grand 'patrician pose'.[62]

In Korda's film this artistic and social hubris gradually turns into a more humble, inward-looking demeanour. Rembrandt's eager greediness to buy things at the beginning of the film is opposed to the miserable little herring with which he feeds himself near the end. In the same vein Saskia's proud, aristocratic posing can be seen against the modest simplicity of Hendrickje's sitting. This reversal is symbolised in the setting and decor by the sharp contrast between his sumptuous studio at the beginning of the film and the scanty garret at the end, where painting is reduced to its most elementary components: paint, canvas, light and the imagination of the artist. Rembrandt's vanity is also illustrated within the context of several Biblical references. In his first monologue to the men of Banning Cocq, Rembrandt, unconsciously alluding to his later downfall, compares himself explicitly with Job ('There was a man in the land of Uz') a pious man, blessed with great wealth and many children, but plunged by Satan into poverty and misery to test his faith in God. And when Rembrandt returns to the mill of his father Harmen and his brother Adriaen[63] there is the association with the parable of the Prodigal Son.[64] In that same context one has to understand the reference to Saul, one of the Bible's most supercilious characters for whose portrayal in *Rembrandt*, significantly, a beggar is picked from the street. In the end, through these Biblical references, the film comes closer to the original meaning of the word 'vanity'. This is clearly shown in the next-to-last scene in which a fledgling painter celebrates his first success in the company of friends and acquaintances. While everyone else is drinking to beauty, money and women Rembrandt proposes a toast with the words of Salomon: 'Vanity, vanity, all is vanity... A man shall rejoice in his own works.' As a general motto to the whole film, in the final scene, in Rembrandt's simple attic, these words from the Book of Ecclesiastes will be repeated once more. [65]

Conclusion

My analysis has tried to demonstrate that within the context of Alexander Korda's historical films of the 1930s *Rembrandt* occupies a special place. Although in this production the typical *London Film*-style of that period is easy to recognise (eg, the 'keyhole' approach to the past and the narrative sequencing of loosely connected 'tableaux'), it is just as easy to see that Carl Zuckmayer's introspective scenario has created a striking contrast to Korda's more comical (e.g., *Henry VIII, Don Juan*) or opulent (*The Rise of Catherine the Great*, 1934) historical films. In order to fully explore the multi-layered significance of *Rembrandt* as a historical film a broader – filmic, cultural and scientific – context was then brought into play. From this perspective the film was shown to be permeated with the Ur-myth of Rembrandt much as the literary fiction of that period was. Especially the Rembrandt novel of Hendrik Willem Van Loon, published in 1930, just before the production of Korda's film, carried quite a lot of weight in that respect. Just like nearly every *vie romancée* on Rembrandt the book was heavily inspired by the image of Rembrandt as it had emerged out of early 'art-historical studies' by the likes of Arnold Houbraken. The legendary discourse on which the narrative structure of *Rembrandt* leans so heavily, can, however, also be traced back to the work of various art historians. Neumann's image of the bipartite Rembrandt and its popularisation by Schmidt-Degener have played a notably central role. Surpassing the immediate context of the Rembrandt discourse as such, many aspects of these legends appeared to reach back to both the earliest artist anecdotes as well as to a number of myths of the gods and heroes of Antiquity. Bringing together that background, the film explores themes that go beyond the specific figure of Rembrandt and bear upon more general issues such as the nature of artistic genius and artistic creation.

At least as significant as this connection is the gap between *Rembrandt* and its cultural-scientific background. Remarkably the film dispenses with several vivid and (from a dramatic angle) very rewarding anecdotes that are closely tied to the Ur-myth (e.g. those about Rembrandt's greed for money). In addition it is striking that in comparison with the literary Rembrandt fiction of those days Korda's film scarcely relies at all on melodrama. This fits in with the fact that, although here too some of the oddities are inevitably displayed historical films seemingly cannot do without (cf. the way Jan Six and Banning Cocq walk about in the costumes Rembrandt has immortalised them in) *Rembrandt* emphatically aims for an adult treatment of its subject. This is borne out by the fact that with respect to the representation of Rembrandt's love life the film follows a much more explicit (and in a sense more authentic) line of action than many 'scientific' studies of that period.

In comparison with the classic biopic, furthermore, there is not much that *Rembrandt* has in common with the triumphant trajectory this 'genre' usually covers. As far as the subgenre of the artist biopic is concerned one can even speak of a pioneering role in the sense that in its filmic representation of artistic genius *Rembrandt* employs textual elements and strategies that, while strongly reflecting cultural norms and ideas of its time, would leave their mark on the mainstream artist film to this day.

Notes

1   Kris, E. and O. Kurz (1979) *Legend, Myth and Magic in the Image of the Artist. A Historical Experiment*. New Haven-London: Yale University Press. This remarkable study was first published in 1934, 'rediscovered' in the 1970s and later published in an English translation with a preface by Ernst Gombrich.

2   Korda was not the first one to make a film on Rembrandt. Arthur Günsburg, with *Die Tragödie eines Grossen* (1920), had the *primeur* of a feature film on the Dutch master. More than twenty years later Nazi director Hans Steinhoff made his *Ewiger Rembrandt* (1942), partly in occupied Holland. During the war years the shooting of a Rembrandt film by Gerard Rutten was interrupted by the Germans; later, several fragments of this aborted project turned up in the documentary *Rembrandt in de schuilkelder* (*Rembrandt in the Air-Raid Shelter*, 1941-1946). Jos Stelling's *Rembrandt fecit 1669*, made in 1977, represents the first and so far the only Dutch feature film on Rembrandt, while Charles Matton's *Rembrandt* (1999) closes the series. Due for 2007 is a Rembrandt film by Peter Greenaway (titled *Nightwatching*).

3   Watts, S. (1933) Alexander Korda and the International Film, pp. 12-15 in *Cinema Quarterly*, 2 (1).

4   Korda, M. (1981) *Charmed Lives*. New York: Avon, p. 107.

5   Cf. Kulik, K. (1975) *Alexander Korda. The Man Who Could Work Miracles*. New Rochelle: Arlington House Publishers, pp. 96-98.

6   Tabori, P. (1966) *Alexander Korda*. New York: Living Books, p. 165.

7   Cf. Drazin, Ch. (2002) *Korda. Britain's Only Movie Mogul*. London: Sidgwick & Jackson, p. 152.

8   This period is extensively treated in Claus, H. (2001) Zuckmayers Arbeiten für den Film in London 1934 bis 1939, pp. 341-411 in Nickel, G. (ed.) *Carl Zuckmayer und die Medien. Beiträge zu einem internationalen Symposion*. St. Ingbert: Röhrig Universitätsverlag.

9   Zuckmayer in a letter to Albrecht Joseph, Henndorf, 7 December 1935, quoted in Claus (2001), p. 369.

10 Claus (2001), p. 375.

11 Besides Zuckmayer, Biró and Wimperis the scenario had the co-operation of June Head. Her main task was to translate Zuckmayer's script from German into English.

12 Zuckmayer's *Rembrandt*-scenario has been posthumously published as *Rembrandt. Ein Film* (1980) Frankfurt am Main: Fischer Taschenbuch Verlag.

13 Slive, S. (1953) *Rembrandt and His Critics 1630-1730*. The Hague: Martinus Nijhoff, p. 4.

14 Emmens, J.A. (1979) *Rembrandt en de regels van de kunst*. Amsterdam: G.A. van Oorschot. This study was defended as a dissertation in 1964 and for the first time published in book form in 1968. Contemporary Rembrandt experts as White and Scheller point out that despite the facts that have come to light in the past century, many obscurities with regard to Rembrandt's life and career still remain, leaving room for all sorts of myths and legends that contribute to make the painter a victim of a Romantic imagination. Cf. White, Ch. (1984) *Rembrandt*, London: Thames and Hudson, p. 7; Boomgaard, J. and R. W. Scheller (1991) In wankel evenwicht. De Rembrandt-waardering in vogelvlucht, in: Brown, Ch., J. Kelch and P. van Thiel (eds) (1991) *Rembrandt. De meester en zijn werkplaats. Schilderijen*. Zwolle: Rijksmuseum Amsterdam-Waanders Uitgevers, p. 120.

15 Knuttel, G. (1956) *Rembrandt. De meester en zijn werk*. Amsterdam: Ploegsma; Benesch, O. (1957) *Rembrandt. Étude biographique et critique*. Genève: Albert Skira; Rosenberg, J. (1964) *Rembrandt*. London: Phaidon Press.

16 Brom, G. (1936) *Rembrandt in de literatuur*. Allard Pierson Stichting, Afdeling voor Moderne Literatuurwetenschap, Universiteit van Amsterdam, No. 10, Groningen-Batavia: J. B. Wolters, p. 30.

17 Brom (1936), p. 31.

18 Zuckmayer, C. (1966) *Als wär's ein Stück von mir. Horen der Freundschaft*. Stuttgart-Hamburg: Deutscher Bücherbund, p. 346.

19 Beebe, M. (1964) *Ivory Towers and Sacred Founts. The Artist as Hero in Fiction from Goethe to Joyce*. New York: New York University Press.

20 In this respect Beebe refers to the Romantic and early-Victorian literature and to the genre of the so-called *apprentice novel*.

21 Beebe situates this tradition in French literature from the second half of the 19th century and in the Aesthetic Movement in England.

22 The classic pattern, traceable to the texts of Duris, is that of a young man of humble origin (in Renaissance versions often a shepherd, cf. Giotto) who displays signs of extraordinary talent, that is coincidentally discovered by a passing master or Maecenas who then introduces him in a circle where he can develop his talents and gain social and artistic glory. Kris and Kurz (1979, p. 38) point out that

the narrative pattern of these legends bears a close resemblance to the way the young manhood of the ancient heroes is narrated in myths.

23 The character of Ludwick is based on the art dealer Lodewijk van Ludick. In the original Zuckmayer script this character bears the name of Ornia, based on the art dealer Gerbrand Ornia. Rembrandt had trouble with both of them because of a loan he had obtained from Jan Six in 1653.

24 Vasari, G. (1996) *De levens van de kunstenaars*. Amsterdam: Pandora, p. 282.

25 Duchateau, M. (1949) *Rembrandt Harmenszoon van Rijn. Fijnschilder*, Leuven: Davidsfonds, p. 97.

26 Kris and Kurz (1979), p. 41.

27 Alpers, S. (1989) *De firma Rembrandt. Schilder tussen handel en kunst*. Amsterdam: Bert Bakker, p. 52 et seq.

28 Wittkower, R. and M. Wittkower (1969) *Born Under Saturn. The Character and Conduct of Artists. A Documented History from Antiquity to the French Revolution*. New York-London: W.W. Norton & Company, p. 157.

29 Dudok van Heel, S. (2001) *Rembrandt van Rijn (Leiden 1606-Amsterdam 1669) De schilder, zijn leven, zijn vrouw, de min en het dienstmeisje*. Amsterdam: Museum Het Rembrandthuis, p. 3.

30 De Vries, Th. (1934) *Rembrandt*. Arnhem: Van Loghum Slaterus, p. 13.

31 Van Loon, H.W. (1947) *The Life & Times of Rembrandt van Rijn*. London: Walter Edwards, p. 319.

32 Kris & Kurz (1979), pp. 66-67.

33 Kris & Kurz (1979), p. 43.

34 Kris & Kurz (1979), p. 48.

35 In the opposite direction the image of God as Creator-Artist develops: first as builder-forger of the world, then as sculptor of mankind (cf. the painting of Jupiter by Dosso Dossi).

36 Shroder, M. Z. (1961) *Icarus. The Image of the Artist in French Romanticism*. Cambridge: Harvard University Press, p. 27 et seq.

37 Shroder (1961), p. 32.

38 Kris and Kurz (1979), pp. 118-119.

39 White (1984), p. 93.

40 Muller, J. E. (1968), *Rembrandt*. London: Thames and Hudson, p. 67. Some art historians have noticed that in the later years the relationship between Rembrandt and Saskia seems to have deteriorated. The question of Saskia's inheritance is sometimes seen as proof of this. Schwartz finds that the will Saskia drew up just before her death put Rembrandt in a difficult financial position (Schwartz, G. (1986) *Rembrandt. His Life, His Paintings*. London: Guild Publishing, p. 223). Schama has no very positive impression of the will either: 'there is something odd, distinctly cautious, about the document, as if in the year of *The Night Watch*, the optimism of their marriage had caught a sudden chill.' (Schama, S. (1999) *Rembrandt's Eyes*. London: Allen Lane, p. 508).

41 Schama (1999), p. 380 et seq.

42 Of the *Flora* of 1634 (St. Petersburg, Hermitage) it is generally assumed that Saskia can be recognised in it and the same goes for the *Flora* of 1641 (Dresden, Gemäldegalerie alte Meister). More doubts exist with regard to the *Flora* of around 1635 (London, The National Gallery).

43 In some mythical versions Flora herself had a past as a prostitute.

44 Brown, Kelch and van Thiel (1991), p. 253.

45 Emmens (1979), p. 200; also Bevers, H., P. Schatborn and B. Welzel (1991) *Rembrandt. De meester & zijn werkplaats. Tekeningen en etsen*. Zwolle: Rijksmuseum Amsterdam-Waanders Uitgevers, pp. 212-214.

46 This character probably refers to Andries Bicker (1586-1652) who for about thirty years was one of the most powerful regents of Amsterdam.

47 Anachronistically enough the painting on display is the cut-up version.

48 In this way the film clearly distances itself from the countless anecdotes of Rembrandt's legendary stinginess and greed.

49 Since Slive has established that there is no proof that Rembrandt's clients were dissatisfied with *The Night Watch* it is *communis opinio* in art history circles that the rejection of the painting is a fable (Slive (1953), p. 5 et seq.; Emmens (1979), p. 31).

50 Scheller, R.W. (1961) Rembrandt's reputatie van Houbraken tot Scheltema, p. 111 et seq. in *Nederlands Kunsthistorisch Jaarboek* 12.

51 Emmens (1979), p. 30.

52 Michel, E. (1893) *Rembrandt. Sa vie, son oeuvre et son temps* (2 tomes), Paris: Hachette. Also: Emmens (1979), p. 30.

53 Emmens (1979), p. 31.

54 Van Loon (1947), p. 99 et seq.

55 Duchateau (1949), p. 100.

56 For example, the last two paintings from the Passion series commissioned by Frederick Henry. Cf. Schwartz (1986), pp. 116-117.

57 Schama (1999), p. 511.

58 Kris & Kurz (1979), p. 41.

59 Emmens (1979), p. 105.

60 Schwartz (1986), p. 362.

61 Schwartz (1986), p. 59.

62 Schwartz (1986), p. 204.

63 An anachronism because both had already died by that time.

64 The Biblical atmosphere of this homecoming is underscored by Rembrandt reading the Bible before supper and later by his breaking the bread.

65 Ecclesiastes I:2 and III:22. Once again Zuckmayer seems to have been inspired by Van Loon who uses the same periscope (Van Loon (1947), p. 101).

Robert Morley as the Earl of Manchester rides into battle in Cromwell (1970) © Columbia Pictures

The World Turned Upside Down: *Cromwell* (1970), *Winstanley* (1975), *To Kill A King* (2003) and the British historical film

James Chapman

While the historical film has been an ever-present production trend within British cinema for many decades, it is only quite recently that the genre has become part of the agenda of British film and cultural studies. The range and extent of recent scholarship has comprehensively put the lie to Alan Lovell's sweeping dismissal of the genre when he unwisely remarked that it 'can safely be ignored as being of little intrinsic interest'.[1] In recent times the historical film has found itself at the centre of debates around the economic and cultural viability of British national cinema, the use of the past as a vehicle for the dissemination of dominant ideology, and its contested place within 'taste wars' between middle-brow critics and commentators on the one hand and the popular preferences of cinema audiences on the other. These agendas have, to a large extent, pushed the old chestnut of the disputed authenticity or accuracy of the historical film into the background, though charges that films present a false and inaccurate view of the past persist in the critical response to major examples of the genre such as *Chariots of Fire* (1981) and *Elizabeth* (1998).

Contexts

A conventional taxonomy of the British historical film sees it in terms of production cycles that are usually related to the main producers and studios. In the 1930s, for example, historical film production was associated particularly with major independent producers such as Alexander Korda and Herbert Wilcox who saw the genre as a vehicle for the creation of a distinctively British national cinema that was culturally different from classical Hollywood. Korda's *The Private Life of Henry VIII* (1933) and Wilcox's *Victoria the Great* (1937) were highly prestigious films that were not only commercially successful but were also acclaimed by critics for their representation of British historical subjects. During the Second World War the historical film became a vehicle for propaganda with a cycle of patriotic epics that drew explicit parallels between past and present, culminating in Laurence Olivier's production of *Henry V* (1944) for the Rank Organisation. In post-war decades the genre responded to the decline of British power by recreating inspiring stories of courage and heroism from Britain's past: *Scott of the Antarctic* (1948) for Michael Balcon's Ealing Studios, *A Night to Remember* (1958) for Rank and *Zulu* (1964) for the American producer Joseph E. Levine. More recently the contraction of the production sector of the British film industry has meant that historical films have become fewer in number, but the genre has still attracted ambitious independent producers such as David Puttnam, whose Oscar-winning triumph with *Chariots of Fire* was seen by many commentators to represent a revival for British film-making in the early 1980s, and Working Title, the most successful British production company of recent times, which enjoyed critical and commercial success with *Elizabeth*, made for Europe's closest equivalent of the Hollywood majors, Polygram Filmed Entertainment, at the time a division of the Dutch electronics corporation Phillips.

Within this taxonomy of production trends and cycles it is possible to identify certain recurring themes and motifs that consistently inform the genre. The British historical film has privileged biopics focusing on the kings and queens of England or on the lives of revered national heroes, statesmen and adventurers.[2] It has represented the British past in accordance with a popular view of history that sees Britain as a liberal democracy leading resistance to foreign tyrants and it has dramatised notable British achievements in various fields such as exploration, aviation and sport. Furthermore, the favourite periods for producers of historical films have tended to be those which give rise to narratives of national greatness. Hence the prominence of films about the Tudor period, which saw the emergence of England as a great power; about the Victorian era, which witnessed industrial progress and imperial expansion; and about the Second World War, which in the popular imagination of the British public still remains 'our finest hour'.[3] In contrast there have been relatively few films about periods of internal strife and conflict such as the Dark Ages or the English Civil Wars.

This essay examines three British feature films: *Cromwell* (directed by Ken Hughes, 1970), *Winstanley* (directed by Kevin Brownlow and Andrew Mollo, 1975) and *To Kill A King* (directed by Mike Barker, 2003) – which collectively represent the sum total of British cinema's historiography of the civil wars of the 1640s and the subsequent period of Oliver Cromwell's protectorate. There have been other films set during the Interregnum period, though these have for the most part been fictional narratives that use the conflict between Cavaliers and Roundheads as a historical background for adventure stories. Two British-made swashbucklers – *The Moonraker* (1958) and *The Scarlet Blade* (1963) – had at most only a casual acquaintance with recorded history. *The Moonraker*, produced by Hamilton Inglis for the Associated British Picture Corporation and based on a play by Arthur Watkyn, featured a fictional Royalist hero, the Earl of Dawlish who rescues Charles II from the Roundheads in 1651. *The Scarlet Blade*, produced by Anthony Nelson Keys for Hammer Film Productions, was one of the economically-produced adventure films that the studio turned out between its horror productions and released during school holidays. It borrowed (unacknowledged) the premise of Alexandre Dumas's *Three Musketeers* sequel *Twenty Years After* in that it was about a secret Royalist plan hatched by one Edward Beverly (Jack Hedley) to rescue Charles I from the scaffold – a scheme which, for obvious historical reasons, ends in failure. Neither film was especially distinguished: they were routine, economy-conscious productions (*The Moonraker* confines much of its action to the interior of an inn, *The Scarlet Blade* used sets left over from 1962's *The Devil-Ship Pirates*) made at a time when the swashbuckling adventure was on its last legs as the genre had moved over to television in the form of ATV's *The Adventures of Robin Hood* (1955-1959), *The Buccaneers* (1956-1957), *The Count of Monte Cristo* (1956), *The Adventures of Sir Lancelot* (1956-1957), *The Adventures of William Tell* (1958-1959), *Sword of Freedom* (1958-1960) and *Sir Francis Drake* (1961-1962). Their representation of the period conforms to the popular view of the civil wars in which the Cavaliers are characterised as handsome, heroic and romantic in contrast to the Roundheads who are dour, ruthless and humourless.[4]

A stronger case could be made for the inclusion of *Witchfinder General* (1968), which at least concerns an actual historical person, Matthew Hopkins, a notorious witch-hunter who operated in East Anglia towards the end of the first civil war, though it is a heavily fictionalised narrative – loosely based on Ronald Bassett's 1966 novel of the same title – that tends more usually to be located within the horror genre.[5] It was the third and last feature directed by the talented Michael Reeves – following *Revenge of the Blood Beast* (1966) and *The Sorcerers* (1967) – who died from an overdose of barbiturates shortly after its release. *Witchfinder General* was produced by Tigon, a small company specialising in horror films, which at the time had a production arrangement with American International Pictures, the leading producer of exploitation films which had enjoyed commercial success with Roger Corman's Edgar Allan Poe series, *The Fall of the House of Usher* (1960), *The Pit and the Pendulum* (1961), *The Raven* (1963), *The Masque of the Red Death* (1964) and *The Tomb of Ligeia* (1964). The casting of Vincent Price, star of those films, suggests that AIP probably saw *Witchfinder General* as similar fodder for the exploitation market, but Reeves and his co-writer Tom Baker turned out a film that was very different both in its content and in its style from the camp melodramatics of the Corman-Poe films.

Although attracting adverse criticism at the time for what many perceived to be its sadistic violence (it includes graphic scenes of torture, and, moreover, the torture of women), *Witchfinder General* is characterised by a degree of moral seriousness and visual beauty that differentiates it from run-of-the-mill exploitation fare and demands that it be taken seriously. It is a study of the consequences of social disintegration and the brutalising effect of violence upon the innocent. The idea that the civil war has created a power vacuum is established by a sober voice-over narration: 'The structure of law and order has collapsed. Local magistrates indulge their individual whims. Justice and injustice are dispensed in more or less equal quantities without opposition. An atmosphere in which the unscrupulous rebel, the likes of Matthew Hopkins, take full advantage of the situation.' The bleak tone of the film is established by the opening sequence where a woman accused of witchcraft is dragged, screaming, across a desolate landscape and hanged from a gallows on a windswept hill. The visual style, with bleak country landscapes photographed in muted colour, is far removed from the elegant pictorialism of contemporary period costume films such as *Far from the Madding Crowd* (1967) or *The Go-Between* (1970): here the countryside is no pastoral idyll but is full of menace and foreboding.[6] The violence of the film, far from being gratuitous, is used legitimately: Matthew Hopkins (an uncharacteristically subdued performance from Price) is characterised as a zealot who has become so obsessed by purging society of witchcraft that he has become corrupted by his own religious fervour into a tyrant and persecutor. Reeves does not sensationalise violence, nor, unlike various other 'witchfinder' films that followed in its wake – *El Juez Sangriento* (*The Bloody Judge*, 1969), *Hexen bis aufs Blut Gequaelt* (*Mark of the Devil*, 1969) and *The Devils* (1971) – does *Witchfinder General* attempt to eroticise sexual violence against women as a form of spectacle. Reeves's representation of violence is objective and detached: this is where the true horror of the film lies. The climax is shocking and sudden: nominal hero, Roundhead soldier Richard Marshall (Ian Ogilvy), forced to watch the torture of his fiancée Sara (Hilary Dwyer), breaks free of his bonds and viciously bludgeons Hopkins to death with an axe, while the last shot of the film is a close up of Sara's face, her screams suggesting that the ordeal has driven her insane.

Witchfinder General uses various devices in an attempt to authenticate its fiction, including the opening commentary which establishes the time (1645) and place (East Anglia) and a brief appearance by 'guest star' Patrick Wymark as Oliver Cromwell. It was *Cromwell*, however, which marked the first historical film proper (as opposed to a largely fictional film set against a historical background) about the events of the civil wars and their aftermath. *Cromwell* was one of a cycle of expensively-produced historical films in the late 1960s and early 1970s that also included *The Charge of the Light Brigade* (1968), *Alfred the Great* (1969), *Anne of the Thousand Days* (1969), *Mary, Queen of Scots* (1971), *Young Winston* (1972), *Lady Caroline Lamb* (1972) and *A Bequest to the Nation* (1973). Most of these films, with the exception of EMI's *Lady Caroline Lamb*, were part of what has been called the 'Hollywood England' trend in that they were backed by American studios which at this time were investing heavily in British production: United Artists (*The Charge of the Light Brigade*), MGM (*Alfred the Great*), Universal (*Anne of the Thousand Days*, *Mary, Queen of Scots*, *A Bequest to the Nation*) and Columbia (*Cromwell*, *Young Winston*). They shared common characteristics: high production values, literate scripts and the use of visual style to assert period authenticity. They were marketed as 'hard-ticket specials', opening at a restricted number of prestigious cinemas before their general circuit release. The levels of capital investment ($6.5 million for *The Charge of the Light Brigade*, over $8 million for *Cromwell*) would suggest that the films were regarded as potential blockbusters, though in the event most of these films were so expensive to produce that they recorded a net loss for the studios involved and helped to precipitate the withdrawal of US investment from the British production sector.[7]

An unrecorded meeting between Cromwell and the King? Richard Harris and Alec Guinness on the set of *Cromwell* (1970). © Columbia Pictures

Cavaliers and Roundheads

Cromwell was produced by Irving Allen, former partner of Bond co-producer Albert R. Broccoli in Warwick Pictures during the 1950s, and written and directed by Ken Hughes, a versatile British director whose previous credits include Warwick's *The Trials of Oscar Wilde* (1960) and Broccoli's *Chitty Chitty Bang Bang* (1968). Hughes's aim was 'to bring to the screen for the first time the full story of Oliver Cromwell and the panorama of events that tore apart a family as well as a kingdom'.[8] Irving Allen and Ken Hughes assembled a cast of notable British actors, headed by Richard Harris as Cromwell and Alec Guinness as Charles I, with Robert Morley as the Earl of Manchester, Dorothy Tutin as Queen Henrietta Maria, Timothy Dalton as Prince Rupert and Patrick Wymark as the Earl of Strafford. *Cromwell* was shot on location in Spain in the summer of 1969, followed by interiors at Shepperton Studios. It was released in Britain in July 1970, opening at the prestigious Odeon, Leicester Square.[9]

The critical reception of *Cromwell* can best be described as one of muted approval. It won praise for its production values and for the acting of Harris and, especially, Guinness, though several critics found it dramatically rather dull. It was seen very much as a traditional exercise in historical film-making. Thus David Robinson in the *Financial Times* averred that it 'conforms loyally to the old traditions of the historical epic genre' and Penelope Houston in the *Spectator* called it 'a thumping return to traditionalism'. Patrick Gibbs in the *Daily Telegraph* thought it was a retrograde step for the genre: 'After such intelligent, small-scale historical films as "A Man for all Seasons" and "The Lion in Winter" it is sad to return to the old, blockbusting pseudo-DeMille style with "Cromwell".' Derek Malcolm in the *Guardian* described it as a 'series of more or less animated historical tableaux that are fitted together between the battles' and felt that Hughes 'might well have done his subject more justice if he had been given less money to spend on it' as the 'production values of such a film have meant too many compromises'. The reviews in the popular press were more favourable. Ian Christie in the *Daily Express* called it 'a historical epic that excites the imagination and stirs the emotions without insulting the intelligence', and Richard Baker in the *Sunday Express* thought it 'a nicely-costumed and authentic-looking historical piece'. The reaction of the specialist film review journals was divided. *Films and Filming* acclaimed it as an 'excellent and exciting epic ... an intelligent and hugely enjoyable film', adding for good measure that the battle sequences 'must rank with the finest ever filmed', whereas the more jaundiced *Monthly Film Bulletin* complained that 'Period atmosphere is almost entirely lacking' and concluded that '*Cromwell* tries to combine serious intentions with the widest kind of popular appeal and falls unhappily between the two. It will offend the purists and bore the kiddies.'[10]

With its linear narrative structure, its emphasis on period detail in sets and costumes, and its spectacular battle sequences, *Cromwell* does indeed exemplify a conventional form of historical film-making. It adheres to the conventions of the historical epic in its focus on a charismatic protagonist, characterised in terms of accepted norms of psychological realism, who becomes an agent of historical change. Cromwell himself is represented as a proponent of 'democracy' (an entirely anachronistic and misleading use of the word) who believes in the 'true representation of the people' through Parliament. In order to safeguard the principle of English liberty he is prepared first to take up arms against the King and then to dissolve Parliament by force when its members have betrayed the cause for which they fought. He is a reluctant leader who assumes power only as a last resort and who resolves to 'give this nation back its self respect'. The motif of the reluctant hero whose life is shaped by destiny locates *Cromwell* squarely within the tradition of international historical epics represented by Anthony Mann's *El Cid* (1961) and David Lean's *Lawrence of Arabia* (1962), though it failed to match either the critical or commercial success of those films.

Cromwell also exemplifies a perennial problem faced by historical film-makers: that historical events rarely, if ever, fit into a coherent narrative pattern. It is generally accepted, even by its most severe critics, that the historical film has to take certain liberties with the past in the interests of dramatic coherence: thus events are often compressed and composite characters are created in order to assist audience comprehension. *Cromwell*, however, was criticised for taking more liberties than most. The *Monthly Film Bulletin* complained that the film 'cannot justify distortion of historical fact even in the service of dramatic effect', and a correspondent in *Films and Filming* called it a 'compound of falsehoods and half-truths'.[11] The film makes Cromwell a much more active participant in events: he becomes one of the 'five members' whom the King's attempt to arrest precipitated the civil war and during the war itself becomes commander-in-chief of the New Model Army, a position in fact held by Sir Thomas Fairfax. The film's most glaring departure from the historical record is that it contrives no fewer than three face-to-face meetings between Cromwell and Charles I (and another three occasions when they are both present at the same time without actually speaking to each other) when there is no reliable evidence that the two men ever met. This, however, was a familiar tactic of historical film-makers: *Mary, Queen of Scots* included two entirely fictitious meetings between Mary Stuart (Vanessa Redgrave) and Elizabeth I (Glenda Jackson). On that occasion the producer, Hal B. Wallis, clearly had no qualms about taking such a liberty: 'Audiences would feel cheated if they never had a scene together. I'd rather face the wrath of a few stuffy historians and get my big dramatic scene.'[12]

There are other instances where the film's version of historical events would seem to have been influenced, perhaps even determined, by external factors. It has been a recurring feature of the British historical film that its representation of the past is also to some extent a commentary on the present: the genre responds to and is informed by the ideological, social and cultural conditions prevailing at the moment of production. Several critics, for example, remarked upon the absence of any reference to Cromwell's brutal suppression of Irish rebels in 1649-50. A sequence was shot but was cut from the finished film on the grounds 'that the Irish episode interrupted the dramatic flow of the film when it needed to be wrapped up quickly after the death of the King'.[13] It is tempting to speculate that another consideration may have been that the film's production coincided with a period of renewed sectarian strife in Northern Ireland. British troops were sent to the province in April 1969 and that summer the Irish Republican Army, relatively quiescent since the Second World War, resumed its campaign of organised terrorist violence. This was not a time to revive memories of such notorious massacres such as Drogheda and Wexford. One clear contemporary reference that was apparent at the time was Cromwell's concluding speech in which he promises that 'I will build schools and universities for all. This will be the golden age of learning.' This has clear echoes of the Labour government of Harold Wilson, elected in 1964, which oversaw radical expansion of the higher education sector with the establishment of new universities such as East Anglia, Essex, Kent, Lancaster, Stirling, Sussex, Warwick and York, culminating with the formation in 1969 of The Open University which did indeed represent a new form of education for all. One commentator was moved to remark that 'far from clearing the House at the point of a sword in order to make a Wilsonian speech about schools, colleges, universities and the birth of democracy in England, all that Cromwell could find to do was to establish a military dictatorship, during which the ordinary people, after suffering worse barbarities than those attributed by the film to the late lamented King, came to long for the return of the Stuart monarchy'.[14]

Another criticism made of the film – made, indeed, of most major historical films by critics on the political left – was that it privileged a 'great man' approach to history at the expense of the wider social context of the past. It was a frequent complaint of Nina Hibbin, long-standing film critic of the *Daily Worker* and its successor the *Morning Star* – the official mouthpieces of the Communist Party of Great Britain – that mainstream historical feature films either marginalised or omitted entirely an engagement with the social conditions and lives of ordinary people. It was a point she made again about *Cromwell*, asking rhetorically:

> 'But where, apart from occasional glimpses of anonymous acquiescing crowds, are the people? What are their conditions and their sufferings? A small episode showing peasants being beaten off the common land by an officer enforcing an enclosure order is a gesture in the right direction. But it is the film's single hint that the seventeenth-century Britain it depicts is in the process of dramatic social change ... Not a word, needless to say (apart from a brief street oratory scene), about the Levellers and the Diggers and the other groupings representing the aspirations of the various classes grouped around the Cromwell cause.'[15]

However, the suggestion that the film should have engaged with the social consequences of the English Revolution was rejected by Dilys Powell, the venerable film critic of the *Sunday Times*: 'The popular cinema is no place for revolutionary interpretations of history.'[16]

Diggers and Dissidents

Yet while *Cromwell* had nothing to say about the emergence of radical movements in the 1640s and 1650s – Levellers, True Levellers, Diggers, Ranters, Seekers, Fifth Monarchists and the rest – Kevin Brownlow and Andrew Mollo were planning a film that did. Brownlow, a film historian and archivist, had already collaborated with historian Mollo in making the 'alternative history' film *It Happened Here* (1965), a documentary-style account of Britain under Nazi occupation. Brownlow and Mollo worked independently, outside the commercial film industry, raising financial backing from friends and supporters such as Tony Richardson and Stanley Kubrick. *It Happened Here* took eight years to complete; *Winstanley* took nine from the initial idea to its eventual release. The film was based on David Caute's historical novel *Comrade Jacob* (1961) and the £17.000 to develop it was provided by the British Film Institute Production Board which had recently changed its policy from backing only short films as a 'ticket' into the industry for new directors to also supporting features by established film-makers on the condition that 'ideas for films should reveal some kind of originality'.[17] *Winstanley*, as the title became, was shot over a year between 1974 and 1975, using a largely non-professional cast which necessitated shooting mostly at weekends. It was made in black-and-white and using both 16-millimetre and 35-millimetre film.[18]

Winstanley is an account of Gerrard Winstanley, a former cloth merchant who turned pamphleteer, arguing for common ownership of the land and for ordinary people to have the same rights as the gentry. Winstanley led a sect known as Diggers and founded a commune at St George's Hill, Weybridge, Surrey. This was one of the radical secular movements that flourished briefly following the temporary disestablishment of the Church of England.[19] The Diggers had been largely written out of history until Winstanley's writings were rediscovered and published in the 1940s. The communal values and opposition to property ownership that Winstanley espoused became particularly relevant in the 1960s when hippie communes were established on university campuses in Paris and Berkeley. Brownlow in fact recruited a group who called themselves New Diggers to appear in *Winstanley*, averring that 'their spokesman, Sid Rawle, became most enthusiastic about the film. He was one of the few people in the country with personal knowledge of Winstanley's kind of commune. He had organised a similar commune on an island off the coast of Kerry, Ireland, which lasted for two years.'

Winstanley can be seen as an example of what, following Robert Rosenstone, we may term 'the New History film'. This a type of film that 'finds the space to *contest* history, to interrogate either the meta-narratives that structure historical knowledge, or smaller historical truths, received notions, conventional

Miles Halliwell played the seventeenth-century dissident in the remarkable *Winstanley* (1975).
© BFI Production

images'.[20] *Winstanley* does this in a number of ways: it has a non-linear narrative structure, its mise-en-scène is crowded with historical detail rather than being used in support of narrative, explanatory inter-titles are kept to a minimum and the historical context is established only through quotations from Winstanley's writings rather than by recourse to traditional voice-overs or rolling captions. The whole film has a rough-edged feel that distinguishes it from the polished products of mainstream cinema. Yet in an odd sort of way this actually works to its advantage. The non-professional actors, for example, give the impression of living history rather than acting out a role which makes their performances seem more authentic. Interestingly, Brownlow revealed: 'We tried first to cast the film with professionals, and either the agents turned us down because we could pay only the Equity minimum, or the actor we selected (i.e. Eric Porter for Parson Platt!) rejected the script. With some relief, therefore, we decided to cast non-professionals (with the exception of the role of Lord General Fairfax, for whom we wanted Jerome Willis).'

Winstanley had only a limited release, restricted for the most part to film festivals and screenings at the National Film Theatre. It nevertheless attracted considerable attention from critics and was generally admired for its boldness and its refreshingly different interpretation of the past. Derek Malcolm thought that 'clearly Brownlow and Mollo are not after creating a film about individuals so much as recreating a feeling for time and place through which their ideas can be effectively formulated'. Alexander Walker called it 'a stark, hard, practical and beautiful film that shows the passion of its makers ... in its period accuracy and almost lyrical use of man and landscape in the pursuit of political ends'. David Robinson averred that it 'exemplifies some of the characteristic strengths of the new British cinema: a sturdy, uncompromising *Englishness*; a peculiar sensitivity to time and place and mood'. He also felt that it exhibited 'a visual style inherited from the classic days of silent American cinema'. John Coleman also admired the visual composition, suggesting that 'you could probably stop it at any frame and come up with a composition reminiscent of the sky-line of the Russians or the intimate Carl Dreyer'.[21]

As well as appealing to cinephiles, *Winstanley* also found a champion in the academy. Brownlow had shown an early cut to Christopher Hill, Master of Balliol College, Oxford, and a renowned social historian of the seventeenth century whose books included the classic *The World Turned Upside Down*

Filming **Winstanley**: Andrew Mollo behind an Arriflex camera. © Kevin Brownlow Collection

(1975) and a collection of essays about Cromwell entitled *God's Englishman* (1970). Hill evidently liked the film, as he went as far as to endorse it in the prestigious scholarly history journal *Past and Present*:

> 'Good historical films are sufficiently rare for it to be worth drawing attention to Winstanley, directed by Kevin Brownlow and Andrew Mollo. Although made on a shoe-string budget, the film's detail is meticulously accurate, down to the shoes which the Diggers wear, the agricultural implements they use, the breed of animals they farm ... But more important than this convincing background is the imaginative reconstruction of the world in which the Diggers lived – still torn by social conflict, but one in which fundamental reform still seemed possible. This film can tell us more about ordinary people in seventeenth-century England than a score of textbooks ... Winstanley is never likely to be a commercial success, but it is a film that readers of Past and Present should go out of their way to see if they get a chance.'[22]

It is rare indeed for a professional historian to offer such a glowing testimonial to a historical film: usually they are only too eager to demonstrate their superior historical knowledge and to list the myriad minor errors they can identify. What is particularly interesting here is Hill's assessment that *Winstanley* was not only authentic in its period detail but also in its evocation of the mood of the times. This is something extraordinarily difficult to achieve.

For all that *Winstanley* was seen as an authentic reconstruction of the past, however, it was nevertheless still informed by the present. John C. Tibbetts avers that it is 'a presentist view of history. Brownlow and Mollo project contemporary concerns and considerations onto the screen of a meticulously constructed past.'[23] There is more to this than just the fact that the film's gestation period in the late 1960s and early 1970s coincided with the emergence of counter-cultural movements whose values of communal living, pacifism and free love were similar to the outlook of the Diggers, though this undoubtedly gave the film a currency that it may not have enjoyed had it been made at a different time. *Winstanley* is a study in failure: the failure of a revolutionary movement. The social experiment of the Diggers is beset by the hardships of communal life (Winstanley learns that his idealism is insufficient to cope with grim economic reality) and by external opposition (the landowners who resent their presence and who eventually destroy the commune by burning it). The late 1960s – and particularly the events of May 1968 in France – had seemed to promise the possibility of both a political and a social revolution in which the catalyst was direct action by students and workers. This did not, of course, materialise, and, as recent research has conclusively demonstrated, had never been very likely to happen anyway, though the myth has persisted amongst a certain breed of Marxist intellectuals about the tragic failure of the 'revolution' of 1968.[24] There are parallels to be drawn here with the failure of the radical movements of the English Revolution. It must be considered, however, that Brownlow disavowed any overt political message in the film:

> 'It isn't really a political film. It is a trip in a time-machine back to the seventeenth century; a glimpse of a heroic attempt to change the way people lived. The fact that Winstanley was a couple of hundred years ahead of his time in his political thinking gives it the political relevance. He was a true communist, but his compassion and his humanity made him a pacifist. The Diggers were nonviolent, despite the violence used against them. The film has resonances for today, but we tried not to make obvious parallels. We even dropped the references to Cromwell's troops fighting in Ireland. Winstanley's own words – and his actions – are eloquent enough.'[25]

This is not to say that *Winstanley* is not open to a presentist reading – clearly it is – but it does suggest that this had not been Brownlow's intention in making it. Few historians, however, would endorse the anachronistic description of Winstanley as a communist.

Rebels and Royalists

The restricted distribution that made *Winstanley* a little-seen film was also a problem that beset *To Kill A King* 27 years later. This film had a troubled production history. It went onto the floor at Shepperton Studios early in 2002 under the title *Cromwell & Fairfax*, but shooting was halted after three weeks when the financial support collapsed. It is an indication of the changing political economy of the British film industry that whereas *Cromwell* in 1969 had been backed by a Hollywood studio, *To Kill A King*, in common with other recent historical films including *Land and Freedom* (1995) and *Elizabeth*, depended on European co-funding. The initial development money of $2.2 million had been provided by Screenland Movieworld of Germany, but this was insufficient to support the film without television pre-sales. Another backer, Banque Internationale of Luxembourg, withdrew after the sales company, IAC Films, revised its financing plan. The production was rescued by British sales organisation HanWay, which agreed to provide $7.5 million with its partners

DZ Bank and Visionview. Other investors included the tax financier Future Film Group and FilmFour, the distribution arm of British television broadcaster Channel 4. Even so the production was only completed when cast and crew agreed to deferral of payments. Producer Kevin Loader, reflecting on the near-collapse of the film, remarked upon the difficulty of making historical films that by their nature were expensive: 'You fall between this cleft stick. If you want to make a period film for a cinema audience ... you have to step up a gear. It does cost.'[26]

The model for *To Kill A King* in many respects was *Elizabeth* to which it bears many similarities in form and style: a mobile camera that moves around static groups of people, a fondness for high-angle shots and a recurring motif of shots through gauze curtains or stained glass windows. It is a visually expressive film that is stylistically different from the somewhat sterile look of the 'heritage' cinema of Merchant Ivory and others that had been the dominant form of British period film-making during the 1980s and 1990s.[27] It is also a highly literate film: Lady Anne Fairfax's reference to her son being born 'into a world his father has turned upside down' suggests that writer Jenny Mayhew may have been familiar with the historical literature. Philip Kemp remarked approvingly in *Sight and Sound* that it 'bids fair to be the first intelligent movie treatment of British history for many a year, while avoiding the staginess and gloss of, say, *A Man for All Seasons* or *The Lion in Winter*'.[28] That it failed to match the popular success of *Elizabeth* is a reflection as much of its subject matter as the qualities of the film itself. The trade journal *Screen International* thought that it represented 'a daunting market challenge' and that it would be a difficult film to sell as 'it is a history lesson propelled by ideas rather than action'.[29]

To Kill A King begins in the aftermath of the Battle of Naseby in 1645 and focuses on the period until Cromwell's proclamation as Lord Protector in 1653 (though seems to imply this occurred shortly after the King's execution in 1649 and before Cromwell's campaigns against the Irish and the Scots). The focus of the narrative is the deteriorating relationship between Sir Thomas Fairfax (Dougray Scott) and his lieutenant Cromwell (Tim Roth) as the latter becomes more extreme in his desire to force through the trial and execution of Charles I (Rupert Everett). Fairfax is portrayed as a reluctant revolutionary and a political moderate, in contrast to Cromwell, a ruthless extremist who desires power for himself (against the mass of historical evidence). In this interpretation Fairfax is the charismatic general of the army, the leader of men and the populist adored by the masses, whereas Cromwell is uncharismatic, unpopular and unloved. Cromwell is resentful of Fairfax's wife Lady Anne (Olivia Williams) who is the only person closer to Fairfax than he, though the film stops short of imposing any sort of homo-erotic interpretation onto their relationship. Given the time when it was made, there is an irresistible, though admittedly highly tendentious, presentist reading of *To Kill A King* as a political allegory of the problems that beset New Labour over issues such as the Iraq War following its landslide general election victories of 1997 and 2001. The narrative of *To Kill A King* charts the deteriorating relationship between the two principal architects of Parliament's victory in the civil war. Is it entirely too fanciful to suggest that it mirrors the growing estrangement between Prime Minister Tony Blair and Chancellor of the Exchequer Gordon Brown over the famous 'broken promise' that Blair would step down for Brown at some point during his second term of office? At the end of the film, as Fairfax visits a dying Cromwell, Cromwell still harbours ill will over what he sees as Fairfax's betrayal: 'I was counting on you. You let me down.'

To Kill A King is no more faithful to the historical record than *Cromwell*, like which it compresses events between the end of the first civil war and the trial and execution of the King. Perhaps to forestall the expected complaints from the academy, the film's closing credits include a more forthright disclaimer than usual: 'This film is based on history; however, certain characters and events have been combined and/or fictionalised for dramatic purposes.' One of the fictionalised events, for example, was Fairfax's intent to assassinate Cromwell upon his proclamation as Lord Protector, though in the event he cannot bring himself to go through with it. On this occasion, however, there was none of the outcry that had greeted *Elizabeth*, which had been severely criticised for its suggestion that the 'virgin queen' was in fact nothing of the sort and had a passionate love affair with Robert Dudley, the Earl of Leicester. Perhaps the failure of *To Kill A King* to excite either public or professional interest was a reflection that Fairfax, unlike Elizabeth I, is hardly a well-known historical figure outside the academy. Or perhaps it was due to the fact that *To Kill A King* did not receive anything like the exposure of *Elizabeth*. As Ian Christie remarked: 'Released on few screens, with short-lived advertising and off-hand reviews, it seems like another *film maudit* in the making – likely to be rediscovered as a brave, forgotten film in decades to come, but now suffering the common fate of British films trying to be properly British and deal with our history.'[30]

The failure of either *Winstanley* or *To Kill A King* to secure anything more than a very limited release suggests that film distributors were sceptical of the box-office appeal of seventeenth-century radicals and Parliamentary generals. The most plausible explanation for the absence of the civil wars from the British cinema – unlike the American Civil War, which has been frequently presented on screen from *The Birth of a Nation* (1915) via *Gone With the Wind* (1939) to *Glory* (1989) – is that it does not give rise to the narrative of national greatness that characterises the majority of historical feature films. The historical events themselves are too complex to represent in a narratively coherent form; the side that was ostensibly fighting for a progressive cause (to end the divine right of kings and defend the liberties of the people) seems less attractive than the romantic Royalists; and the eventual outcome was the imposition of a military-theocratic dictatorship more authoritarian than the monarchical regime it had deposed. It is significant that the most widely-distributed of the major civil war films, *Cromwell*, was also the most conservative, both culturally and aesthetically, whereas the more revisionist and, to an extent, radical narratives of *Winstanley* and *To Kill A King* were less successful in finding a receptive audience. The fate of these films would, therefore, tend to support Dilys Powell's contention that popular cinema is no place for revolutionary interpretations of history.

Notes

1 Lovell, A. (1969) 'British Cinema: The Unknown Cinema', p. 6, paper presented to the Education Department of the British Film Institute on 13 March 1969, typescript held by the BFI National Library, London. Since then there has been an ever-expanding body of scholarly literature on the genre, including, but not limited to: Chapman, J. (2005) *Past and Present: National Identity and the British Historical Film*, London: I.B. Tauris; Cook, P. (1996) *Fashioning the Nation: Costume and Identity in British Cinema*, London: British Film Institute; Harper, S. (1994) *Picturing the Past: The Rise and Fall of the British Costume Film*, London: British Film Institute; Higson, A. (2003) *English Heritage, English Cinema: Costume Drama Since 1980*, Oxford: Oxford University Press; Landy, M. (1991) *British Genres: Cinema and Society, 1930-1960*, Princeton: Princeton University Press; Monk, C. & A. Sargeant (eds) (2002) *British Historical Cinema*, London: Routledge; Richards, J. (1997) *Films and British National Identity: From Dickens to 'Dad's Army'*, Manchester: Manchester University Press.

2 The royal biopic includes, but is not limited to, *The Private Life of Henry VIII* (1933), *Tudor Rose* (1936), *Victoria the Great* (1937), *Sixty Glorious Years* (1938), *Alfred the Great* (1969), *Anne of the Thousand Days* (1969), *Mary, Queen of Scots* (1971), *Henry VIII and His Six Wives* (1972), *Lady Jane* (1986), *The Madness of King George* (1995), *Mrs Brown* (1997) and *Elizabeth* (1998). Biopics of national figures include *The Life Story of David Lloyd George* (1918), *Nelson: The Story of England's Immortal Naval Hero* (1919), *The Iron Duke* (1934), *Drake of England* (1935), *Rhodes of Africa* (1936), *The Prime Minister* (1941), *The Young Mr Pitt* (1942), *Lawrence of Arabia* (1962), *Khartoum* (1965) and *Young Winston* (1972).

3 The war film tends to be seen as a genre in its own right and is usually discussed separately from the historical film. While the war film also includes fictional treatments, factually-based treatments of historical incidents include *The Colditz Story* (1954), *The Dam Busters* (1955), *Above Us the Waves* (1955), *The Battle of the River Plate* (1956), *Sink the Bismarck!* (1960), *Battle of Britain* (1969) and *A Bridge Too Far* (1977).

4 See Richards, J. (1977) *Swordsmen of the Screen*. London: Routledge & Kegan Paul, pp. 132-133.

5 See Halligan, B. (2003) *Michael Reeves*. Manchester: Manchester University Press, pp. 107-194; Hardy, P. (ed.) (1985) *The Aurum Film Encyclopedia: Horror*. London: Aurum Press, pp. 201-202; Hutchings, P. (1993) *Hammer and Beyond: The British Horror Film*. Manchester: Manchester University Press, pp. 144-151; Petley, J. (2002) 'A crude sort of entertainment for a crude sort of audience': the British critics and horror cinema, pp. 33-38, in Chibnall, C. and J. Petley (eds), *British Horror Cinema*. London: Routledge; Pirie, D. (1973) *A Heritage of Horror: The English Gothic Cinema 1946-1972*. London: Gordon Fraser, p. 105; and Rigby, J. (2000) *English Gothic: A Century of Horror Cinema*. London: Reynolds & Hearn, pp. 148-149. The title of the film is sometimes given as *Matthew Hopkins: Witchfinder General*; it was released in North America with the inexplicable title of *The Conqueror Worm*.

6 An illuminating discussion of landscape in British horror films of the late 1960s and early 1970s is provided in Hutchings, P. (2005) Uncanny Landscapes in British Film and Television, pp. 25-40 in *Visual Culture in Britain*, 5 (1).

7 See Murphy, R. (1992) *Sixties British Cinema*. London: Routledge; Walker, A. (1986) *Hollywood, England: The British Film Industry in the Sixties*. London: Harrap.

8 Anon. (1 March 1969) Directing 'Cromwell', p. 17, in *Kinematograph Weekly*.

9 The film's production was reported in Cooper, C. (10 May 1969) 'Cromwell' ready for locations in Spain, p. 16 in *Kinematograph Weekly*, and Pearson, K. (8 June 1969) Cromwell, warts and all, p. 21 in the *Sunday Times*. See also the studio press releases, declaring that '[the] production will be one of Columbia's biggest in 1969', on the microfiche for *Cromwell* held by the National Library of the British Film Institute (hereafter BFI Lib.)

10 Robinson, D. (16 July 1970), *Financial Times*; Houston, P. (25 July 1970), *Spectator*; Gibbs, P. (17 July 1970), *Daily Telegraph*; Malcolm, D. (16 July 1970), *Guardian*; Christie, I. (16 July 1970) History lives - and it kept me enthralled, *Daily Express*; Baker, R. (19 July 1970) Cromwell the reluctant hero, *Sunday Express*; Walker, J. (1970), pp. 52-53 in *Films and Filming*, 16 (12); Davies, B. (1970), p. 180 in *Monthly Film Bulletin*, 27 (440). (Reviews without a page number are taken from the BFI Lib. microfiche on *Cromwell*.)

11 Ollenshaw, N. F. (1970) Fact and fiction, p. 4 in *Films and Filming*, 17 (3).

12 Quoted in Clarke, S. (25 March 1972) King Hal and the Queens of England, p. 26 in *CinemaTV Today*.

13 Eyles, A. (1970) Ken Hughes and Cromwell, p. 22 in *Focus on Film*, 4.

14 Ollenshaw (December 1970), p. 4.

15 Hibbin, N. (18 July 1970) What was this revolution all about?, *Morning Star*.

16 Powell, D. (19 July 1970), *Sunday Times*.

17 Wilson, D. (1972) New Directions, p. 143 in *Sight and Sound*, 41 (3).

18 On the production of the film, see Brownlow, K. (1972) Before the deluge, pp. 186-187 in *Sight and Sound*, 41 (4); Glaessner, V. (1976) Winstanley: An Interview with Kevin Brownlow, pp. 18-23 in *Film Quarterly*, 30 (2); Houston, P. (1975) Winstanley, pp. 232-233 in *Sight and Sound*, 44 (4); Rubenstein, L. (1980) *Winstanley* and the Historical Film: An Interview with Kevin Brownlow, pp. 22-25 in *Cineaste*, 10 (4); and Tibbetts, J. C. (2000) Kevin Brownlow's Historical Films: *It Happened Here* (1965) and *Winstanley* (1975), pp. 227-251 in *Historical Journal of Film, Radio and Television*, 20 (2). The most detailed account of the making of the film is a seven-page typescript by Brownlow on the BFI Lib. microfiche for *Winstanley*. All unattributed quotations from Brownlow in the main body of the text are from this source.

19 The classic study of the various sects and movements is Hill, C. (1975), *The World Turned Upside Down: Radical Ideas during the English Revolution*. London: Penguin, from which this chapter unashamedly borrows its title.

20 Rosenstone, R.A. (1995) 'Introduction', p. 8 in *Revisioning History: Film and the Construction of a New Past*. Princeton: Princeton University Press.

21 Malcolm, D. (14 June 1975), *Guardian*; Walker, A. (14 October 1976), *Evening News*; Robinson, D. (29 October 1976), *The Times*; Coleman, J. (18 October 1976), *New Statesman*. Same question as in note 10.

22 Hill, C. (1975), Notes and Comments, p. 132 in *Past and Present*, 69.

23 Tibbetts (2000), p. 244.

24 See Marwick, A. (1998) T*he Sixties: Cultural Revolution in Britain, France, Italy and the United States, c.1958-c.1974*. Oxford: Oxford University Press, pp. 584-675.

25 Rubenstein (1980), p. 25.

26 Quoted in Anon. (12 April 2002) UK budgets face the chop, p. 14 in *Screen International*. For reports on the production of the film see: Anon. (25 January 2002), p. 16 in *Screen International*; Anon. (9 August 2002), p. 17 in *Screen International*; Jeffries, S. (26 July 2002) Heads on the block, pp. 10-11 in *The Guardian* Section 2.

27 The heritage film cycle includes, but is not limited to, *A Passage to India* (1984), *A Room With A View* (1986), *Maurice* (1987), *Howards End* (1992), *The Remains of the Day* (1993), *Sense and Sensibility* (1995), *Emma* (1996) and *The English Patient* (1996). See Hall, S. (2001 rev.) The Wrong Sort of Cinema: Refashioning the Heritage Film Debate, pp. 191- 199 in Murphy, R. (ed.) *The British Cinema Book*. London: British Film Institute; Higson (2003), pp. 9-45; Monk, C. (2002) The British heritage-film debate revisited, pp. 176-198 in Monk and Sargeant (eds).

28 Kemp, P. (2003) Love of the common people, p. 36 in *Sight and Sound*, New Series 13 (6).

29 Hunter, A. (2 May 2003), p. 28 in *Screen International*.

30 Christie, I. (2004) British Cinema - A View from (Elsewhere in) Europe, p. 120 in *Journal of British Cinema and Television*, 1 (1).

Waterloo: Napoleon (Charles Vanel) realises that he has lost his cause. © Emelka

'A truly fatherlandish epic'?
Karl Grune's *Waterloo* (1928)

Uli Jung

In 1928, the German director Karl Grune made the film *Waterloo*. The historical epic centred on the 1815 battle in which Napoleon and his troops were defeated by an international coalition. This essay frames Grune's nearly forgotten film in its historical and cinematographic context in order to consider how far it blends with the patriotic ('fatherlandish') tendencies so clearly present in many German historical films of the interwar era.

Waterloo (1815)

The defeat of Napoleonic France by an international coalition led in March-April 1814 to the abdication of Napoleon Bonaparte. He was exiled to the island of Elba, the French monarchy was restored and the victors gathered at the Congress of Vienna (1814-1815) where they reversed the achievements of the French Revolution and the Napoleonic Wars. The Congress brought about a rearrangement of the European states and fostered the idea of the nation state which was to be a decisive factor in European and world politics throughout the nineteenth and twentieth centuries.

When, after a period of confinement of nearly 18 months, Napoleon escaped from Elba and resumed power (March 1815) the other European powers formed a coalition and declared war. Great Britain, Austria, Prussia and Russia were planning to invade France from various directions and seize Paris in order to force Napoleon to step down again. However, only Britain and Prussia had their armies ready in time to do battle with the French army. Napoleon's strategy was to attack and defeat these allied armies separately. He therefore deployed his troops to present-day Belgium[1] where the British and Prussian armies were gathering. Napoleon moved two armies, which engaged the Allied forces on

16 June 1815 in the *Battle of Quatre-Bras* and the *Battle of Ligny*. Napoleon thus succeeded in keeping the Prussian and British armies apart but was misled into believing the Prussians were defeated. He regrouped his troops just opposite the British troops commanded by the Duke of Wellington. Since the French outnumbered the British, who had withdrawn near Waterloo, Wellington did not attack Napoleon but rather tried to hold his position until the Prussians arrived.

At Waterloo on June 18, Napoleon launched his attack. The *Battle of Waterloo* remained undecided for some time with severe casualties on both sides. Despite these casualties the Guards succeeded in breaking through Wellington's front line. They were surprised by the British troops which Wellington had kept in reserve and which forced the Imperial Guard – for the first time in its history – to retreat. At this very moment the Prussian army commanded by General Blücher reached the battlefield. In the evening Wellington and Blücher met while the fresh Prussian cavalry pursued the retreating French. This ended Napoleon's one hundred days of reign. He abdicated on 22 June 1815, committing himself to British protection. He was exiled to the island of St. Helena in the South Atlantic where he died on 5 May 1821. The Congress of Vienna reconvened and continued working on the new map of Europe.

'Napoleonic films' and Karl Grune

International film history is rife with reconstructions of Napoleon's biography, especially his ultimate downfall. This started early on: Ursula von Keitz, in her account of Napoleon as the 'ideal hero for monumental films',[2] counts at least sixteen films produced in France, Great Britain, the United States, Russia, Belgium and Italy prior to 1921, the year commemorating the 100th anniversary of Napoleon's death. Every single stage in his biography, from childhood to his death, was seen and continues to be seen as a fit topic for films. Von Keitz maintains that there was no unified cinematic discourse on Napoleon but rather, she explains: 'For each film it is decisive for the ideological ground colour if the character can be identified with, that is, seen and conceived of from the perspective of the historical Napoleon, or if it is presented from the point of view of the political or military adversary. [...] The material is thus patriotically impregnated.'[3]

Starting with Ferdinand Zecca's *Napoléon Bonaparte* (1903), probably the first Napoleon film, the medium's preoccupation with the French emperor never lessened, but it was, as von Keitz rightly states, Abel Gance's *Napoléon* (1927) which created Napoleon as a cinematic myth. Gance conceived of his film as the first of six episodes which were to cover the entire biography of Bonaparte. This plan did not materialise, partly because of the sheer size of the project, partly due to the coming of sound which rendered the first instalment commercially unsatisfactory. Lupu Pick's *Napoleon auf St. Helena* (*Napoleon on St. Helena*, 1929) is widely recognised as the 'sixth episode' of Gance's project.[4] It melodramatically narrates the last years of the fallen emperor who turns away from the remaining followers who accompanied him into exile when he is told that his former wife is expecting a child by another man. It is easy to see that the perspective has changed: Gance's film focussed entirely on the young genius who, with his domineering, hypnotising gaze alone could bring entire armies under his spell. Pick deals only with the ageing emperor: 'Nothing else, only this growing old, this waiting for death, this fading away in exile', as one reviewer remarked,[5] who at the same time characterised the film as a 'documentary rendition [...] handed down from history'.

This short account of Pick's film indicates that the German approach to the topic was somewhat different from the French; it was not designed to glorify a war leader but rather to create an 'objective' historical version which meant that the filmic devices he applied tended to play down the content. Many German reviewers pointed out how dispassionate and neutral the narrative was: 'No etching-like poses, no thrilling visions of war, no falsely imposed heroic epics,'[6] wrote Hans Sahl. The film critic of the *Neue Berliner Zeitung* spoke of the 'impressiveness' which Pick achieved by avoiding pathos and heroic gestures: 'No reminiscences of battle, no memories of a pompous court'.[7] Rudolf Arnheim praised it as: 'Clean, objective historical painting without nationalistic distortion,'[8] before he went on to mock the film for its 'deadly boredom'. *Film und Volk* was also very critical of *Napoleon on St. Helena*. Its reviewer maintained: '[Pick] deliberately declines to stage a real drama, a conflict-laden, affecting storyline which the subject of Napoleon would certainly have afforded. What Pick shows one might call a historical *Kammerspiel* [chamber play]'.[9]

Napoleon meets Ney on his way to Paris © Emelka

Pick made his film in 1929 in Berlin; it is mentioned in nearly all histories of German film, though it is rarely shown today since the only non-commercial distribution is through the Bundesarchiv-Filmarchiv, Germany's national film archive. Only ten months prior to the premiere of Pick's film, another version of Napoleon's downfall had hit the German screens: Karl Grune's *Waterloo* (1928) which today has been generally forgotten even among film scholars specialised in German silent film history. In fact, for decades the film was thought to have been lost until in the early 1990s the late Fred Junck, then the director of the Cinémathèque Municipale de Luxembourg, obtained a print from an anonymous French collector. Shortly afterwards another print turned up in the vaults of the Cinémathèque Suisse. It was restored in a joint venture by the Cinémathèque Municipale de Luxembourg, the Cinémathèque Suisse and the Belgian Royal Film Archive under the auspices of the Lumière Project of the Media Programme of the European Union.[10] It had a new premiere with a new musical score by Carl Davis on 24 March 1995 at the Conservatoire de Musique de la Ville de Luxembourg. It has rarely been shown since.

Waterloo (1928), a film about Blücher

In a style typical of its time, *Waterloo* attempts to combine historical epic with individual melodrama. Historical events and romantic entanglements are skilfully interwoven. Since 1814 Napoleon has been living in forced exile on the island of Elba, while the Congress of Vienna is attempting to reshape Europe. Countess Tarnowska is spying for Napoleon in Vienna, applying her female charms. She meets Lieutenant Fritz Reutlingen, the personal adjutant to Marshall Blücher who has withdrawn from active duty after the wars of liberation and has retired to his Saxon estate. Reutlingen shows an interest in the Countess's advances and starts a romance with her. Meanwhile Napoleon has decided to return to France and overthrow the Bourbon government. The news of his escape reunites the quarrelling Congress member states which then form a new coalition against their common enemy. They command the French Marshall Ney to bar Napoleon's way and to disarm him. But when the would-be opponents meet, Ney succumbs to Napoleon's notorious charisma and defects to him with his entire army.

Wellington and Blücher meet before the battle of Waterloo. © Emelka

In Prussia, Marshall Blücher is upset by the developments in Vienna. At the point when he is ready to resign, Blücher receives word that Napoleon has landed in France and at once accepts reappointment as commander-in-chief of the Prussian army. He meets with the troops of the Duke of Wellington and both commanders promise to stand side by side and come to the other's aid if need be. Near Ligny, the French troops prevail in their first encounter with the Prussian army who are forced to retreat to Wavre where Reutlingen's fiancée, Rieke, is visiting relatives. A little later, Countess Tarnowska, who has followed Reutlingen from Vienna, appears on the scene. She intercepts an important message sent by Blücher to Wellington, but her messenger, sent to warn Napoleon of the British-Prussian schemes, is arrested by Blücher's guards. Thus Tarnowska's act of espionage is discovered and she commits suicide.

Near Waterloo, Wellington and Napoleon are engaged in battle. Wellington is under heavy pressure, but on accounts of a message that Blücher's army is approaching he does everything to hold his stand despite many casualties. At last the Prussian army intervenes, and the joint British and Prussian troops defeat the French. Reutlingen, though, who had fought heroically during the battle, has sustained serious injuries. When she learns of this, Rieke realises she truly loves Reutlingen and looks for him in the sick bay. Reutlingen wakes up from his deep unconsciousness and sees the victorious British and Prussian soldiers marching by. His happiness is thus complete.

From this synopsis of *Waterloo* it is clear that the focus of the film is not Napoleon but Marshall Blücher. The Prussian is depicted as an ageing, dotty, good-natured character who has foregone all his military attitudes and now lives on his estate as a landowner-farmer respected by his peasants but no longer cares about social hierarchies. He is first introduced while inspecting a new horse he is thinking about buying. He is seen from the back while bending forward to look at the horse's hoof; his large bottom almost fills the screen. His wife cares for the household herself instead of leaving the work to domestics. The relationship of the couple is fond if wisecracking. Blücher calls his wife 'Olle' (old hag) and sometimes dances with her in the kitchen when a busker passes by. Blücher's eminence is signified by the sheer mass of mail he receives daily. Although he has promised his wife not to re-enlist, all it takes is a royal order for him to resume his prior position of commander-in-chief of the Prussian army.

Even as a commanding officer Blücher is a down-to-earth character. His soldiers look up to him, as he calls them 'Kinder' (children). Although he is anything but an intellectual – the film makes fun of his poor spelling – he is an ingenious strategist. In Wavre, he makes do with a run-down roadhouse for his headquarters. When Countess Tarnowska arrives, he lets her have his room and the film uses the opportunity once again to mock him for the untidiness of his bedroom. Blücher is anything but vain. He is the only one who does not fall for Tarnowska's charms and it is he who realises that the note taken from the secret messenger smells of Tarnowska's perfume. Thus her role as a spy for Napoleon is revealed.

Blücher is played by Otto Gebühr, an actor popular with German audiences from his role as Frederick the Great (in a short flashback he is seen in his most famous role).[11] Audience expectations were disappointed in so far as Gebühr took a completely different approach as an actor. While his Frederick the Great was stern, burdened with responsibility, surrounded by an air of un-approachability and the loneliness of the born leader, Gebühr's Blücher is a lively, humorous, unassuming character whose qualities as a leader are founded on his natural authority and personality. He does not need to surround himself with a pompous lifestyle and is thus the one character in *Waterloo* with whom the audience can fully identify; they tend to perceive him – contrary to the historical events – as the only true adversary of Napoleon.

This is not the case with all the characters. Lieutenant Reutlingen, for instance, who is responsible for most of the physical action of the film, is presented as the exuberant young hero, but there are other sides to his character. Although engaged to be married to Rieke, once he is sent by Blücher on an important mission to Vienna, it only takes the sight of a woman's ankle for him to forget about both his assignment and his engagement. He falls immediately for the Countess Tarnowska. In his defence it should be said that he does not know, nor does he ever learn, about her secret scheme. Still, he is the one who endangers the victory of the Allied troops. He loses Blücher's written message to Wellington, which Tarnowska then intercepts. When her messenger to Napoleon is in turn caught by Blücher's guards, Reutlingen is suspected of changing sides and betraying the Prussian cause. Although he is proven innocent he must make amends for his failure. In battle he turns out to be a brave soldier who rallies the retreating Prussian soldiers and leads them once more against the enemy. By this act he acquires his fatal or near fatal injuries. Surprisingly, the film's ending is not quite clear as to whether Reutlingen dies or not. Waking up from his unconsciousness, he sees the Prussian and British troops marching by in triumph, but his view is dominated by the shadow of a huge cross. There is the final fade-out before Reutlingen collapses.

In *Waterloo*, the Duke of Wellington, who is known in history as the victor over Napoleon, is a rather stern, unemotional character. His courteous manners make him suitable for the high society events in which the film shows him more than once. He receives intelligence of Napoleon's military formation while he is attending a ball in Brussels. But he does everything to prevent panic. Other than that he remains rather colourless nor does he have all that much exclusive screen time, which once more underscores the fact that *Waterloo* is centred essentially on Blücher.

Obviously, Napoleon is one of the decisive characters in *Waterloo*. He is first seen in the garden on the island of Elba where he whiles away his time drawing in the sand strategic formations for imaginary battles. The moment a messenger arrives to inform him about the quarrelling at the Congress of Vienna, he puts on the jacket of his uniform before deciding to go back to France and take over the government again. In exile he never accepts that his political eminence in Europe has faded. Rather, he constantly waits for an opportunity to resume his former role. Napoleon is depicted in the film as a solemn, solitary leader; he keeps his thoughts to himself and makes his decisions without counsel from other people. Accustomed to giving orders, he never seeks advice from his officers. At the same time, he has a strong sense of the historical moment. His landing on the French coast is depicted by the film in terms of a shadow play. Grune cuts from Napoleon's huge shadow walking over the planks down to his boots. Before he steps onto French soil he hesitates for a moment, apparently contemplating the historical dimension of this one step. On his march into Paris he meets with the citizens' unanimous jubilation. When Marshall Ney confronts him and threatens him with an entire army, he proudly presents himself to the soldiers with outspread arms, asking them: 'Do you really intend to shoot at your emperor?' Naturally, the soldiers lower their guns and approach him in an outburst of enthusiasm. Napoleon's powerful personality is enough to bring the common crowd under his spell; it does not take political or ideological rhetoric to convince the soldiers. His presence alone reassures the soldiers that he knows what to do.

In battle, Napoleon never leaves his post overlooking the battleground and is thus never in harm's way (unlike Blücher who at a certain point comes under enemy shelling and suffers an injury to his leg while his horse is killed under him). Napoleon does not seem to be emotionally involved in the development of the combat. Only when informed that his elite troops, the Imperial Guards, are retreating does he realise that his cause is lost. He stands for a moment in a pensive mood, then sits on a canon and covers his eyes as if he were weeping (which, of course, he is not).

There are certain parallels between Napoleon and Blücher which suggest that they are built up as complementary characters. Both seem to be born leaders, although they go about their leadership in different ways. At the core of their respective personalities is their charisma that appears throughout the film. While Napoleon is marching towards Paris he encounters straggling soldiers who, as soon as they recognise him, burst into spontaneous cheers and immediately come forward to enlist with him again. On his march to (present-day) Belgium Blücher comes upon a few peasants working in the fields. When they recognise the Marshall they tell him that they once served in Lützow's battalion and immediately join ranks with Blücher's soldiers. In contrast to Napoleon, though, Blücher is the more dynamic character; he is more often seen in close connection with his men to whom he usually talks with tongue-in-cheek humour. Also, when reappointed, his first decision is to invite the Prussian strategist Gneisenau to join his personal staff. Thus Blücher is seen more than once in professional consultations with his officers bending over maps and discussing strategies.

Waterloo's production and reception

The production company, Münchner Filmkunst AG (Emelka), Germany's second largest film trust during the Weimar Republic, decided to cast international stars for the most important historical roles. Marshall Blücher, as mentioned, was played by the popular Otto Gebühr. Wellington was played by

Humberstone Wright, a veteran British actor who had appeared in more than sixty films, if mostly in important supportive roles. Likewise, Charles Vanel, who was cast in the role of Napoleon, was well known to French audiences from his appearance in roughly thirty-five films. Moreover he had played the role of Napoleon already in the two-part German film *Königin Luise* (*Queen Louise*, 1927-1928) that Grune also directed. Between 1927 and 1929 he appeared in seven German films; German audiences were likely to have seen his face on the screen.

In the light of this cast it is clear that with *Waterloo* Emelka was aiming at international markets. The production had been decided upon at a time when the company was still very prosperous. Its capital reserves made it possible to sign a prestigious director like Karl Grune who had established himself in the Weimar film business with *Die Straße* (*The Street*, 1923). Moreover, the company planned to celebrate its tenth anniversary in 1929 by assigning Grune to make a so-called *Großfilm* (epic film) to highlight the company's ability to achieve a production that displayed cultural prestige. This decision proved utterly wrong in the long run and was, in retrospect, the first nail in the company's coffin. In the words of Petra Putz: 'It was not the artistic risk that made *Waterloo* advance to Geiselgasteig's [the company's studios outside Munich] Waterloo, but rather the fact that Emelka missed with this film the demands of the market. While the company was spending massive amounts of money on this silent film spectacle, the competitive Ufa management was already working on the introduction of sound. Early in 1929, when *Waterloo* was presented to the public, a Ufa study commission was visiting the United States learn about the latest developments in sound film, the talkies. As early as April 1929, Ufa struck a deal with the Klangfilm company. They bought cameras for four sound studios and projectors for all the Ufa theatres; moreover they started building the new studios.'[12]

Emelka's management soon became aware of the consequences of their mistaken decision. The company report for the first six months of 1929 indicated a total loss of more than 950.000 RM and made responsible the problematic transition from silent to sound, which 'unfavourably influenced the profits from of our monumental film *Waterloo* which we have finished early in 1929'.[13]

Der Kongreß tanzt: The Congress of Vienna engaged in an evening's entertainment. © Emelka

The coming of sound hampered the international distribution of *Waterloo* considerably; the film did not recover its investment. A shortened version of the film appeared in France; distributed by the Albert Company, it is fifteen to twenty minutes shorter than the German version.[14] The cuts do not significantly affect the characterisation of the protagonists (although Blücher receives less screen time in the beginning of the film) but serve to trim some of the more atmospheric scenes. The entire last scene of the German version, though, with Reutlingen watching the victorious troops, is missing from the French version. Instead, it cuts from Napoleon sitting on the canon to a title which does not have an equivalent in the German version: 'True, the eagle was vanquished, but its glory and genius have carved the most beautiful pages in the monument of history.' The final image is a graphic sketch of the Arc de Triomphe on which the names of Napoleon's famous battles are superimposed. The name Waterloo is conspicuously missing from the list.

It is clear that the French version attempts to turn the focus away from Blücher and onto Napoleon. This becomes plausible since Grune's film looks at Bonaparte without nationalistic malice. Therefore, with a few minor omissions, the French *Waterloo* version depicts an Emperor who is still great despite his defeat. In the last images Napoleon no more concedes victory to history than he does to the Allied forces. He shrugs his shoulders knowing that he must forsake his ambitions. The reception of the film in France has not yet been researched. The only authoritative book on Napoleon in the movies, which mentions that Grune's film shows no great concern for historical accuracy,[15] merely states: 'The film came out in France in a modified and abridged form, with apocryphal inter-titles (the words of Victor Hugo) and with an ending in which the French defeat at Waterloo is diminished to the level of a 'minute detail' as compared to all the battles that the Emperor has won and which the epilogue lists in an apotheosis.'[16]

What both versions have in common is their negative image of the Congress of Vienna. It is clear that all participants in the negotiations are driven by their own selfish agendas. Their disputations are very emotional, passionate, nearly to the point of physical palpability. The Congress is clearly disunited beyond description; nobody seems to expect positive results. In stark contrast to this, the socialising events, the nightly extravagant balls, are conducted in all ceremoniousness and seem to cover up the severe conflicts that the Congress is not able to overcome. The shallowness of this entire conference is displayed when Wellington receives word of Napoleon's escape from Elba. He makes the announcement to the dancing courtiers during one of the balls. Immediately everybody leaves in utter panic, and a little later an elaborate trick shot reveals the diplomatic envoys hastening to leave Vienna in every direction: the Congress is shown up as an assembly of cowards and fun-loving egotists.

Emelka announced Karl Grune's *Waterloo* as a 'monumental jubilee film' that was to commemorate the production company's tenth anniversary. Referring to the enormous budget, Emelka even named it a 'jubilee million film'.[17] At the same time, the producers seemed to have certain apprehensions that their film might be misunderstood. More than once, Wilhelm Rosenthal, a member of the management, went public stating *Waterloo* was to be an 'image of its time' (*Zeitbild*) 'which would not entail political controversy since the Prussians, the British and the French were to be treated with the utmost objectivity.'[18] The film was not about politics, Rosenthal insisted. As if to furnish proof of this, Emelka publicised the hiring of young British actor Dene Morel (who died at an early stage in the shooting). Dene Morel was introduced as the son of British politician E.D. Morel, who had created a scandal with his pacifist speeches in the British parliament during World War One and gone to prison for his convictions.[19] This was a way of indicating the politically neutral position of Emelka's film.[20]

But it was precisely political one-sidedness which critics held against the film upon its premiere. The liberal press was especially harsh in its criticism. Ernst Jäger, editor-in-chief for *Der Film-Kurier*, accused Emelka of catering to 'fatherlandish sentiment' with *Waterloo*; he called it a 'German-national campaign film': 'It commits itself openly to the Prussian ideals symbolised by the military march, by Lützow's wild, audacious chases, by Blücher's driving spirit, by the national Europeanism.'[21]

'Also, Leo Hirsch saw in *Waterloo* a politically questionable film, since it had not depicted the peoples' war against Napoleon, but rather a 'duel between him and Blücher': 'The battle between the two parties is limited to the two heroes [...]. One cannot recognise fatherlands anymore, only heroes, each uniform a hero and the soul of a man. Because this is a jubilee film, and during an anniversary every sin of the past is absolved, everybody receives a moral medal [...] Thus we have militarism instead of nationalism.'[22] The reviewer for the *Berliner Börsen-Courier* also pointed to certain problems: 'Of these human beings, of this people one sees only a military reflection. A sweeping battle scene, an exciting saber-rattling parade of uniformed film extras.' Karl Grune, the reviewer goes on, 'at last shows us here his true face'.[23] In a like manner Ernst Jäger had earlier chided Grune for his pacifism that was only a facade,[24] and Leo Hirsch had called Grune a 'former pacifist'.[25]

The conservative press was much tamer with its criticism of the film. *Der Kinematograph* admitted that *Waterloo* surely would not 'find grace in the eyes of historians and aesthetes', but described it as 'a compositional unity of gripping effect'. For the journal's reviewer it was Blücher who was at the centre of the film: '[Otto Gebühr] is once again bedecked with all the charms of historical authenticity, with all the little traits which made the 'Marshall 'Forward'' so popular.' *Waterloo*, the critic continues, 'revolves around an episodic popular action which does not provoke historical objections'.[26]

Another anonymous reviewer pointed to Grune's 'widely known humanitarian convictions' and claimed he had depicted history 'objectively, honestly and excitingly'. He sees in him 'predominantly a sculptor of human beings, a narrator of states of minds – we do not have many like him today.' What other critics saw as depictions of militarism this reviewer perceived as 'role models of true character and generosity'. He did see the political aspect of the material but in his opinion *Waterloo* had mastered these problems: 'This film could easily have become just another hoorah-film; that this did not happen, despite the vast array of battles and the fact that human life is not treated squeamishly, is thanks to Karl Grune who is once again moved primarily by the figures of men who changed their time.'[27]

Yet another reviewer saw in *Waterloo* a humanitarian film in which the 'pacifist Karl Grune' had displayed his 'desire for peace'. In its commercialism, though, it attempted to cater to all political tendencies.[28] On the other hand, Fritz Olimsky, one of the eminent film reviewers of the Weimar period, recognised a 'truly patriotic film work', which had managed to treat the action

King Friedrich Wilhelm's and Hardenberg's conversation is overheard by a spy.
© Emelka

'as apolitically as possible on a purely human level'. He saw the meaning of the film in the 'revival of a piece of national history'. For Olimsky, *Waterloo* could have served as a lesson in social studies: 'Especially in our time, politically confused as it is, such a film must deal with a great task, since it induces the audience involuntarily and inevitably to think about our political problems, especially about the problem of political unity. And that is a great deal!'[29]

The reviewer of the *Deutsche Filmzeitung* put his discussion of *Waterloo* in the broader context of the historical epic: 'Historical renditions draw their actual power and effectiveness not from the object, but rather from the subject, from the personality of the one who shapes and interprets the material, from the artist in the historian.' It was not possible to narrate history without having a political agenda, without wanting to affect something. *Waterloo*, he contended, did not have this will to be effective. Anyone who wanted to create an apolitical historical film would inevitably end up with 'a character sketch, an idyll'. The reviewer criticised the film precisely for its lack of a definitive political standpoint. He could only praise the technical brilliance of the film.[30]

In the United States, where *Waterloo* could be received without a struggle over the historical and ideological background, the technical and aesthetic qualities were what impressed the critics most (all in all their response to the action remained reserved). The *New York Times*, for example, wrote: 'In several sequences Herr Grune reveals marked ability with the camera, especially when he divides the screen in half and shows troops on the march contrasted with people dancing. He also gives some excellent scenes of the gathering of Napoleon's forces, and the episode between Marshal Ney and Napoleon is effectively sketched.'[31]

A 'fatherlandish' epic?

From the brief overview of the first reception of the film, it is apparent that *Waterloo* divided the professional critics into two camps. The dividing line ran along the ideological boundary between conservative and liberal points of view, since the battle of Waterloo was widely seen as a part of the national or, depending on the ideological bias, 'fatherlandish' history, a long tradition in German film history. Nineteen thirteen is described by many film historians as a decisive year, since it is known as the year of the so-called 'Autorenfilme' (auteur films) in which 'literary standards' were applied to film in order to elevate the new medium in a cultural sense. At the same time, another set of films emerged from the German studios which have until recently escaped the scholars' attention: historical epics. As some significant events in 'fatherlandish' history had their hundredth anniversaries, they became topics for films which were largely geared to bourgeois and petty-bourgeois audiences. A film like *Richard Wagner* (1913), directed by Carl Froelich and William Wauer, celebrated German musical culture. Others, like *Theodor Körner* (1913) or the trilogy *Der Film von der Königin Luise* (*The Film of Queen Louise,* 1913) were encouraging awareness of the efforts to prevent French dominance over Europe in the wake of the French Revolution. What sets these films apart from later productions is their preoccupation with historical authenticity. The producers were careful to get original objects from museums to use as props and to shoot on original locations to persuade the audience that they were watching, if not real historical events, at least exact reconstructions of them. The scheme of these historical reconstructions was to give their audience an impression of how things must have happened; they should be viewed, therefore, not as feature films but as non-fiction which showed the 'world' as it was, or at least as it was to be imagined.[32]

To be sure, these early filmic accounts of 'fatherlandish' history were also ideologically charged. They exclusively narrated stories of heroic deeds. There is not a single film known to commemorate the history of social advancement, to glorify social or even revolutionary movements or to take issue with the living conditions of workers or the middle classes. The German film industry prior to the First World War was exclusively in the hands of producers with strong national affiliations; thus the point of view of the ruling classes was predominant on German – and probably on international – screens.

During the Weimar Republic the cinematic preoccupation with Prussian and thus national history in general and especially with the history of so-called wars of liberation did not go away. Many of the relevant films were announced as 'Großfilme' and their premieres were staged as huge social events, as was the case for Grune's *Waterloo*.[33] What is different about Grune's film is that it does not play the chauvinistic tune of the time. In Germany, France was seen as the 'hereditary enemy', and not only among conservatives. It was still widely felt that the unification of the German Reich in 1871 was the result of a war against and victory over France. The rivalry of the two countries had never subsided, although with Wilhelm II's ascent to the throne in 1888 the German focus changed to Great Britain and its sea power. The outcome of the First World War fostered additional biases against France among German conservatives and the petty-bourgeoisie. The peace treaty of Versailles not only encouraged right-wing sentiments that the German troops had not been overcome in battle but were rather 'stabbed in the back' by German politicians who had surrendered to the Allied forces without sound military justification. The French occupation of the Ruhr valley, Germany's foremost industrial region, added to the anti-French sentiments of wide parts of the German population. The German-French rapprochement in the Treaty of Locarno in 1925 did not affect the broad strata of the German society because it more or less affirmed the stipulations of the peace treaty of Versailles as far as the German Western border and the de-militarization of the Rhineland were concerned. On the contrary, the German, French and Belgian decision not to insist in the future on the forceful alteration of borders (by which Germany de facto accepted her territorial losses to France and Belgium as a consequence of the war) was widely seen as the ultimate manifestation of the status quo. This is an important source for what German conservatives and nationalists called the 'German Disgrace'.

In 1928, a film centring on Napoleon, the man who had changed the entire map of Europe, could easily be perceived in this very light. It is all the more surprising that *Waterloo* did not attempt to exploit this issue. It is perfectly clear that the film is much more about Blücher. His face (Otto Gebühr) was not only featured in most of the advertisements in the trade press[34] but also on the cover of the official film programme.[35] The purpose of the film is to present Marshall Blücher as a popular hero of German history. His heroic leadership caters to the national sentiment of the Germans. Which is not to say that *Waterloo* does not give Napoleon his due. The Emperor is certainly shown to have strong leadership qualities. In contrast to Blücher he is the lonely leader who keeps his distance from his officers and men. But at the end of the battle he realises that he has taken too high a risk and lost. The film depicts his downfall without malicious glee. Napoleon retains his honour. What we see is a great historical figure at the moment of his decline. This depiction makes

Napoleon confronts Ney's troops who will defile before him. © Emelka

it possible for the French version to turn the ending of *Waterloo* around and make it into a national icon of French history. Grune's film thus does not cater to the anti-French sentiment of conservative Germans. In his film Napoleon is not only an eminent historical figure, but someone who plays a pivotal role, if involuntarily, in ending the political quarrels at the Congress of Vienna and thus helps to create a new unified notion of a European order. Although the role of Prussia is significantly highlighted against the British endeavour, the film is decidedly not 'fatherlandish' in its ideological orientation.

Six years after *Waterloo*, Napoleon's hundred-day reign would hit the German screens again. This time it was a German language version of Gioacchino Forzano's *Campo di maggio* (*Field of May*, 1935) which was based on a 1930 stage play of the same title by Forzano and Benito Mussolini. Franz Wenzler's version, *Hundert Tage* (*Hundred Days*) , was produced under the auspices of the Italian company Consorzio 'Vis' in Rome and premiered in Hamburg on 15 March 1935.[36] This film covers the period between Napoleon's escape from Elba and his death on St. Helena. But the film's discourse focuses more on the character of Joseph Fouché (Gustav Gründgens), the French minister of internal security under the reign of Louis XVIII. Fouché is a careerist and opportunist who had sided with Bonaparte during his first reign. Now that Napoleon is back in power, Fouché once again changes sides and serves Bonaparte as a minister while at the same time conspiring with royalists, just to be on the safe side. Indeed, after Napoleon's abdication Fouché is appointed prime minister of the provisional government. In this position he works towards the restoration of the Bourbon reign, under which he once more serves as minister of internal security.

Compared to Gustav Gründgens' ideally matched rendition of the slimy intriguer Fouché, Werner Krauss' Napoleon appears more stern, serious and brooding. Unlike Fouché, Napoleon has a vision which he expresses twice in the film. His historical mission is to conquer Europe in order to unite it and thus to prevent future wars. In the light of the expansionist plans the Nazis were already entertaining at the time, this historical borrowing appears to be all the more cynical.

Notes

1 Independent state since 1830, Belgium was administered by France after 1795 and annexed by it from 1795 until 1813. The Congress of Vienna (1813-1815) following the defeat of Napoleon at Waterloo united the region with its northern neighbour (formerly the Dutch republic) into the United Kingdom of the Netherlands, which was ruled by the House of Orange. In 1830, a revolution broke out in Brussels and the kingdom was eventually divided in two independent states: Belgium and the Netherlands.

2 Von Keitz, U. (1998) Der Idealheld des Monumentalfilms: Napoleon in der Kinematographie, pp. 250-266 in Rother, R. (ed.) *Mythen der Nationen: Völker im Film*. Berlin: Deutsches Historisches Museum.

3 Von Keitz (1998), p. 252.

4 Von Keitz (1998), p. 255.

5 Sahl, H. (11 November 1929) Napoleon auf St. Helena, in *Der Montag Morgen*, quoted from [www.filmportal.de].

6 Sahl (1929).

7 Anonymous (8 November 1929) Napoleon auf St. Helena, in *Neue Berliner Zeitung*, quoted from [www.filmportal.de].

8 Arnheim, R. (1929) Kinematographisches, pp. 774-777, in *Die Weltbühne* 25 (47).

9 Dr. M.B. (1929) Kritischer Filmbericht, pp. 16-18 in *Film und Volk* (11/12).

10 Surowiec, C. (ed.) (1996) *The Lumière Project: The European Film Archives at the Crossroads*. Lisbon: Associação Projecto Lumière, p. 156.

11 Gebühr would continue to play that role for the rest of his career, for instance also in Veit Harlan's *Der grosse König* (The Great King, 1942).

12 Putz, P. (1996) *Waterloo in Geiselgasteig: Die Geschichte des Münchner Filmkonzerns Emelka (1919-1933) im Antagonimus zwischen Bayern und Reich*. Trier: WVT, p. 74.

13 IHK-WA V5/V441 Geschäftsbericht für das Zwischengeschäftsjahr 1929, quoted in: Putz (1996), p. 74.

14 The exact length of the French release version is not known.

15 Matei, J.-P. (ed.) (1998) *Napoléon & le cinéma: Un Siècle d'images*. Ajaccio: Editions Alain Piazzola, p. 327.

16 Matei (1998), p. 328.

17 Cf. an advertisement for the film by the Bayerische Filmgesellschaft, the German distributor for *Waterloo*, reprinted in Jung, U. and J.-L. Scheffen (eds) (1995) *Waterloo. Programme booklet of the world premiere of the film*. Luxembourg: Cinémathèque Municipale de Luxembourg, p. 2.

18 Rosenthal, W. (10 January 1929) Film und Literatur, in *National-Zeitung*.

19 For an account of Morel's anti-colonial activities, see Hochschild, A. (1998) King Léopold's Ghost. A Story of Greed, Terror and Heroism in Colonial Africa. Boston: Houghton Mifflin.

20 S. (6 October 1928) Interviews in München: Dene Morel, in *Der Film-Kurier*.

21 Jäger, E. (11 January 1929) Waterloo, in *Der Film-Kurier*.

22 Hirsch, L. (19 January 1929) Es ist der Geist, der sich den Film verbaut, in *Das Blaue Heft*.

23 Anonymous (13 January 1929) Der Waterloo-Film, in *Berliner Börsen-Courier*.

24 Jäger (1929).

25 Hirsch (1929).

26 Anonymous (13 January 1929) Filmkritische Rundschau: Waterloo, in *Der Kinematograph*.

27 Anonymous review in the *Waterloo* files in the archives of the Stiftung Deutsche Kinemathek, Filmmuseum, Berlin.

28 Cf. Gong (1929) Sturm über Asien und Waterloo. (Anonymous review in the *Waterloo* files in the archives of the Stiftung Deutsche Kinemathek, Filmmuseum, Berlin.)

29 Olimsky, F. (1929) Waterloo. (Anonymous review in the *Waterloo* files in the archives of the Stiftung Deutsche Kinemathek, Filmmuseum, Berlin.)

30 Sp. (1929) Waterloo, p. 10 in *Deutsche Filmzeitung*.

31 Hall, M. (16 April 1929) Wellington and Bluecher, quoted in: *New York Times Film Reviews, vol. 1: 1913-1931* (1970). New York: *New York Times* and Arno Pr, p. 521.

32 Jung, U. (2005) Fiktionale Historienfilme als 'patriotische' Dokumente, p. 357-367 in Jung, U. and M. Loiperdinger (eds) *Geschichte des deutschen Dokumentarfilms. Vol. 1: Kaiserreich, 1895-1918*. Stuttgart: Reclam.

33 For a more systematic overview of Prussian topics on film, see Marquardt, A. and H. Rathsack (eds) (1981) *Preußen im Film: Eine Retrospektive der Stiftung Deutsche Kinemathek*. Reinbek: rororo.

34 Jung and Scheffen (1995), p. 2.

35 *Illustrierter Film-Kurier* (1929), 1067.

36 Apparently, the play was given at the Berlin 'Staatsbühne' to packed houses when Wenzler's film was premiered in Berlin on 22 March 1935. Both versions were said to be a mere shadow of the play's effectiveness. Wendtland, K. (1989) *Geliebter Kintopp: Sämtliche deutsche Spielfilme von 1929 - 1945, Jahrgang 1935 und 1936*. Berlin: Medium Film, p. 38.

Sybill Thorndike as Miss Cavell during the final walk to the rifle range. The scene was shot at the prison of Saint Gilles, Brussels. © British & Dominions Film Corporation

Reframing the Past to Change the Future. Reflections on Herbert Wilcox's *Dawn* (1928) as a Historical Documentary and War Film

Liesbet Depauw

'Those connected with the picture
have had an unexpected responsibility thrust on them.
They made it in the ordinary way as a commercial offering.
Now its release has become a national question.'[1]

Dawn (1928) is in many ways a forgotten film. The film tells the story of the British nurse Edith Cavell who, during the Great War, helped to smuggle Allied soldiers across the Belgian-Dutch border. She was captured, tried and shot by the German occupiers and has been remembered as a heroin ever since. Although *Dawn* was one of the few truly successful British movies of the 1920s, it is now only known by a few scholars and/or film fans. Due to its banning and the principal questions on film censorship that arose from it, the film has entered the history books as a classic example of a controversial movie. But there are other interesting aspects to this film that have often been ignored. In this article, I want to move beyond the mere description of the controversy surrounding the film by regarding *Dawn* as a war film and an historical film. *Dawn* is a fine example of a reconstruction of the past through an emerging medium that would considerably influence the perception of history in the years to come. So even if writing about *Dawn* inevitably means describing the history of its censorship, the main focus of this essay lies elsewhere. I will try to reconstruct the discourse about *Dawn* starting from genre theory by showing that genre expectations, even unspecified, played a crucial part in the various debates about whether or not the film could be shown.

As Robert Altman has stated, generic discourse can be problematic since generic terms do not have a fixed meaning and the way they are used by exhibitors, scholars, producers, critics, the public and politicians may well differ.[2] For the purposes of this chapter, I will consider primarily the discourses of these last four.

The making of: bringing British myth to life

'And that is what makes Dawn,
A page of history, a slice of life,
Quintessential cinema, pure cinema.'[3]

During the 1920s British cinema went through a competitive struggle with American films which had gained a dominant position in the British market since the war. After years of pressure from various film market actors, the *Cinematograph Films Act* was passed in 1927. The Act introduced quota for distributors and exhibitors and was described as 'an act to restrict blind booking and advance booking of cinematographic films and to secure the renting and exhibition of a certain proportion of British films, and for purposes connected therewith.'[4] British distributor C. M. Woolf[5] claimed that the underlying thought behind the quota was that England had to be shown to the world as she really was, and not systematically caricatured and belittled.[6] The story of Edith Cavell would have fit perfectly in this scheme. She was a British nurse who moved to Brussels in 1906 to be the head of a training school for nurses, the *Berkendael Institute*. During the First World War, she used that institute to hide Allied soldiers and eventually get them across the Dutch border. She was caught by the Germans and executed. Her death has been used by Allied propaganda forces and she has been worshiped ever since. But for some British opinion leaders (such as Lord Chamberlain and Lord Birkenhead), using Edith Cavell on the silver screen, was tasteless and improper. Apparently, Britain was not quite ready to use its most recent heroes or heroines to spread a positive image of itself.

Ready or not, the film industry quickly sensed that change was on its way, and from the beginning of 1927 new companies emerged and nearly all existing ones were reorganised. The film industry gained self-confidence and in this exciting, sometimes overconfident period, Herbert Wilcox, who already had several years of successful filmmaking behind him, set up the company that would eventually produce *Dawn*. He founded the *British and Dominions Film*

Corporation (BDFC) in June 1927. *Dawn* was the second BDFC film and became a huge success thanks largely to the controversy that surrounded it.[7] A critic once commented that the strength of *Dawn* as a film lay in the fact that 'it tells a straightforward story straightforwardly.'[8] As I will explain, the Cavell story was anything but straightforward, and yet that is not to suggest that the movie of her life, thus focusing on only a small part of a complex truth, cannot be appreciated for the sobriety and clarity with which it is told. *Dawn* had nothing of the great impersonal spectacles with enormous casts that Wilcox had made before, but was a beautifully shot, realistically acted, credible movie. The décor was realistic since Wilcox preferred to shoot on the historical sites rather than rebuilding them in a British studio. In November 1927, he moved his film crew to Belgium. As described in a Belgian newspaper, Wilcox filmed on location in the Rue de la Culture in Ixelles, where the *Berkendael Institute* was situated; in the prison of Saint Gilles where she spent her last days and on the national rifle range were she was shot.[9]

Convinced of the need to portray the actual occurrence of events, Wilcox tried repeatedly to obtain information about the execution from the German Embassy, but without success.[10] Undoubtedly concerned to seek the truth, Wilcox was still a filmmaker who had to follow the rules that govern the telling of a story without speech. The only way to make a strong movie out of a complicated event was to single out one person's story and leave out every unnecessary detail and character. Obviously, the primary purpose of *Dawn* was to make money. But the author of the script, Reginald Berkeley, was convinced that the movie contained a higher message: 'The German Officers responsible stood for the state, the laws of which had been broken by Miss Cavell. Nurse Cavell stood for the higher service of humanity and these two big interests clashed and Nurse Cavell went under.'[11]

Evidence that Wilcox did not regard *Dawn* as an exclusively commercial venture can be found in the way he depicted the scene of her execution. As the legend went, a German soldier called Rammler refused to shoot at Cavell and was therefore shot by his officer in command. Seeing this, Cavell fainted and received the *coup de grace*. Wilcox filmed this violent scene very indirectly. In the original version the scene goes as follows:

'On the command "Firing party, Ready", the incident with Private Rammler, where he refuses to shoot is played...to [the point] where the officer steps towards him. The actual shooting [...] is not shown. It is merely reflected in the eyes of Nurse Cavell who faints. While she is on the ground [...] the officer in charge realises that he must do his duty. As he moves from his position [...] the scene is transferred to the face of the Lutheran Chaplain and so from his expression the scene that takes place is indicated.'[12]

If Wilcox had merely been concerned about making money, he could have chosen to shoot more explicit scenes to enhance the sensationalism and probably the film's success. Or he could have done what most British directors had done by that time and, responding to the exciting rumours of change in the cinematic world, dedicated himself to the new and rapidly accepted medium of the sound film. Wilcox did not do so, and largely for that reason, in an age of technological change, *Dawn* was soon to be forgotten.

Genre expectations: *Dawn* as a historical documentary and war film

The focal point of this paper is to look at *Dawn* as a historical film, and yet to describe *Dawn* in this way is not as obvious as it might at first appear. First of all, it is difficult to come up with a satisfying and exclusive definition of historical film. Agreeing with the opinion of Altman, genres are not stable over time nor space and most films cannot be pinned down to one particular genre but exhibit the characteristics of multiple genres.[13] In addition, as Kilpi points out, researchers do not always agree whether historical film should be understood in the strictest sense, or as a broad umbrella-term for every movie, including melodrama or war films, that sets the action in a past represented as historical.[14] Furthermore, contemporary critics did not label *Dawn* as a historical film, but systematically, both in Great Britain and abroad, described it either as a documentary or as a war movie. It can be argued that most of the discussion about the intention, meaning and value of the movie was the logical consequence of genre expectations. The term 'genre' is never used, but that does not mean there were no such expectations, for as Altman points out, genres can simply be regarded as broadly recognized public categories.[15]

When we realise that some contemporary critics saw *Dawn* as a documentary, the emphasis and criticism concerning historical veracity seems more logical. On the other hand, if we consider that *Dawn* could be regarded as a war movie (which had its propagandistic purpose during and even after the war), it is easy to understand how the Germans, without ever seeing *Dawn*, could act out of an expectation of what *Dawn* as a war movie would contain. The two genres are not mutually exclusive since the division between the genre of documentary on the one hand, and war movies on the other is based on completely different arguments: in the first case, the aim of the movie, and in the second, the presence and presentation of war. Finally, Dawn could also be categorized as an historical film, for the obvious reason that by 1928 World War One had become an historical fact.

Dawn as a historical documentary

Documentary as a genre in film was first described in the late 1920s by John Grierson who stated that a documentary should be 'the creative treatment of actuality'.[16] This definition is in itself contradictory, since it is difficult to suppose there is any 'actuality' left after 'creative treatment'. But it is interesting that in the decade that *Dawn* was released, Grierson explicitly connected documentary with actuality.

Documentary, as derived from the Latin word *documentum* (a tale), carries a connotation of evidence[17] and, as a result, one of the main expectations of a documentary is that what it depicts is the truth and nothing but the truth. Whether this expectation is desirable or even possible is a complex question over which researchers today are still debating. And yet it is clear that this is what both the manufacturers of the movie – politicians, critics, journalists and audience – expected of *Dawn*. Historical truth turned out to be a crucial factor in the debate that surrounded the film's release.

Based upon a true story, but which one?

Historical inaccuracies became a weapon of the British Foreign Office to bring the movie into discredit, and everybody agreed that documentaries, as *Dawn* was categorized, had to be 'true' from beginning to end. But what the truth might have been was not exactly clear in 1928 and now, nearly ninety years

THE MURDER OF MISS CAVELL
INSPIRES GERMAN "KULTUR"

Propaganda Postcard by the Italian artist Tito Corbella entitled Miss Cavell and German Kultur. A welcome gift for Kaiser's Birthday. © G. Pulman & Sons, Ltd.

later, there still are some mysteries in the Cavell story. It is not my aim to tell the 'real history' of Miss Cavell. It is necessary, however, at least to point out the main issues in the Cavell Myth in order to come to a better understanding of the reception of *Dawn*.

As stated earlier, Edith Cavell was a British nurse who came to Belgium in 1906 and was offered a position as head of a training school for nurses in Brussels a year later. In those days it was unusual for nurses to be trained and Cavell, who was taught at London Hospital, was a pioneer in trying to lift the profession of nursing to a higher level by replacing nuns with professionally trained nurses. The war interrupted her mission though.[18] As the popular version of the story goes, Cavell used the training school building to hide and care for wounded Allied soldiers and eventually to smuggle them across the Dutch border, together with Belgians and Frenchmen willing to join the Allied army. Perhaps she was betrayed by one of the men she helped, or maybe her name was deciphered from a coded list. In any case, she was captured by the Germans on 5 August 1915, court-martialed on 7 and 8 October, sentenced to death and, by command of the new governor of Brussels, General von Saubersweig, was shot at dawn on 12 October.

Many articles and books have been written about the activities and death of Cavell during the Great War, but few of them have tried to look beyond the myth that surrounds her.[19] Most of the authors, including the scriptwriter of *Dawn*, Reginald Berkeley, drew up an unambiguously heroic picture of Edith Cavell. In their stories and essays, Cavell becomes an extraordinarily capable nurse, without fear or regret, who rescued hundreds of men nearly single-handedly. In Britain, this romanticised image of Cavell was still very much alive in 1928, due to the fact that during the war her life story had been widely exploited and disseminated by Allied propaganda.

Although the trial and execution of Cavell were in accordance with the German Imperial Military Penal code and hence perfectly legal; the decision of General von Saubersweig to execute a woman was an extreme measure and, given the circumstances of the war, distinctly unwise.[20] According to her lawyer Sadi Kirschen, Cavell was the first woman to be executed by the Germans on the charge of recruiting soldiers for the allies.[21] Additionally, the short time span between trial and execution left international forces too little time to demand a reprieve from the German emperor. The Allies were shocked and for weeks newspapers echoed the sentiments of disbelief and outrage. The general opinion was that a perfectly charitable woman had been shot by a bunch of barbarians.[22] By shooting Cavell the image of the bloodthirsty Prussian Hun was enforced and the Cavell case was used by the Allied governments to recruit thousands of (mostly British) men for the army.[23]

Portraits and postcards of the death of the British nurse soon went on sale in Brussels along with photographs of the body of the so-called disobedient German soldier Rammler. The postcard of the dead soldier suggests that what Wilcox portrayed in his film might not have been the entire truth, but was commonly accepted as fact. The movie *Dawn* and the protests of the German government surrounding it would open up the debate over what really happened. In the light of a publication in 1965 by A. E. Clark-Kennedy, it is now fairly safe to assume that Cavell was simply shot by the entire firing squad and that no soldier disobeyed the order. Although Kennedy-Clark can hardly be cleared from the charge of partisan and subjective writing, his efforts to reconstruct the historical truth about Cavell proved that her history, as with any history, is far more complex than is usually passed on by myths and stories. Despite his overt admiration for Cavell, he does acknowledge certain additional or alternative aspects of the case. Edith Cavell was no leader of the resistance; she was a mere link in the chain. She sheltered soldiers in her hospital who were assigned to her by other people and passed them on to yet other people who tried to get them over the border. When Cavell was arrested on 5 August, she believed the German police when they falsely told her that they already knew everything, and so she betrayed every single person of the network. Twenty-seven people appeared before the military court on 6 October, and five of them were sentenced to death. All except for Cavell lodged an appeal for clemency, but General von Saubersweig decided on 11 October 1915 that in the interests of the State at least two executions had to take place. Edith Cavell and Philippe Baucq, a Belgian architect and member of the same resistance network as Cavell died at dawn.[24]

By means of propaganda and the construction of myth, the story of nearly thirty people all involved in a network of heroic resistance, has been reduced to the story of a single woman, and it is important to note that whatever discussion there might have been over the details of Cavell's life as portrayed in *Dawn*, no critic suggested that history might not be as simple and straightforward as a (silent) movie could possibly portray.

The execution of an execution scene: the demand and search for historical accuracy

The *Dawn* controversy, as reflected in mainly British newspapers started in early February 1928 and lasted for about a month, after which interest in the movie faded due to other important news facts.[25] The first articles about *Dawn* were all about the German demand to suppress the movie due to historical inaccuracies, referring to the disobedient Rammler. *The Daily News*, as did practically every other British newspaper of significance, stated on 9 February that, 'The German point of view is that if the film is to be shown it should be in such a way as to keep within historical facts and avoid injustice to Germany and the officials who played a part in the tragedy of Miss Cavell's execution.'[26] *The Times* agreed with the German opinion and wrote that the very fact that the film was not consistent with official reports of the execution placed the conduct of the German officer and his firing party in a bad light and could therefore be seen as a *Hetzfilm* (rabble-rousing film).[27]

As history was to reveal, Germans were right in their statement that no soldier had refused to shoot, but in February 1928 there was a lot of evidence that Herbert Wilcox had indeed tried to portray the actual events. The scriptwriter Reginald Berkeley testified that he and Wilcox, when visiting Belgium to investigate the circumstances, had decided that the real facts offered material so much more dramatic that they scrapped the fiction (*Dawn* was originally meant to be a fictional account) and decided to confine themselves to telling the true story of the last days and death of the British nurse.[28] In addition, Wilcox stated on various occasions, that they really 'went into the whole thing, sifting the evidence with the greatest possible care.'[29] He further maintained that 'so far as details were concerned, the story, […], is taken from entirely reliable sources on the spot, partly from the evidence of Mr Kirschner [sic], a Belgian lawyer, to whom the scene of Nurse Cavell's death was described by a Lutheran pastor who was there.'[30]

Ada Bodart (right) greeting Sybill Thorndike during the filming of Dawn. © British & Dominions Film Corporation

It is interesting to note that evidence of the accuracy of the historical images, as in the tradition of the documentary, was mainly based upon the testimony of eye-witnesses. Ironically enough, these eye-witnesses turned out to challenge Wilcox's vision of the past. Unlike other films that focus on a historical event, many eye-witnesses were still alive and the *Dawn* controversy encouraged them to tell their story to the press. The four main witnesses were Ada Bodart, the doctor Benn, the lawyer Kirschen and the Lutheran pastor Paul Le Seur to whom Wilcox referred.

Ada Bodart, who worked with Cavell in the resistance network, had been condemned to death as well, but the Germans reduced her sentence to lifelong labour, due to the fact that she was a widow and mother of two. Madam Bodart acted as herself in the movie and thus increased its credibility. She strongly believed that everything in the movie was true, and felt personally insulted when the British Conservative leader and Minister of Foreign Affairs, Austen Chamberlain, described the film as 'repugnant'. As a token of her disagreement, Ada Bodart sent him back her OBE, insisting that the execution scene was absolutely true and that the director had always urged the actors to do nothing to distort the facts.[31] Bodart's testimony and actions were rather emotional and did not have a great impact on providing a piece of the puzzle we call truth, but the other testimonies did. Both Benn, the official doctor at the shooting of Cavell, pastor Le Seur, who accompanied Cavell to the execution, and Cavell's lawyer Kirschen, declared in the press that no officer refused to shoot and that Rammler was a fictional character.[32]

Wilcox's movie did indeed turn out to be historically incorrect. One of the film's merits, though, was that it led to a renewed interest in Cavell's death and helped the historical truth to emerge a bit further from the myth.

The newspaper accounts seem to suggest that the accuracy of the execution scene was merely a matter of principle, but official documents of the British government reveal that the debate came close to being politically orchestrated for the sole purpose of discrediting the movie and thus pleasing the German Government. As Robertson proved, the *Dawn* controversy started much earlier in official circles.[33] Austen Chamberlain was informed of Germany's worries about *Dawn* as early as December 1927 and the Foreign Office tried to find a way to discredit *Dawn* without being accused of political censorship. One of the first solutions they came up with was to abuse the possibly false sense of historical truth as portrayed in the film. The reason why they did not, or at least not openly, was the fact that neither the War Office nor the Imperial War Museum were able to give proof beyond all doubt that what Wilcox showed in the film and was the generally accepted version in 1928 was inaccurate. The Foreign Office knew it was on shaky ground and Chamberlain himself warned his cabinet colleagues that to try to discredit *Dawn* in public on grounds of historical inaccuracy was not without serious risk. Robertson concluded that it was likely that Chamberlain was ordered by the Foreign Office to discuss the historical facts with the president of the British Board of Film Censors (BBFC), T. P. O'Connor, on an informal basis. The BBFC did ban the movie on 20 October, claiming that the film was 'inexpedient' in the present time, without commenting on what the inexpediency might have been.[34]

The only critic who questioned the necessity of absolute truth seems to be E. A. Baughan, dramatic critic of *The Daily News*: 'Even if it were not a fact [the shooting of Rammler] I cannot see that the incident is anything more than a reflection on the military discipline of the German war machine…Whether she [Edith Cavell] actually fainted on seeing the soldier shot and had to be dispatched by the officer commanding the firing party, I do not know. It may have been so, or it may not have been so. But the incident as shown in the film does not deserve Chamberlain's declaration that it was an 'outrage on a noble woman's memory'.[35] Apart from this one opinion, virtually everyone else expected *Dawn* to be entirely true. The London City Council (LCC), that would be the first authority in Great Britain to give permission for *Dawn* to be shown in theatres, tried to fulfil those expectations by demanding that every possible historical inaccuracy be cut out of the movie. They asked cuts to be made of the scene depicting the threat of shooting private Rammler, of the firing squad for refusing to obey orders, and of his grave beside that of Nurse Cavell.[36] All the cuts were made by Wilcox who simply claimed that he had never refused to change the film, but that he who demanded such alterations should at least have seen the movie beforehand.[37]

Film as a new medium of passing on history

Dawn provided another topic for serious consideration. People started to question the film medium as a source of historical events. The main problem with film as a medium was that it is highly commercial and that a producer, distributor and eventually exhibitor can make a lot of money by using history.

Austen Chamberlain, as chief proponent of the banning of *Dawn*, opened the public debate about the desirability of the commercial exploitation of the death of a national heroine by publicly turning down Wilcox's personal invitation to attend a private viewing of the film. The Belgian ambassador in London, Baron de Cartier de Marchienne (further referred to as de Cartier), described Chamberlain's feelings to the Belgian Minister of Foreign Affairs, Paul Hymans: 'The overall impression here is that the tragic death of Miss Cavell is far too noble and beautiful to be exploited in a commercial and lucrative manner. Sir Austen has made this idea his own and has expressed it in an eloquent way that is supported by a great many people.'[38] In *The Daily Telegraph*, the Secretary of State for India, Lord Birkenhead, described the exploitation of the movie: 'And what is the purpose of this adventure? [...] Is it to preach a holy message? Are the profits to be devoted to some charitable purpose? [...] Or are they intended to bring in profit to the producer and those associated with him? If this, indeed, be the purpose, is it decent so to exploit the agony and the sacrifice of the noblest woman whom the war produced?'[39]

To this accusing letter, Reginald Berkeley responded: 'In the name of common sense, if it is not illegitimate for a publisher to make a profit by selling Bibles…why should it be illegitimate for a film producer to make a profit out of a reverent and unexaggerated picturisation…?'[40] As the debate raged on, Wilcox sensed the widespread anxiety for exploitation and, to calm his critics, promised to donate a portion of the profits to the Edith Cavell Rest Homes for Nurses.[41] In Belgium, the first country to screen the picture, the newspapers announced for weeks that five percent of the profits made in Belgium would be given to *La Fédération Nationale des Combattants* (The National Federation of Servicemen) and *Les Ecoles d'infirmières de Belgique* (The Nurses Training Schools of Belgium); in France, the profits from a special exhibition at the *Théâtre des Champs-Elysées* went to the Belgian disabled veterans of the war.[42]

Dawn as a war movie

'To show a war-time horror in all its shame revealed
To rake up facts that peace allows to sleep
Betrays a beaten country, bursts a wound that time had healed
And cheapens every memory we keep.'[43]

Cinema, as a relatively modern invention in 1928, already had a history of portraying not only the First World War, but other conflicts as well, such as the Boer War (1899-1902) and the battles in the Balkans in the 1910s.[44] Although critics regarded the generic characteristics of war films as clear, the definition of a war film is neither unambiguous nor consistent over time. The first aspect of the genre is whether or not it emphasises combat. According to Neale's definition it does: 'War films are films about the waging of war in the twentieth century; scenes of combat are a requisite ingredient and these scenes are dramatically central.'[45] *Dawn* was labelled a war film, but the emphasis on combat does not apply, so I prefer Shain's broader definition of the genre: 'A war film deals with the roles of civilians, espionage agents, and soldiers in any aspects of the war'.[46]

The second problem is that the generic aspects of a war film change over time. Propagandistic as they were at first, they altered to become peace-time movies that used the portrayal of war as a warning against future wars. But such alterations were not always perceived by the public at the time they took place. During the 1920s, the reputation of war films persisted for some years after the actual changes in the genre.

Dawn in the tradition of propagandistic war films

During the war, Britain, France and the United States all used film to support their cause. But films depicting war and revealing an often demonised enemy were certainly not a monopoly of the Allied forces; Germany, after noticing the success of films as propaganda and as a means of dealing with low troop morale started producing its own war films by 1916.[47] Besides official propaganda films such as the British *Battle of the Somme* (1916), commercial war films were also being produced. War films thus were known, used and feared by nearly every country involved in the First World War. And after 1918, war films continued to stir international emotions. Commercial films as *The Four Horsemen of the Apocalypse* (1921), *Mare Nostrum* (1926) and *The Flight Commander* (1927), caused diplomatic riots because they were said to stereotype Germans as barbarians, and in fact they often did. The German government, during the 1920s and 1930s, looked anxiously for images that ridiculed, caricatured or insulted the country, and they were justified in thinking that Germans were generally the villains in war films made by their former enemies.[48]

Debauche stated that war films in the 1920s were told from the soldier's point of view and featured battle over any other wartime experience. In addition, they usually eliminated or significantly reduced the role of women as causal agents in their narratives.[49] *Dawn*, as a movie which is completely based on the actions of a woman and in which no actual combat scenes are shown, can hardly be seen as a typical war film of that period.

Yet, according to the discourse concerning *Dawn*, we can assume that war films as a genre were defined quite broadly and that *Dawn*, even with all its atypical aspects, was recognised as a genuine war film. Consequently, when the German government heard that the story of the execution of Edith Cavell, was to be turned into a major production for international consumption, they assumed that it would be a vicious war film and did what they always did in such cases: they protested strenuously. It was not the first film they had objected to[50] and considering one of the earlier films on Cavell, *The Martyrdom of Nurse Cavell* (1915), they had cause to be suspicious. The scriptwriter himself, Edgar Wallace, described it as a purely anti-German propaganda film.[51] So instead of reacting to a screening of the film, the German government contacted the British Foreign Office as early as September 1927, five months before the film was finished. In addition, genre expectations of war films were so strong that journalists, politicians and civilians were able to discuss the desirability of the film for over a month without having seen it. The debates that swirled around *Dawn* were heated and shed an interesting light on how war films in the inter-war period were being conceived by contemporaries. The most striking observation is that Belgium and Great Britain had different views on the desirability of depicting war memories.

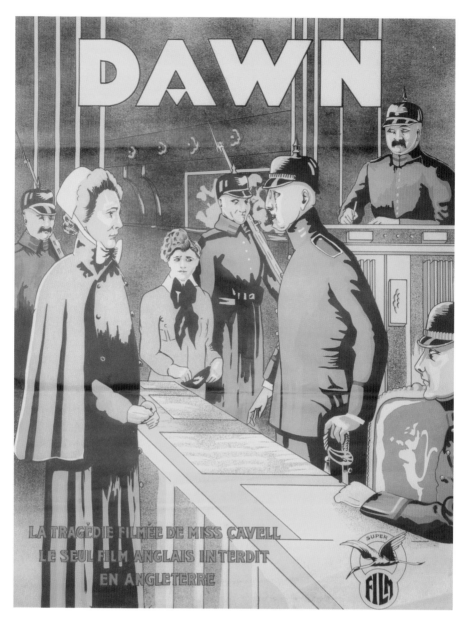

Presumably French movie poster of Dawn explicitly mentioning the banning of the film: 'the filmed tragedy of Miss Cavell. The only English film forbidden in England'. Source: Depauw

Neither the British nor the Belgian government had any official means of banning a film, but Great Britain did take steps to prevent the film from obtaining a BBFC certificate, and some politicians (albeit unofficially or through the words of Austen Chamberlain) protested vigorously against the film. Most British newspapers agreed with their government and editorialised on the purpose of war movies. Without having seen the film, British newspapers generally agreed that films with a malicious and inflammatory character were to be avoided in peacetime.[52] The conservative *Daily Telegraph* pointed out that war films had served a useful purpose, but went on to say that people now realised that a war film presupposed an enemy. If the primary concern of a modern society was to live together in harmony with other nations, the author concluded that war films should be discontinued if peace was to be maintained. The same newspaper resumed the debate two days later by noting that the *Dawn* film might be historically accurate and in that sense no injustice would be done to the German nation, but that the present was a time for forgetting things that belonged to the past. [53]

Judging by the many letters received and published by the British newspapers, public opinion agreed with this line of thinking. But there were some dissident voices in the press and some opinion leaders urged that the truth must not be concealed, even if the truth about the war was likely to be unpleasant: 'If truth were to be sacrificed…then indeed it would mean an end to all serious discussion.'[54] *The Evening News* even dared to state that one could hardly conceive of a more practical contribution to the cause of peace than a demonstration of the horrors and crimes of war to a generation that was being brought up in a conspiracy of silence towards the experience of the war.[55] By claiming that war movies were necessary in maintaining peace, *The Evening News* Owen disagreed with the German, British and even Dutch view that war movies were likely to revive feelings of hate, and agreed with the general Belgian opinion that Edith Cavell's death should be made available for everyone to see.

Belgium's reaction was the opposite of Great Britain's. The susceptibilities of the German government were carefully considered, as with any diplomatic request, but Minister of Foreign Affairs Paul Hymans stated clearly that the Belgian government had no authority to ban a film.[56] Hymans took a special interest in the controversy over *Dawn* and during the whole of February and March he received almost daily letters from Belgian ambassador de Cartier in London and the Belgian ambassador Everts in Berlin. Thanks to these letters, we can state that the Belgian government had no intention of complying with the German request.

One of the first letters written by Everts to Hymans revealed that the German Government had asked Everts to make it clear that they considered the banning of *Dawn* a highly important matter. He did so, but in the same letter he wrote that as long as the conservative German press continued to write insulting articles about the Belgians, it would be hypocritical of them to ask for *Dawn* to be suppressed. Hymans underlined these last sentences and wrote in blue pencil 'Très juste'.[57] The Belgian ambassador in London took the same point of view, writing that the German request might be understandable, but in this case misplaced. Germany was not free of propaganda itself and as long as they published articles like *Der Belgische Volkskrieg* (the Belgian civil war) or produced movies like *The World War through German Spectacles* (original title and date unknown), they had no right to ask for *Dawn* to be banned.[58]

The Belgian Press mainly agreed with its government. The quality newspaper *Le Soir* treated the *Dawn Affair* as front page news for more than a month. They contended that the number of war films in Germany could no longer be counted, and that the Germans, before asking for *Dawn* to be banned could be a bit more scrupulous about their own film production. Belgium would not tolerate German interference and the debate over war films concentrated mainly on whether they should ever be suppressed at the request of any other nation. In most cases the answer was a clear 'no' and Belgian commentators even found the interference of Germany insulting.[59]

But Belgians did not want *Dawn* to appear on their movie screens just to take revenge on Germany and its propaganda; they were convinced that *Dawn* was not a *Hetzfilm*. The fact that Wilcox did not show the actual execution led a journalist for *Le Soir* to conclude that the film was not an incitement to hatred, but simply a document made by an honest British director who wished to make a contribution to history.[60] The memory of Cavell was to be honoured and according to the Belgian World War One veterans, people needed a reminder of their heroes and heroines whom they were only too quick to forget. In an open letter to Hymans published in the press, they declared that to forget would be an insult to the past and a threat to the future.[61] The Belgian opinion that *Dawn* was an anti-war movie and that portraying war atrocities to the youth was the best way to prevent war from happening in the future, was widely shared in the French press.[62] The German press, on the other hand, saw this approval for the exhibition of *Dawn* as a typical example of the efforts of Belgium to maintain a war psychosis.[63]

In conclusion, it is clear that while Germany, Great Britain and the Netherlands expected war films to serve the war aims, Belgium and France altered those expectations by believing that portraying war in times of peace might prevent war and serve peace. In *Dawn*'s case, Belgium and France had understood its true nature, although the film obviously did not prevent war. *Dawn* actually portrayed the Germans in quite a favourable light and the inclusion of Rammler would have shown that even the enemy could be human and that war only made victims on both sides of the conflict. Ironically, the demand of the British LCC to cut Rammler out of the movie to please the Germans, failed in its purpose. It made *Dawn* a harsher, far more unambiguous film that portrayed the Germans as cruel and insensitive.

Locarno and the ending of make-belief

> 'As for the Locarno spirit, it is clear to us that its very existence
> has been threatened by this crass blunder of Germany,
> reinforced as that has been
> by official pressure in this country'.[64]

Genre expectations played an important role in the content and structure of the controversy, but context seems to be the key to explain why the debate took on such enormous proportions. The late 1920s by and large are regarded as a period in which the European diplomatic climate improved and serious efforts to maintain peace were made. Due to such international agreements as the Locarno Treaties (1925) and the Kellogg-Briand Pact (1928), a sense of peace and security gradually came over Europe. The three protagonists of the *Dawn* controversy, Chamberlain, Hymans and the German Minister of Foreign

Affairs Stresemann, all played an important role in the drawing up of either one or both treaties. To say the least, the *Dawn* debate was carried on among some of the top politicians of the time. They all signed the Kellogg-Briand Pact and Chamberlain and Stresemann played a decisive role in the completion of the Locarno Treaties. The Kellogg-Briand pact was to be signed after the *Dawn* controversy had ended, but the Locarno Treaties did play an important role in the perception of the events happening around Wilcox's film.

The Locarno Conference (5-16 October 1928) united representatives of Belgium, France, Germany, Great-Britain, Italy, Poland and Czechoslovakia. The treaties settled the Western borders between France, Germany and Belgium as stipulated in the Treaty of Versailles, and the contracting parties made a number of promises to avoid further wars. Belgian participation in the Locarno Treaties meant an important change in foreign policy, which moved further away from the existing bilateral political and military solidarity with France. The Locarno Treaties even stood for an overall reorientation of European politics, where the Anglo-Saxon opinion that the German economy had to be restored gained strength over the post-war French and Belgian view that its economy should be kept as low as possible. The treaties led to a common approach among all European powers, including Germany.[65] Chamberlain, Stresemann and the French Minister of Foreign Affairs of that time, Aristide Briand, all received the Nobel Peace Prize for their achievements at Locarno.[66]

Despite the positive message of the Locarno Treaties, in hindsight it was certainly naïve to think that all sources of friction between Germany and the Allied nations had simply vanished. Evidence of lingering resentments in Europe are to be found in the *Dawn* controversy. The public debate over the interference of the German government's attempt to ban the film eventually led to a closer, more critical look at the so-called spirit of Locarno. Although British public opinion generally was in favour of the Locarno Treaties and such conservative newspapers as *The Daily Telegraph* and the *Daily Express* continued to support the actions of Lord Chamberlain, dissident and more critical voices began to be heard. *Dawn*, as a controversial movie, made people think about how to interpret the present. Commenting on the *Dawn Affair*, the *Evening Standard* wrote:

'[...] the German attitude in this matter has done Germany herself and the "Spirit of Locarno" far more harm than a thousand films could have done. The Foreign Secretary's interference has made millions of people in this country wonder whether, if we have to make such concessions in order to keep Germany in a good temper, whether the "Spirit of Locarno" is really worth preserving.'[67]

Other critical voices concerning the desirability, or not, of preserving the Spirit of Locarno at the expense of principle appeared in articles in *The Referee* and *The Morning Post*, among others.[68] In France and Belgium, where response to the Locarno Treaties had at first been favourable, the old mistrust of Germany was still noticeable. In France, one of the most important quality newspapers, *Le Temps*, dedicated an extensive article to German propaganda films in Greece. The author concluded that 'despite the beautiful declarations made by the Germans at Locarno, Geneva and Berlin, the French living outside France can inform their countrymen [...] as to the true spirit of the Germans'.[69] Furthermore, Georges Clemenceau, co-author of the Versailles Treaty and a proponent of harsh treatment for Germany, stated in the press that 'if the situation is so delicate that a film [*Dawn*] based on reality can strain friendly relations, then they are not founded on sincerity.'[70]

The Belgian press, which had always been in favour of showing *Dawn*, soon started to criticise the actions of the German government in the light of Locarno. The Socialist newspaper *Le Peuple* stated that 'appeasement of the spirits cannot be unilateral'[71], while the neutral *Le Soir* gave a more thorough analysis of the influence of Locarno on the *Dawn Affair*. The author stated that the banning of *Dawn* was a typical British thing to do and coincided completely with their pragmatic commercial policies. While the British, in the author's view, signed Locarno to re-establish international trade, the Belgians' primary concern was security. German interference in a domestic affair, especially in Belgium, inspired a sense of insecurity and heightened scepticism about the Locarno Treaties.[72] Resentment against the way the Germans used or even abused the spirit of Locarno can also be found in official documents. For example, the Belgian ambassador in London de Cartier wrote to Hymans that the Germans, wrongfully invoking the spirit of Locarno, forced Chamberlain to openly condemn *Dawn*.[73] A good example of the different attitudes of Belgium and Great Britain is the fact that the former Minister of Foreign Affairs, who had signed the Locarno Treaties, reacted in sharp contrast to his co-signer Austen Chamberlain by publicly attending the first showing of *Dawn* in Belgium.[74]

Edith Cavell (Sybill Thorndike) awaits her death sentence at the prison of Saint Gilles, Brussels.
© British & Dominion Film Corporation.

Conclusion

Dawn is one of the most hotly debated films of the 1920s, and yet remarkably few people have ever seen it. One possible explanation for why some people were so eager to condemn the film is that they acted out of genre expectations. There were those who saw *Dawn* as a historical documentary, while others labelled it a war film, or both. If they thought of *Dawn* as a documentary, they expected the film to tell the truth about the Cavell case, without considering that the absolute truth might not exist, and certainly cannot be portrayed in a silent film, or any film for that matter. *Dawn* opened up the debate and made people wonder whether history should or should not be used on the screen or, more specifically, whether war was ever a suitable topic for a film. War films had the reputation of being sheer propaganda that provoked hatred towards the old enemy. *Dawn* was rather the opposite; by trying to use the depiction of the atrocities of war to prevent future wars. Since people had not seen the film and genre expectations had not yet caught up with actual genre characteristics, many opinion-leaders panicked and tried to stop what they considered a threat to the Spirit of Locarno. That Spirit, referring to the overall efforts to attain and preserve peace, heated the controversy. But the Dawn controversy reached further than the film and soon the Spirit of Locarno itself was questioned. German interference in a strictly domestic matter, such as the making of a film, led some people to wonder whether the Spirit of Locarno was really worth preserving, especially when Germany itself made no effort to restrain its own propaganda. In conclusion, we can state that *Dawn* was a film that made many people think about their past, present and even their future; a film that made people see not only the meaning of what had happened, but also shed a light on what was going on in interwar Europe.

Notes

1 Anonymous (1 March 1928) Dawn as I saw it, in *Daily Herald*.
2 Altman, R. (2004) 95 theses about film genre. On the generic applications of studio publicity, pp. 31-58 in Biltereyst, D. and Ph. Meers (eds) *Film/TV/Genre*. Ghent: Academia Press.
3 Anonymous (1 December 1928), Dawn, p. 14 in *Cinéa-Ciné*. (My translation.)
4 Balcon, M., Lindgren, E., et. al. (1947) *Twenty Years of British Film*, 1925-1945. London: Falcon Press, p. 14.
5 C.M. Woolf was the British distributor of *Dawn*.
6 Anonymous (16 February 1928) Nurse Cavell Film, English distributors view, in *Daily Telegraph*.
7 Low, R. (1973). *The History of the British Film, 1918-1929*. London: Allen & Unwin.
8 Richard Watts, cited in Low (1973), p. 178.
9 Anonymous (25 February 1928) La projection du film de Miss Cavell, in *Le Soir*.
10 Anonymous (8 February 1928) Dawn, the ambassador's letter, in *Daily News*.
11 Anonymous (13 February 1928) Defence of Dawn, Author of Cavell Film replies to Sir Austen, in *Daily Herald*.
12 Anonymous (28 february 1928) Execution scene in 'Dawn', in *The Times*.
13 Altman, R. (1999). *Film/Genre*. London: British Film Institute.
14 Kilpi, H. (2001, January). British historical film: history and generic classification. *Wider Screen, Internet movie magazine*, [http://www.film-oholic.com/widerscreen/2002/1/british_historical_film.htm].
15 Altman (1999).
16 Winston, B. (1995). *Claiming the real: the Griersonian documentary and its legitimations*. London: British Film Institute, p. 11.
17 Winston (1995).
18 De Weerdt, D. (1993). *De vrouwen van de Eerste wereldoorlog*. Gent: Stichting Mens en Kultuur, pp. 164-165.
19 Rosseels, M. (12 October 1965) Vijftig jaar geleden te Brussel gefusilleerd. Edith Cavell: levensbeeld werd door myte misvormd, in *De Standaard*.
20 Clark-Kennedy, A.E. (1965). *Edith Cavell, pioneer and patriot*. London: Faber and Faber, pp. 177-179.
21 Tytgat, Ch. (1919). *Nos fusillés (recruteurs et espions): Philippe Baucq, Edith Cavell, J. Corbisier, Pitje Bodson, Le grand procès de Mons*. Bruxelles: Bulens, p. 63.
22 Tytgat (1919), p.65; De Weerdt (1993), pp. 169-170.
23 De Weerdt (1993), pp. 169-170.
24 Clark-Kennedy (1965).
25 Belgian Office of Foreign Affairs. Central Archive. File 452/26-31: Film "Miss Edith Cavell", 1928-1939. De Cartier de Marchienne, E. (Belgian Ambassador, London), letter to Hymans, P. (Belgian Minister of Foreign Affairs, Brussels), 1 March 1928.
26 Anonymous (9 February 1928a) Nurse Cavell Film, German government seeking a ban, in *Daily News*.
27 Anonymous (9 February 1928b) Nurse Cavell Film, German protests, in *The Times*.
28 Anonymous (9 February 1928a).
29 Anonymous (9 February 1928a).
30 The Belgian lawyer referred to in this article, is probably Cavell's lawyer Sadi Kirschen, assuming that his name was misspelled in the Morning Post. Anonymous (9 February 1928c) Cavell Film Protest, Statement by the producer, in Morning Post.
31 Anonymous (15 February 1928) Le film de Miss Cavell, ce que dit madame Ada Bodart, in Le Soir. Anonymous (16 February 1928) Champion of Cavell Film, Why Mme. Bodart returned her O.B.E. medal, in *Morning Post*.
32 Anonymous (2 March 1928) Nurse Cavell, the last minutes in Brussels, in *The Times*.
33 Robertson, J. C. (1984) Dawn (1928): Edith Cavell and Anglo-German relations, pp. 15-28 in *Historical Journal of Film, Radio and Television*.
34 Anonymous (21 February 1928) Censor bans the Cavell film, in *Morning Post*. Anonymous (21 February 1928) Official Ban on Cavell Film, in *Daily Telegraph*.
35 Baughan, E. A. (1 March 1928) The facts about 'Dawn', in *Daily News*.
36 Anonymous (6 April 1928) Dawn' passed for exhibition, in *The Times*.
37 Anonymous (30 March 1928) LCC and Dawn, committee favour exhibition, in *Daily Telegraph*.

38 Belgian Office of Foreign Affairs. Central Archive. File 452/26-31: Film "Miss Edith Cavell", 1928-1939. De Cartier de Marchienne, E. (Belgian ambassador, London), letter to Hymans, P. (Belgian Minister of Foreign Affairs, Brussels), 13 February March 1928, my translation.

39 Anonymous (25 February 1928) Lord Birkenhead on Cavell Film, in *Daily Telegraph*.

40 Anonymous (27 February 1928) New Restrictions on Cavell Film, in *Daily Telegraph*.

41 Anonymous (27 February 1928) Dawn again held up, in *Daily News*.

42 Anonymous (5 March 1928) announcement for Dawn, in Le Soir. Anonymous (3 November 1928) La sortie de Dawn, p. 13 in *La cinégraphie française*.

43 Anonymous (28 February 1928) A schoolboy cited in Letters to the editor, War horrors on screen, in Daily Telegraph.

44 Low, R. (1949) *The History of the British Film, 1906-1914*. London: George Allen & Unwin Ltd., p. 149-151.

45 Neale, S. (2000) *Genre and Hollywood*. London: Routledge, p. 125.

46 Shain, R. E. (1976). *An Analysis of Motion Pictures about War Released by the American Film Industry, 1930-1970*. New York : Arno, p. 20.

47 Curry, R. (1995) How Early German Film Stars Helped Sell the War(es), pp. 130-148 in Dibbets, K. and B. Hogenkamp (eds) *Film and the First World War*. Amsterdam: Amsterdam University Press, pp. 139-148.

48 Engelen, L. (2005) Cinematic Representations of the Enemy in Belgian Silent Fiction Films, pp. 359-378 in Purseigle, P. (ed.) *Warfare and Belligerence. Perspectives in First World War Studies*. Leiden: Brill

49 Cited in Neale (2000), p. 129.

50 For instance, they had objected to the screening of *The Four Horsemen of the Apocalypse* in both Belgium and Great Britain.

51 Percy Moran's *The Martyrdom of Nurse Cavell* obtained a BBFC certificate in 1919 on condition that the name of Nurse Cavell appear neither on the screen, in posters nor in any publicity matter used in connection with the film. The film was renamed *Nurse and Martyr*. When rumours appeared in the press that the movie was to be reissued in 1928, Wilcox's company, the British and Dominions Film Corporation, purchased it and suppressed the negative. Anonymous (22 February 1928) Banned Cavell Film, in *Daily Telegraph*.

52 Anonymous (9 February 1928) Nurse Cavell Film, German protests, in *The Times*.

53 Anonymous (23 February 1928) War Films, in *Daily Telegraph*. Anonymous (25 February 1928) War films and War memories, in *Daily Telegraph*.

54 Anonymous (14 February 1928) Mistaken Meddlesomeness, in *Daily Mail*.

55 Owen, H. (14 February 1928) A film before our eyes, in *Evening News*.

56 Anonymous (12 February 1928) A propos du film sur Miss Cavell, in *Le Soir*.

57 Belgian Office of Foreign Affairs. Central Archive. File 452/26-31: Film "Miss Edith Cavell", 1928-1939. Everts, R. (Belgian ambassador, Berlin), letter to Hymans, P. (Belgian Minister of Foreign Affairs, Brussels), 11 February, 1928.

58 The article *Der Belgische Volkskrieg* was written by Professor Meurer and was published in 1927 in the official German publication '*Volksrecht im Weltkrieg 1914-1918*'. Office of Foreign Affairs. Central Archive. File 452/26-31: Film "Miss Edith Cavell", 1928-1939. de Cartier de Marchienne, E., (Belgian ambassador, London), letter to Hymans, P. (Belgian Minister of Foreign Affairs, Brussels), 27 February 1928.

59 Anonymous (1928) Ceux qui se plaignent, ou la paille et la poutre, in *Le Soir*. Anonymous (12 February 1928) La consigne est d'oublier, in *La Gazette*.

60 deGodart, A. (2 March 1928) Le film Dawn à Paris, in *Le Soir*.

61 Anonymous (24 February 1928) Le film Miss Cavell,in *Le Soir*.

62 deGodart (2 March 1928).

63 Anonymous (12 March 1928) Le film Dawn, appreciations allemandes, in *Le Soir*.

64 Anonymous (27 February 1928) Darkness and Dawn, in *Morning Post*.

65 Coolsaet, R. (1998) *België en zijn buitenlandse politiek, 1830-1990*. Leuven: Uitgeverij Van Halewyck, pp. 233-258.

66 The Nobel Prize Internet Archive, [http://www.almaz.com/nobel/].

67 Anonymous (23 February 1928) The Film Affair, in *Evening Standard*.

68 Anonymous (26 February 1928), What is behind? in *The Referee*; Anonymous (28 February 1928) The false Dawn, in *Morning Post*. Anonymous (27 February 1928) Darkness and Dawn, in *Morning Post*.

69 Bertland, R. (14 February 1928) Lettre de Grèce, la propagande allemande, in *Le Temps*.

70 Anonymous (23 February 1928), Will the Germans admit they regret the shooting of Miss Cavell? in *Evening Standard*.

71 Anonymous (20 February 1928) A propos de films, in *Le Peuple*.

72 Anonymous (5 March 1928) Locarno et 'Dawn', in *Le Soir*.

73 Office of Foreign Affairs. Central Archive. File 452/26-31: Film "Miss edith Cavell", 1928-1939. de Cartier de Marchienne, E., (Belgian ambassador, London), letter to Hymans, P. (Belgian Minister of Foreign Affairs, Brussels), 13 February, 1928.

74 Anonymous (11 March 1928) 'Dawn', la tragédie filmée de Miss Cavell, in *Le Soir*.

Bruno Ganz is Adolf Hitler. His excellent performance is the only thing about *Downfall* virtually all reviewers and critics agree on. © Constantin Film GmbH

Hitler's *Downfall,* a film from Germany (*Der Untergang,* 2004)

Roel Vande Winkel[1]

An empire meant to last a thousand years collapses in the thirteenth year of its existence. As enemy forces encircle the capital, the uncrowned emperor and his entourage hide in a fortified shelter. Aboveground all hell breaks loose. Soldiers and civilians, some of them children, risk their lives in fruitless attempts to hold back the enemy. Others have lost all hope and, for better or for worse, just wait for the end. Underground, their leader shows no interest in the fate of his subjects. Sometimes calm, sometimes outraged, the dictator awaits the arrival of liberation troops in vain. In an apocalyptic finale, determined to remain out of enemy hands and concerned to safeguard his place in history, he takes his life. His wife, married to him only a few hours before, after spending most of her life in his shadow, dies with him. Some of his closest collaborators follow their example. Some of his inner circle even take the lives of their children as well. Others make a final attempt to escape. Some succeed, some fail. It is zero hour: the end of an era, the beginning of a new one.[2]

The events unfolding in Berlin during the final days of the Third Reich have the narrative quality and dramatic potential of a Greek tragedy. It is not surprising that, in the age of film and television, various attempts have been made to reconstruct this episode on film or tape. And yet it was nearly sixty years before the first German mainstream film solely dedicated to this subject was made. *Der Untergang* (*Downfall*, 2004) premiered in Germany (Munich) on 9 September 2004 and was presented internationally with a gala screening (14 September) at the Toronto International Film Festival. *Downfall*, released in Germany on 16 September, became an international hit. The film received an Academy Award nomination (2005) for best foreign language film and won the British Independent Film Award (2005) for best foreign film. In Germany, the film attracted over four and a half million cinemagoers while an extended version, aired in two parts on consecutive nights, was viewed by over seven million Germans.[3] The production was sold by EOS Distribution / Beta Cinema to more than forty countries, including Poland and Israel. (For its American release, the film was re-titled *The Downfall: Hitler and the End of the Third Reich.*)

Downfall is estimated to have grossed nearly 87,000,000 USD.[4] Like any major mainstream production, *Downfall* was released in various DVD editions[5] which increase its audience day by day, as will future television broadcasts at home and abroad.

Shortly after its German release, *Variety* wrote: 'That a German filmmaker, of all people, would dare attempt a drama about the madman post-war generations learned to loathe has become an irresistible topic for historians, tabloids, magazines, talk shows, political leaders, editorial writers and schoolchildren'.[6] *Downfall* was indeed a controversial film. Critics were divided and internationally respected historians had contrasting opinions.[7] *The Hollywood Reporter* saw 'one of the best war movies ever made', enthusiastically describing it as 'a film that will set new standards in the art of committing history to celluloid' and concluded '*Downfall* could be the most important movie ever made about World War II.'[8] The German *Filmdienst* journal, on the other hand, described it as 'the bad kind of producers' cinema': 'at best it sticks to the clichés of war cinema – during which it often embraces pure kitsch.'[9] German film directors were also divided: Volker Schlöndorff praised the movie even before he had seen it[10] while his colleague Wim Wenders hated it intensely.[11]

The controversy did *Downfall* no disservice. The number of viewers the film attracted in and outside Germany was by and large the effect of the heated debates it stirred up. A keen marketing strategy, fuelled by ardent advocates and angry objectors alike turned *Downfall* into a phenomenon. But there is much more to this film than commercially exploited controversy. Ridley Scott's *Gladiator* (2000), which is much less concerned with being historically correct than the film under discussion, inspired academics to write an entire book on that particular film and related sword and sandal films.[12] The same could easily be done for *Downfall*, a production that evokes more questions than any one article can answer.[13]

Much of the debate surrounding *Downfall* centred on the historical correctness of its narrative and/or on the relevance of the film. This chapter wants to contribute to those debates by addressing some key questions raised by *Downfall*. Some are only relevant to this film, but others are relevant to our understanding of historical mainstream films in general. First, an attempt is made to understand why it took Germany so long to produce this particular historical film. Second, the movie's main storyline and narrative techniques are analysed. Third, against the background of that analytical sketch, some choices that *Downfall* producer/scriptwriter Bernd Eichinger made are evaluated. Aiming to interconnect with larger debates surrounding the possibilities and limitations of mainstream cinema to 'do' history, it will be argued that, because of the symbolic ways in which film works, it can often do historical reality more justice by slightly altering historical 'facts' than it can by trying to recreate them 'as they really happened'. Finally, an attempt is made to grasp the relevance of this particular historical film.

Previous Führer bunker films

On 16 April, 1945, twenty Soviet armies, comprising two and a half million soldiers, opened the offensive against the capital of Nazi Germany. The battle for Berlin had begun. One day later, propaganda minister Joseph Goebbels addressed his staff. Many of his collaborators were eager to leave Berlin before the Red Army entirely encircled it. Referring to Veit Harlan's colour film, *Kolberg* (1945), a textbook example of Nazi *Durchhaltepropaganda* (endurance propaganda),[14] Goebbels urged his staff to carry on and delivered one of his most frequently cited speeches:

> 'Gentlemen, in a hundred year's time they will be showing another fine colour film describing the terrible days we are living through. Don't you want to play a part in this film, to be brought back to life in a hundred year's time? Everybody now has a chance to choose the part that he will play in the film a hundred years hence. I can assure you that it will be a fine and elevating picture. And for the sake of this prospect it is worth standing fast. Hold out now, so that a hundred years hence the audience will not hoot and whistle when you appear on the screen.'[15]

As Goebbels knew only too well, history is always written by the victors. The first feature film about the battle of Berlin was produced by *Mosfilm*, the major production unit of the Soviet Union. *Padeniye Berlina* (*Fall of Berlin*, 1949) was devoted to glorifying Joseph Stalin (who handpicked the actor that was to play him and gave detailed instructions as to how he should be filmed)[16] and did not even try to portray Hitler and his inner circle in a remotely accurate manner.[17] In the following years and decades, various feature films were made about the collapse of the Third Reich, but the first German feature film dealing exclusively

Adolf Hitler (Albin Skoda), Joseph Goebbels (Willy Krause) and Heinrich Himmler (Eric Suckmann) in a German promotional leaflet for Georg Pabst's *Der letzte Akt* (*The Last Ten Days*, 1955). The script was written by Erich Maria Remarque and based on a book by Michael Musmanno, who made Pabst hire Traudl Junge as his assistant. The Austrian film flopped in Germany but was quite successful elsewhere. Source: Vande Winkel

with this subject was a long time coming. *Downfall* was produced by the Munich-based *Constantin Film GmbH* in collaboration with German, Italian and Austrian television networks[18] and released in late 2004. (In fact, one could argue that *Downfall* is more of a European than a German production.)

Downfall was directed by Oliver Hirschbiegel, a television director with only a few films to his credit. But above all it was the brainchild of producer Bernd Eichinger.[19] Born in 1949, Eichinger, like many Germans of the post-war generation, is concerned with the Third Reich and its legacy, 'a past which will not pass away'.[20] For decades, Eichinger wished to make a film on the subject, a wish that was clearly apparent after his production of Hans Syberberg's experimental film, *Hitler, ein film aus Deutschland* (*Hitler, a film from Germany*, 1978).[21] Eichinger's idea to make a more mainstream film only became a viable project after he read Joachim Fest's 2002 *Der Untergang*.[22] The book focused on the last days of Adolf Hitler and his entourage in the Führer bunker beneath the new Reich Chancellery, including the onset of the Russian offensive (16 April, 1945) to Hitler's suicide (30 April) and the flight of the remaining bunker inhabitants on the night of 1-2 May.[23]

It is not hard to see why Eichinger found in this particular historical episode the 'dramaturgical key'[24] to realise his long-cherished dream of a film about Nazi Germany. The limited time span and confined topography of what may be considered the ultimate downfall of the Nazi regime made it an attractive subject. As a matter of fact, the concept was so attractive and feasible that it had been done several times before.[25] As early as 1955, Georg Wilhelm Pabst, whose own activities in the Third Reich film industry had not gone unnoticed, directed the Austrian production, *Der letzte Akt* (*The Last Ten Days*), the first feature film solely devoted to Hitler's demise. Other films about the Führer bunker were Ennio De Concini's feature, *Hitler: the Last Ten Days* (1973; an American production starring Alec Guinness), and George Schaefer's television film, *The Bunker* (1980; a French-American co-production starring Anthony Hopkins).[26] Each of these productions was based on books that primarily used eye-witness accounts to reconstruct the microcosm of the Führer bunker. Pabst's *The Last Ten Days* leaned on the work of later State Supreme Court Justice and Congressman Michael Musmanno (Pennsylvania), who also presided over a panel for the second set of trials at Nuremberg. As the former leader of the American investigation to determine how Adolf Hitler had died, Musmanno had had access to many eye-witnesses and related documents.[27] De Concini's film was based on a similar, even older book, authored by Hugh Trevor-Roper, former member of a British intelligence group entrusted with reconstructing the circumstances of Hitler's death.[28] *The Bunker* was also based on interviews with dozens of eye-witnesses conducted by James P. O'Donnell, former *Newsweek* editor in Berlin.[29]

As these examples indicate, Fest's book was certainly neither the first nor the most detailed study of Hitler's last days. Many more have been published since Trevor-Roper's work, a pioneering study admired by leading historians, including Fest.[30] All of these publications were scrupulously analysed and compared by Anton Joachimsthaler in a book of his own. [31] Other authors have indirectly helped to expand what is basically a rather limited field of research by writing accounts of the battle for Berlin from a military as well as a civilian viewpoint.[32] What made Fest's own book to some extent innovative were not his four narrative chapters (a sketch of what happened during those final days, including some minor corrections and new information),[33] but the four interspersed reflective ones. It was chapters like 'Hitler in German history: Consistency or Catastrophe?' that tried to connect the micro-(hi)story of Berlin and the Führer bunker with broader philosophical questions and historiographical debates. When writing his script, as will be explained in further detail below, Eichinger made no attempt to integrate such questions or topics into his film. This leads us to the crucial question of what made Eichinger want to produce this film, the essential source materials for which had been available for decades and even been turned into a number of feature films.[34]

A film from Germany

It was undeniably a combination of factors that led to the production of *Downfall*, which was shot in August-November 2003. There is no reason to doubt that Fest's book, which Eichinger and many Germans first read as a prepublication in the magazine, *Der Spiegel*, inspired the producer to make a film on this specific subject. The book can be used to write a plot outline, but is too sketchy to form the basis for a complete script. More important than the actual book, which is a good introduction to more in-depth studies and related archive documents, was probably the persona, if not the brand name, of its author. As the former editor-in-chief of the respected newspaper, *Frankfurter Allgemeine Zeitung*, and the author of voluminous studies on the Third Reich, including an internationally acclaimed biography of Adolf Hitler, Joachim Fest (1926-2006) enjoyed high academic and social status in Germany.[35] Associating Fest, who had a keen interest in cinema,[36] with the project guaranteed Eichinger at once a superb historical adviser and all the credibility his film could ask for.[37] Teaming up with Fest, 'a central figure in his country's postwar debate about the origins and consequences of the Nazi catastrophe',[38] was a brilliant move, especially with regard to the German home market where schools formed an important target audience for the film.[39]

A second impetus to make the film was given by Traudl Junge, née Gertraud Humps (1920-2002).[40] Junge became at the age of twenty-two one of Hitler's personal secretaries and stayed with him from late 1942 until his death. Because Hitler dictated his political testament to her shortly before his suicide, Junge had for decades been familiar to scholars interested in this period. After the war, she was interviewed by many researchers and historians, including Michael Musmanno who several years later convinced Pabst to hire her as his assistant for the filming of *The Last Ten Days*.[41] She was and remained, however, an insignificant player in the story of the Führer bunker and certainly in the broader context of Hitler's rise and fall. This perception partially changed when Anne Frank's biographer, Melissa Müller,[42] residing in Munich, was introduced to her fellow-townswoman, Junge. Informed that Junge still possessed unpublished memoirs of her service with Hitler, typed in 1947-1948, Müller began a project that eventually led to the 2002 publication of Junge's annotated manuscript.[43] Also through the intermediary of Müller, Junge was extensively interviewed by André Heller (who, incidentally, played a role in *Hitler, a film from Germany*) and Othmar Schmiderer. Both men turned her testimony into the documentary *Im toten Winkel – Hitlers Sekretärin* (*Blind Spot – Hitler's secretary*, 2002), which by chance premiered a couple of hours after her death. The simultaneous release of the book and the film nearly coincided with the publication of Fest's monograph.

In the documentary as well as in the book chapter written by Müller, 'Confronting Guilt – A Chronological Study', Junge talked openly about her past and about the time it took her to realise the problematic nature of her wartime job. Junge explained how she had been a young and naïve follower of Hitler with a 'blind spot' for the many dark sides of his regime, but refused to be too apologetic while acknowledging that she had made mistakes. This attitude of critical self-reflection gave Eichinger the chance to introduce a new perspective. Moreover, her original manuscript contained many details absent from the existing, rich corpus of documentation about life in the Führer bunker. Junge's account does not reveal so much that is new about the meetings Hitler had with his ministers and generals – conferences Junge usually was not required to attend – as it does about the little things that happened in between or elsewhere. Not the kind of information post-war investigators or historians were likely to look for or ask after, but just the kind of background detail one needs to picture what 'everyday life' was like during those final days. Junge's observations, in 1947-1948 still impregnated with an unspoken affection for Hitler, provided Eichinger with a fresh angle. Although, as discussed below, he did not fully exploit its potential, Eichinger jumped at the opportunity to acquire the rights and eventually listed Junge's manuscript as the second major source for his script.

The third and major factor that made *Downfall* possible was the Zeitgeist, that opportune moment in time in which the film was released. A project such as *Downfall*, with an enormous budget by European standards of an estimated 13,500.000 Euros,[44] is not launched unless financial backers are convinced the film has a potentially large audience. The German box office numbers, DVD sales and television viewing figures proved them right. German society's *Vergangenheitsbewältigung* – its coming to terms with the (Nazi) past – has, as Eichinger and his financers correctly assessed, apparently reached a stage that allows German audiences to welcome a film on the final days of the Third Reich. For decades, this had been far from the case. In the former Democratic Republic of East Germany, where the Communist party and state doctrine propagated a one-dimensional interpretation of the Nazi past, the 'cornerstone'[45] of national film culture had for decades been formed by anti-fascist films. The conventions of that genre prescribed the glorification of communist anti-fascist resistance before and during the Second World War, but certainly did not encourage films about the upper classes of fascist society, which is how the inhabitants of the Führer bunker were categorised in accordance with the Marxist-Leninist world view.

In former West Germany, where coming to grips with the Nazi past was less conditioned by the state, a Führer bunker film, a biopic of Hitler for that matter, was initially neither needed nor welcomed. Pabst's *The Last Ten Days*, already suspect in the eyes of many Germans because the script (based on Musmanno) had been written by Erich Maria Remarque,[46] was not successful in 1955 West Germany, but did well in many other countries. In a society that had barely begun to come to terms with its past, it was 'too early for Hitler films', as one German newspaper put it.[47] Even films commemorating the 20 July, 1944, assassination attempt on Hitler, films that supported what was at the time a widely accepted image of a 'clean' Wehrmacht that was not guilty of Nazi war crimes, received a mixed audience response. This fate also befell the film Pabst made immediately after *The Last Ten Days*. *Es geschah am 20. Juli* (*Jackboot Mutiny*, 1955) reconstructed the assassination attempt and was, just like the rival film, *Der 20. July* (*The Hitler Assassination Plot*, 1955), not very successful.[48]

As the West German *Vergangenheitsbewältigung* matured, so did West German films about the Third Reich. In the 1970s and 1980s, exponents of the 'New German Cinema' such as Rainer Werner Fassbinder started questioning, as many of their contemporaries did in other sections of society, the complicity of the older so-called *Tätergeneration* ('generation of culprits').[49] Film and television became important forums for such debates, as they still are today. In January 1979, *Holocaust*, the mediocre American mini-series (1978) that in retrospect is memorable mainly for its pioneering role, was broadcast for the first time on West German television. By stirring up sociological debate overnight about the complicity of ordinary Germans in the Shoah, *Holocaust* 'did more than the countless academic studies in print at the time to lay bare the psychological scars of a country that, for decades, had avoided confronting head-on the full horror of the murder of the Jews and the role of ordinary people, not just Nazi leaders, in those terrible events'.[50] The production of *Holocaust* and of innumerable other foreign films and television series about the Third Reich (and about the German involvement in the Second World War) also prompted debate about the need for German filmmakers to 'take back narrative possession of their own past'.[51] Whether persuaded or not by such arguments, German film and television responded to increasing public interest in German productions about the Hitler era. This trend continued after German reunification (1989-1990).

Having 'given back national continuity to German history',[52] the reunification of West and East Germany reinforced public interest in the history that both Germanies shared and for the Hitler era in particular. As the so-called 'Goldhagen debate' (1996)[53] made very clear, German historical consciousness was in those days more than ever preoccupied with the dark legacy of the Shoah. The cruelty of the occupation of eastern territories and the large-scale responsibility of the German army for these crimes – facts that were not new to readers of scholarly works – had also increased public awareness, especially since the controversial *Wehrmacht Exhibition* which visited thirty-three German and Austrian cities in the second half of the 1990s.[54] In a more recent trend that does not necessarily contradict the others, there is a growing German interest in Third Reich historiography focusing on the Germans who can also be seen as victims. This is demonstrated by the success of Jörg Friedrich's best-sellers which, without minimising Nazi Germany's war guilt or the actions of its own air force, describe and show in detail the devastating results of the Allied bombardments of German cities.[55] Stories of citizens that in some way or another went against the National-Socialist tide have also encountered increased public interest, e.g. the renewed interest in the White Rose resistance group (*Weiße Rose*) commonly identified with Sophie Scholl; for the *Rosenstraße* protest (German women protesting against the 1943 arrest of their Jewish husbands) and for individuals such as Lily Wust, a German woman who during the war engaged in lesbian relations with her Jewish partner. Each of these three examples forms the subject of one or more publications, but also from relatively recent German historical films: *Sophie Scholl* (2005), *Rosenstraße* (2003) and *Aimée & Jaguar* (1999). German television history programmes also highlight both sides of the picture, without minimising the crimes against humanity committed in the name of Nazi Germany. In 2005, for instance, Guido Knopp, the German trendsetting producer of internationally successful series such as *Hitler, eine Bilanz* (*Hitler – A Reckoning*, 1995) and *Holokaust* (2000), produced *Das Drama von Dresden* (*The Drama of Dresden*, 2005), a documentary about the controversial Allied bombing of the German city in February 1945.[56] In 2006, German public broadcaster ZDF produced the TV drama *Dresden* (2006).

As these examples indicate, German society has reached a new phase in its *Vergangenheitsbewältigung*. A stage of maturity that not only allowed for the production and marketing of a non-satirical mainstream feature film in which Hitler is portrayed by an actor, but also for a film that portrayed 'ordinary'

Germans, in this case Berliners, as perpetrators and as victims. Moreover, *Downfall*'s international success as well as the International Emmy Award that was given to Knopp's *The Drama of Dresden* in 2005, indicate that the historical consciousness of the international community has evolved. Whereas the export, even the very production of *German* films or documentaries on such topics only a couple of decades ago would have been considered politically incorrect by the international community,[57] today it is welcomed and rewarded.[58]

Berlin 1945 – *Downfall*'s storyline and narrative techniques

The DVD release of both the theatrical and the television version as well as the publication of its script (theatrical release)[59] make it unnecessary to describe *Downfall*'s storyline in detail. The following paragraphs will mainly sketch out the overall structure and point out recurring narrative techniques. None of these techniques is challenging or innovative, which also goes for many stylistic aspects of the film. Like virtually any mainstream (historical) film with international ambitions, *Downfall* safely plays by the rules of classic Hollywood cinema. The limited topography of the film and the majority of interior scenes – it has been suggested that Hirschbiegel was asked to direct the film[60] because his *Das Experiment* (*The Experiment*, 2001) also had a claustrophobic setting[61] – reminded various reviewers of the *Kammerspiel* genre. The solid but average look of this production is one of the main reasons why, though recognising that films are complex audiovisual artefacts, a complete analysis of which must take into account many other parameters, the rest of this chapter will mainly focus on *Downfall*'s script (theatrical version).

Downfall's opening and closing sequences are framed by short statements by the aged Traudl Junge, excerpts from the above-mentioned documentary *Blind Spot*. The first sequence of the film, showing how Hitler hires the young Traudl as his secretary in November 1942, is introduced by Traudl, explaining how hard it is to forgive herself for not having refused to do the job interview, for not having recognised 'the horror' and 'the monster'. The last sequence of the film, showing how Traudl (and the boy Peter) escape from Berlin, fades out to titles commemorating the final capitulation of 8 April 1945, the death of 50.000.000 people in World War Two and the murder of 6.000.000 Jews in

Eva Braun (Juliane Köhler), Adolf Hitler (Bruno Ganz) and Albert Speer (Heino Ferch). © Constantin Film GmbH

concentration camps. Short biographies of several protagonists follow. The final biography is that of Traudl and cuts to another interview fragment of the aged woman, expressing how shocked she was to learn about the genocide from the Nuremberg trials. She then goes on to explain that for a very long time afterwards, she soothed her conscience with the fact that she was so young at the time and completely unaware of such cruelties. Until, she adds, many years later she noticed a memorial plaque for Sophie Scholl. This plaque directly confronted Hitler's secretary with the fact that Sophie Scholl, who had been executed in the same year Traudl went working for Hitler, was the same age as Traudl. 'And at that moment I actually sensed that being young was not an excuse, and that it would have been possible to find things out'.[62]

This framework, similar to the interview scenes inserted in other historical films and television series such as *Reds* (1981) and *Band of Brothers* (2001), serves several purposes. On the one hand, it anticipates criticism that the horror of the Shoah and global war are excluded from the film's plot. On the other, it introduces a protagonist the viewer can empathise with, a character that through her final statement offers the kind of moral message and closure her younger self in 1945 could never have provided. Thus the old and the young Traudl supply the closed narrative that is essential to mainstream cinema. Moreover, the clear message that Traudl came to terms with her past without totally absolving herself from any guilt has great symbolic strength and can be interpreted as a representation of Germany's *Vergangenheitsbewältigung*. Conveniently, the reference to Scholl brings to mind that at least a small minority of Junge's contemporaries dared to resist.

Apart from the introductory sequence (Traudl's 1942 job interview in East Prussia, now Poland), *Downfall*'s entire story is set in Berlin, from 20 April until 2 May, 1945, from Hitler's 56th birthday until the break-up of a group of bunker occupants that managed to leave the chancellery safely. Rather uncommon for a mainstream film is the fact that *Downfall* has no real main character in the usual sense of the word. Hitler obviously plays an important role, but dies half an hour before the film ends. The character of Traudl, mostly an observer rather than a participant, ties together many of the bunker scenes where Hitler is absent, but has so little dialogue that she cannot qualify as a protagonist. In the end, one could argue that the only constant or true main character is the war itself, the 'downfall' of Nazi Germany as experienced by a number of Germans from the centre of the capital.

SS Leader Heinrich Himmler (Ulrich Noethen, right) and his representative with Hitler, Hermann Fegelein (Thomas Kretschmann, left). Constantin Film GmbH

Nevertheless, the spotlight is largely on what went on down in the Führer bunker. Having gathered once more in the Reich Chancellery on the occasion of their Führer's birthday, with the Soviets virtually at the gates of the capital, many of Hitler's closest collaborators (Heinrich Himmler, Hermann Göring, Albert Speer) leave Berlin hastily. Hitler agrees that they can be of greater use to him elsewhere, but remains in the capital with a number of generals, collaborators (Martin Bormann, Joseph Goebbels), representatives, personal aides and lower-ranking personnel. Communicating with the outside world by telephone and telegraph, Hitler regularly withdraws with his staff to a small conference room to discuss the military situation that is becoming more and more hopeless. And yet Hitler keeps on 'moving' army battalions that scarcely exist anymore and giving orders that cannot be carried out. It takes him a long time to admit that the 'final victory' will never be achieved. On 22 April, the Führer is informed that no German army force will break through the Soviet lines and rescue him from the bunker. Hitler breaks down in an outburst of frenzied anger. Accusing the army and the SS of betrayal, Hitler shocks the entire bunker population by declaring that the war is lost, but that he would rather shoot himself than leave Berlin. Everyone is declared free to go, but most decide to stay.

In the following days, hope sometimes flares up but is each time crushed again. In the meantime, several more crises arise, as when Hitler realises that both his closest advisers, SS leader Heinrich Himmler and Reich Marshal Hermann Göring, have separately tried to go behind his back and seize power. Himmler's betrayal costs his representative with Hitler, Herman Fegelein, his life, even though he is Eva Braun's brother-in-law. The Führer displays a profound contempt for the lives of his own soldiers and people. People who cannot win his war are in his eyes not worthy to live. On 30 April, Hitler marries Eva Braun. A couple of hours later both commit suicide. (It is noteworthy that *Downfall* does not reconstruct Hitler being informed – on 29 April 1945, the day before his suicide – of Mussolini's execution the day before, at the hands of Italian partisans.)[63] Their example is followed by Joseph Goebbels and his wife Magda. Assisted by a doctor, Magda kills her six young children first. Some other bunker occupants commit suicide too, but most try to escape. The group that Traudl is part of manages to break out. While the men eventually surrender to Soviet soldiers, Traudl can walk away, together with the boy Peter.

Adolf Hitler decorates members of the Hitler Youth with the iron cross on 20 March 1945 (above) and on 20 April (below). The boy actor who performs the role of Peter Kranz has clearly been selected for his physical resemblance to the boy shown here being stroked by Hitler. The boy's name is unknown whereas the boy on his left (Alfred Czech,, right corner of the picture) and the one on his right (Wilhelm Hübner) were identified.. © Constantin Film GmbH and Ullstein-bild

The character of Peter Kranz is fictional, but his appearance is modelled on an historical agent who is so often shown in World War Two documentaries that he may be considered part of the collective memory. On 20 March 1945, Hitler was filmed and photographed while decorating members of the Hitler Youth with the Iron Cross in the garden of the Reich Chancellery. This footage, in which Hitler strokes the cheek of a young blond Hitler youth member, was a few days afterwards inserted in one of the last newsreels (*Deutsche Wochenschau* issue 755) released in Nazi Germany. Exactly one month after that ceremony, Hitler on his birthday (20 April) again decorated Hitler Youth boys and other 'Reich capital defenders' in the garden of the Chancellery. After this ceremony, which was not captured on film, Hitler returned to the bunker.[64] He would not come out alive again and the footage of the March ceremony became the last moving image of Hitler. Therefore, the footage is to this date often used by historical documentaries which suggest or state that it was filmed on Hitler's birthday. It is interesting to note that *Downfall* not only reconstructs the decoration of 20 April by imitating the ceremony of 20 March, but explicitly refers to the original footage by having 'Peter Kranz' played by a look-alike (Donevan Gunia) of the unidentified boy and having Ganz's Hitler accompanied by a newsreel cameraman. Incidentally, the idea of reconstructing this decoration and inventing the family history of this boy (named 'Richard' by Pabst and Remarque) to create an extra storyline, was already used in *The Last Ten Days*.

Peter is only one of the plot devices that are skilfully used to create a second, more fragmented storyline reconstructing what went on aboveground in the parts of Berlin that are not yet occupied by the Soviet troops. Interwoven in the greater narrative are various scenes reflecting the apocalyptic atmosphere that characterised the besieged capital. Soldiers, aided by the so-called *Volkssturm* (People's Militia) that even includes children like Peter, vainly try to defend the city. The 'organisation' of the defence is so chaotic that it becomes self-defeating. The People's Militia, commanded by Goebbels, often operates separately from the Wehrmacht, which causes both to hinder each other. General Helmuth Weidling is nearly executed on Hitler's orders, only because he is rumoured to have transferred his command post unauthorised. (Having convinced Hitler that the rumour is false, Weidling finds himself appointed commandant of the 'Berlin defensive sector'.) Some give up fighting and spend what they believe to be their final hours in bacchanalian revels. As we see through the eyes of Fegelein, military and SS men too participate in these excesses. But most 'war resisters' just try to take care of their family. As experienced by Peter, such persons, like his father, run the risk of being summarily executed for 'defeatism'. Other scenes testify to the general despair; for instance, by showing how Ernst Grawitz blows up himself and his family with hand grenades.[65] Another recurring character, tying loose ends and scenes together, is SS doctor Ernst-Günther Schenck. Through this person, the viewer is repeatedly brought in contact with the civilian wounded who have been left entirely to their own devices, and with the military victims who are not much better off, due to the lack of sufficient medical equipment.

As indicated above, the limited time span and confined topography of life in and around the Führer bunker made the final days of the Nazi reign a filmable subject. But the number of people involved, whose antecedents are important to understand certain events, tended to complicate matters. *Downfall* sometimes tries to remedy this shortcoming by introducing explanatory dialogue. In the first scene between Himmler and Fegelein, the SS leader reminds his subordinate of his marriage to Eva Braun's sister. A similar scene has Himmler confiding to Fegelein his secret attempts to negotiate (behind Hitler's back) a separate peace with the Western Allies. Such scenes, the main purpose of which is to inform/remind the viewers of background information, are rather exceptional. In general, the audience is assumed to have some knowledge of the Third Reich and World War Two. Additional background information on Nazi elite members such as Joseph Goebbels, Albert Speer, Hermann Göring and Martin Bormann is also implicitly required. It is not crucial in order to follow the film's main narrative, but strongly contributes to a better understanding of various scenes.

The Hitler of 1945, probably suffering from Parkinson's disease, was physically a shadow of the charismatic Führer many Germans once considered the saviour of their nation, the man who had the world at his feet in 1939-1940. Psychologically, too, the Hitler of 1945 had gravely deteriorated. Hitler had been shocked by the failed attempt on his life by German officers (20 July, 1944). Ever since the attempt on his life, Hitler was more than ever consumed by distrust towards many members of his entourage, his generals in particular. Understanding the loyalty this man inspired in his inner circle in April 1945 can be difficult for viewers who do not realise how persuasive and hypnotic Hitler had been before. Viewers unfamiliar with the strength of the Führer cult and with the interaction between Hitler and his general staff (members of which had for years been kicked downstairs if not obedient enough) during the previous war years may also have some difficulty understanding why his generals do not contradict Hitler, even when it is overtly clear that their Führer is building castles in the air. Also, viewers unaware that Soviet troops did not know that Hitler was still in Berlin, or that the Soviets had chosen the ruined Reichstag instead of the Reich chancellery (they knew nothing of the bunker) as the symbolic primary target of the battle,[66] will wonder why no Soviet attempt was made to capture Hitler alive. On a smaller level, background information helps the viewer to understand specific scenes. It is, for instance, never mentioned that General Hans Krebs served as a military attaché in Moscow before the German invasion of the USSR. Without that knowledge, this 'historically correct' scene has an alienating effect, as it makes viewers wonder why a German general needs no interpreter during negotiations and addresses a Soviet general (Vasili Chuikov) in fluent Russian.

As the paragraphs above already indicate, *Downfall* tells its story by making use of various techniques so often encountered in historical films: invention, compression, condensation, alteration...[67] A couple of examples will further clarify this matter. The opening sequence shows how Traudl meets Hitler together with other candidates for the vacancy of secretary, but is the only one of the candidates immediately required to take a dictation test which results in her obtaining the position. This sequence condenses and partially invents a process that in reality took several weeks.[68] The following sequence shows how, on Hitler's 56th birthday, the Reich Chancellery is for the first time under artillery fire. Hitler and his entourage are awakened by the sound of artillery grenades. Hitler flies into a rage when he hears that the Soviets are not only within shooting range, but no more than twelve kilometres from the city centre. The next sequence shows Hitler meeting about fifty people at a reception for his birthday. Many of them, including SS leader Heinrich Himmler, can't wait to flee the capital and discreetly discuss the possibility of convincing Hitler to join them. Historically, both sequences are shown in reverse chronological order: the 'artillery incident' took place the day after Hitler's birthday and reception.[69] However, slightly changing this order of events makes the story and dramatic structure more straightforward (the artillery sequence helps to explain why most people want to leave Berlin as soon as possible) without fundamentally altering the viewer's perception of what happened during those

The aged Traudl Junge in *Blind Spot* (2002), the young Traudl in 1942 and Alexandra Maria Lara as Traudl Junge in *Downfall*. © Dor Film Produktionsgesellschaft GmbH and Constantin Film GmbH

days. This technique is repeated throughout the film.[70] Things Hitler or others said at a particular time and place are often moved to another but related setting.[71] Sometimes this is taken one step further, arguably one step too far, as when Himmler asks Fegelein whether it would be more appropriate to greet the American General Dwight Eisenhower with a handshake or with the Hitler salute. The historic Himmler indeed wondered about meeting Eisenhower but hesitated between a handshake and a *bow*[72] – a meeting, by the way, that never took place, but says much about his idle hopes of being treated as the important statesman he fancied himself. In general, however, such liberties are avoided. Nevertheless, the question as to how historically accurate a picture *Downfall* paints deserves more attention.

Downfall and the difficult balance between historical and symbolic realities

In the huge press campaign that launched the film, *Downfall* was invariably presented as a historically accurate reconstruction that had no ambition to evaluate the historical agents it brought back to life. In interviews and press conferences, Eichinger and Hirschbiegel stressed over and over again that the sole purpose of this film was to show what had happened, not to explain why and certainly not to judge anyone involved. As its creators constantly repeated, *Downfall* was 'to tell' (hi)story,[73] not 'to comment on' or 'interpret' history.[74] Or, as Eichinger was quoted as saying: '… if the film has one value, it is the fact that it contains no judgement'.[75] Several people have questioned or viciously attacked this promotional mantra of 'showing historical events without further interpretation or judgement'.[76] Admittedly, it was a very weak statement. The presentation of the film as an unbiased reconstruction -- in other words, as a historical source on the Führer bunker instead of an interpretative representation -- was based on a superseded concept of history. The nineteenth-century German historian Leopold von Ranke's commitment to writing history 'as it essentially was' comes to mind, for it is based on a similar understanding of history as ontology, history as the absolute, indisputable and therefore unproblematic truth about social events that took place in the past. Such views may have been shared by many historians in the past,[77] but it is now commonly accepted that history should be understood as discourse: a signifying practice in which historical events are reworked and re-signified from a contemporary perspective.[78] Or, to put this newer paradigm more simply when applying it to the genre of historical films: it is impossible to write about history (articles, books, film scripts) without interpreting it, to make historical films without interpreting the events and people represented.

The question as to how the makers of *Downfall* interpreted and represented their historical subject(s) is difficult to answer, in particular because answers can only be truly relevant if taking into account (empirical research on) the reception of that film. To paraphrase Marc Silberman: *Downfall's* discourse is not constructed only or most pertinently on its representations of the past but rather on the relations of its spectators to history and to the past represented in the film.[79] I will therefore not attempt to deconstruct the film's entire discourse, but limit myself to focusing on the self-declared main target of Eichinger and Hirschbiegel: to show history 'as it really happened'. To verify this promise, which is of course also a problematic statement, I will compare some of the film's storylines and dramatis personae to authoritative historical studies on what went on in the Führer bunker. What I will *not* do is point out the many things that took place during World War Two , but are not mentioned or represented in *Downfall*. For instance, it has been pointed out very often that *Downfall* pays no attention to the suffering that went on elsewhere in the Spring of 1945 in the concentration camps, on the 'death marches' from those camps or on what was left of the eastern and western fronts. True, the film has a rather limited perspective. But accepting the genre of the historical feature film and the rationale of its existence implies accepting the basic rules of mainstream cinema. It implies understanding that within the scope of one film, one can never show all sides of history.

Admittedly, the film sometimes paints a painfully incomplete picture. This is particularly true for Doctor Ernst-Günther Schenck (1904-1998) who, like Albert Speer (1905-1981), didn't miss the post-war opportunity to write a self-serving memoir[80] that helped to reinvent his own role in the years of Nazi Germany. In April 1945, Schenck, as we see in the film, stayed where he was needed most, instead of fleeing Berlin like most SS members. This was a brave gesture and it is not improbable that in those days Schenck actually behaved as valiantly as he is portrayed throughout the film. What viewers do not see or learn is that Schenck also had a much less heroic personal history. This is background information that one may not need in order to understand what happened in Berlin in April 1945. But it is background that gives another or at least a more complete view of the 'St Francis of Assisi figure on display', as one reviewer described Schenck's film persona.[81] As pointed out by various historians, Schenk was tried after the war for having used concentration camp prisoners as guinea pigs in 'frivolous' medical experiments.[82] The same goes for Waffen-SS General Wilhelm Mohnke (1911-2001). As David Cesarani and Peter Longerich have pointed out: 'Mohnke is depicted as a humanitarian pleading with Hitler to evacuate civilians and arguing with Goebbels against the suicidal deployment of poorly armed militia against the Red Army. This is the same Mohnke whose Waffen-SS unit massacred 80 captured British soldiers outside Dunkirk in May 1940. He later led a Waffen-SS regiment in Normandy that murdered more than 60 surrendered Canadian troops.'[83]

The criticism is well founded. At the same time, one cannot ask a film like *Downfall* to document everything in the space of a feature film. Acknowledging its limited topography and time span, it is more useful to focus on that time and place, and to ask whether *Downfall* really reconstructs events more or less as they took place. Formulating a definitive answer to such questions is obviously impossible. The availability of sources is often problematic because there are either too many or too few witnesses. The monopoly position of some witnesses, as indicated above in the case of Schenck, is questionable by nature. The same goes for scenes featuring Albert Speer. In *Downfall*, when Speer privately says good-bye to Adolf Hitler, he confesses to having disobeyed Hitler for months by safeguarding industries and cities the Führer had wanted destroyed as part of his scorched-earth policy. This scene, which gives Speer a hero-like allure, is purely based on his own post-war accounts and is therefore unreliable. As many critics have noticed,[84] the favourable light in which Speer is depicted is influenced by the rather sympathetic image Joachim Fest painted of him in his biography.[85] (Fest, who shortly before his death published a more critical appreciation of Hitler's collaborator,[86] helped Speer write his memoirs[87] and leaned heavily on his recollections for his own Hitler biography.)

In many other cases the historical events are documented by statements that give conflicting versions. While one would assume that the traumatic impact of that moment would have marked all the witnesses with vivid and therefore identical recollections, there was no agreement even about the positions in which the bodies of Hitler and Eva Braun were found by people who entered their room directly after their double suicide. There are even various examples of specific incidents where the same people gave differing accounts depending on the times at which they were interviewed.[88] Furthermore, some incidents remain insufficiently documented because there were no witnesses at all. This applies to the death of Joseph and Magda Goebbels who committed suicide after making sure orderlies would ignite gasoline over their bodies. In his authoritative biography, Ralf Georg Reuth concludes that both probably killed themselves outside the bunker and certainly did so by swallowing the same kind of cyanide pills they gave to their children. Reuth adds that Goebbels possibly shot himself in the head. The possibility that he shot Magda first is not mentioned.[89] In *Downfall* one sees Goebbels and Magda leaving the bunker, passing by a number of orderlies. Outside the bunker, Goebbels points a gun at his wife. The next scene cuts back to the orderlies, who after hearing two shots run outside with jerry cans (to burn the bodies). This sequence, in which the use of pills remains unmentioned (but is not excluded), suggests that Goebbels shot his wife before taking his own life. One can ask: does this sequence show us 'history as it happened'? But who is to provide the answer to that question? I would argue that it is history as it may have happened, which is probably the best that historical films can offer. Also, one must ask whether it is really so important whether Magda was shot by her husband or 'only' died by swallowing poison? I consider it to be of greater importance to know that both identified so fanatically with the Nazi regime and the positions they occupied in that society that they preferred to kill themselves and their children rather than outlive the Third Reich. And is that not exactly what *Downfall* is showing us?

A comparison between *Downfall* and some of its major sources teaches us that there is a substantial difference between 'reconstructing particular events as they have been documented' and 'being historically correct'. This has much to do with the way film works, through the symbolic, generalising value that may be attached to particular scenes. Various examples can be given of scenes that do not fully reconstruct events as they have been documented by witnesses, simply because to do so would have changed the overall tone of the film. In *Downfall* one sees Bormann, Goebbels and others carrying the bodies of Hitler and Eva Braun out of the bunker. (The bodies are wrapped in blankets. The fact that the bodies remain invisible infuriated film director Wim Wenders.)[90] The corpses are put into a pit, gasoline is poured over them and they are set on fire with a piece of burning paper. The action is interrupted once when gunfire drives the participants back into the bunker before the corpses are ignited. In reality[91] the corpses had to be rushed back and forth several times until gunfire ceased long enough so that they could be lowered into the pit. Also, setting the bodies on fire was not as easy as the film suggests. Various attempts were made by tossing matches on top of them, but the matches kept going out. One of Hitler's orderlies even wanted to use a hand grenade (!) but eventually some papers were twisted into a torch that had the desired effect. Once the fire started, the participants did not make the Hitler salute together before being driven into the bunker by another explosion, as *Downfall* indicates. Instead, from inside the stairwell of the bunker, they stepped forward one by one to salute the corpses. Before closing the door behind them, they witnessed the bodies moving and rising up, a normal physiological reaction during the process of cremation. Would it have been more historically correct to reconstruct this 'as it happened'? To show them running around with the corpses, the clumsy bungling with the matches and the sudden resurrection of the corpses? Strictly speaking, yes. Would such have contributed to recreating the atmosphere of that moment? Obviously not: it would at best have turned the whole incident into a morbid comedy, a horror spoof ('it's alive!') that in no way reflected the tragedy that the moment represented for those involved. In other words, by leaving out historically documented details, the historical reality of the entire scene was done justice.

Other examples of this kind could be given, such as the scene where General Krebs informs Soviet General Chuikov of Hitler's death and vainly tries to negotiate a peace treaty with him. What *Downfall* compresses into a short scene was actually a meeting that lasted nearly twelve hours. During this meeting, the Soviet general forgot that, just before Krebs entered, someone had been hidden in an armoire. What happened after a couple of hours, and would therefore have been 'historically correct' to show, was that the man lost consciousness and fell out of the wardrobe into the conference room.[92] Again, I would argue that the historical accuracy of the scene and the textual coherence of the entire film were done a great service by leaving out this historically accurate detail.

These observations, mainly based on a comparison of the film to the book it was named after, is not to suggest that *Downfall*'s script only left out bits and pieces that could have turned into another *Springtime for Hitler*.[93] Comparing the film to the book Traudl Junge published in collaboration with Melissa Müller reveals other more relevant choices that Eichinger made when writing his script. Many critics have pointed to the opening sequence in which a charming Hitler does not mind Traudl making mistakes during the dictation test. Scenes like this are believed to portray Hitler too sympathetically, as too avuncular. But how would they have reacted if Eichinger had shown the actual conversation in which Hitler definitely hired Traudl as his secretary? The young woman expected to be questioned about her belief in National-Socialism, to be asked for oaths of secrecy and allegiance. Instead, an uncomfortable Hitler expressed his concern that the men in his entourage might have a bad influence on her virtue. Fatherly advice for her to keep her distance and to inform him whenever a man bothered her concluded the interview, which did not require any form of swearing-in.[94] Would critics have preferred this to the slightly fictionalised scene *Downfall* features? I suggest that the 'historically correct' reconstruction would have led to even stronger criticism of the 'humaneness' of Bruno Ganz's Hitler.

Ironically, the potential of Traudl Junge's memoirs to paint an intimate, indeed human picture of Hitler and his inner circle is at his strongest when she describes the final days in the Führer bunker. Eichinger partially exploited this potential, but not as much as he could have done. During those final days, the social barriers and conventions were replaced by feelings of a shared fate. The Bunker occupants, the women probably even more so than the men, formed a tighter group than ever before. All became equal, even Hitler lost some of his status. For instance, no-one refrained any longer from smoking in front of the Führer, who despised that habit.[95] Eva Braun even reprimanded Hitler in public because his uniform jacket was stained, a reprimand that left the otherwise very neat Führer aggrieved.[96] The women stayed together whenever they could and Eva Braun confided in Traudl, telling her how afraid she was of dying.[97] Traudl also had long conversations with Magda Goebbels, for whom she felt very sorry: 'this woman is in bigger pain than any of us'.[98] Since Hitler had given up all hope and did not schedule any more military conferences, he too became more accessible. Traudl told him that since he seemed determined to die, the German people would expect him to fall in battle at the head of his troops. Hitler agreed, but pointed out that he was physically unable to fight, that his shaking hands could barely hold a gun.[99] Scenes like this, which one can easily imagine being integrated into the film, again confront us with the difficult concept of cinematic historical correctness. The events as such did take place, which justifies recreating them. But are they so important that they deserve to be singled out? Should the conversation between Hitler and Traudl have been shown because it revealed just how tired and vulnerable the dictator had become? Or would it have been intellectually incorrect to highlight this facet of his personality during that particular phase of his life, because such might draw attention away from the cruelty and ruthlessness that were his more determinant and persistent characteristics? Apparently Eichinger considered the second option more plausible.

To conclude this argument, let us take a look at how the story 'ends'. In the last sequences of *Downfall*, Traudl and most of the people she escaped with end up in a brewery from which they cannot escape because the Red Army has arrived. The men remain there, some of them commit suicide but most surrender to the Soviets. Traudl, taking the hand of the young Peter, manages to walk out without being stopped. Like other civilians, Traudl and Peter leave Berlin. The bright sunlight and the fact that Peter finds a bicycle on which they can ride together gives this final sequence a glint of hope.[100] Is this a historically correct ending? No, because Peter is, as explained above, rather a plot device than a historical agent. Not surprisingly, the film was attacked for this sequence: 'This way, the otherwise authenticity pretending film finds the reconciling final image of a self-liberation and a rebirth from the destruction that went ahead. Here, *Downfall* conforms to the positive views of the prospects for the future we encounter in other retro-films on National-Socialism.'[101]

True, the final image is a hopeful one. But what would a more 'authentic' ending have looked like? According to her memoirs, Traudl left the brewery in the company of other adults, including Hitler's cook, Constanze Manziarly. Traudl saw Manziarly, a woman obviously attractive to Russian men, for the last time when she was led away by two Soviet soldiers who 'wanted to see her papers'.[102] Manziarly was never seen again. In light of historical evidence on the conduct of Soviet soldiers in that era it is likely that she was raped. A scene of Manziarly being led away by two Soviet soldiers would undoubtedly have been interpreted as a hint at, and judgement of, the maltreatment of German civilians by Soviet soldiers. It would, because of the symbolic ways in which film works, not have been seen as the reconstruction of one incident, but as the symbolic representation of the rape of many German women by soldiers of the Red Army. There is no doubt that such would have led to heavy criticism

Traudl Junge (Alexandra Maria Lara) and Peter Kranz (Donevan Gunia) walk away from the Soviet soldiers, away from the war and into the new future. © Constantin Film GmbH

which could only have been anticipated and warded off by having the film pay attention to the horrors previously committed by German soldiers in Eastern Europe, horrors that indeed help us to understand the attitude of many Soviet soldiers towards German civilians. This in turn would have made an additional storyline necessary. In other words, the ways in which the historically accurate scene of Manziarly being led away could have been interpreted, made it simply impossible to film or include it. The same goes for what actually happened to Traudl after she walked away from the brewery. Having left Berlin, walking from one village to another and hoping to reach the American-occupied sector of Germany, Traudl encountered a former concentration camp prisoner wearing his striped uniform.

> 'At that moment, this man and I shared the same fate, we were both afraid of the Russians and we walked together awhile. We didn't discuss our recent past. At the time I did not realise what had actually gone on in the concentration camps [...] Nowadays it is hard to imagine, but at the time I did not ask that prisoner any questions. And I certainly didn't ask myself any questions.'[103]

Truth is stranger than fiction and that certainly goes for Traudl's march out of Berlin. Hitler's secretary and a refugee from a concentration camp walking side by side through a devastated Germany... One cannot even begin to imagine what this must have looked like, let alone what it would look like in reconstruction, for instance as the closing scene of *Downfall*. There is no doubt that such a scene, if only by suggesting the kind of 'shared fate' Traudl Junge said she experienced, would have been trashed as a trivialisation of the Shoah, a tasteless gesture even the most commercial Hollywood company would not have indulged in. Again the symbolic meanings attached to film scenes would have turned an historical fact into a historic lie.

'Does Germany need this?'
Downfall and the relevance of historical cinema

The release of *Downfall* was meticulously staged as an 'event' not only abroad, but particularly in Germany.. The day before the film premiered, the *Frankfurter Allgemeine Zeitung*.[104] published a lengthy piece by Frank Schirrmacher, who had succeeded Joachim Fest as one of the *FAZ* editors in 1994. The article contained moderate criticism but was altogether very enthusiastic. According to Schirrmacher, *Downfall* was 'a masterpiece – there is no other term for it', 'not only a great work of art, but an important date in our *Verarbeitungsgeschichte*'. Eichinger was eulogised and described as 'a great artist' who had not only 'managed to write a script that itself has become literature' but also 'realised what no-one had pulled off before: to invent Hitler again'. That *Downfall's* script qualifies as literature is, at least in my opinion, nonsense. But, as this essay is meant to demonstrate, as a script it is certainly very intelligent. Eichinger clearly found a way of translating historical data into a script that acceded to the conventions of mainstream (historical) cinema by altering many details without betraying the larger narrative. This script, together with all the other factors so important in making a film successful (convincing actors, authentic-looking sets, etc.) have turned *Downfall* into a very good historical film. But does this make the film relevant?

This question was asked by several reviewers, one of whom reminded Eichinger that 'a screening room is after all not a wax museum'.[105] A similar question was asked by Ian Kershaw, author of the internationally renowned Hitler biography.[106] Shortly after the German premiere, Eichinger personally invited Kershaw to a private screening. It was a brave or at least a self-confident move. Brave because it exposed the film to the potential criticism of an internationally respected authority, whose judgement would resonate in the international press.[107] Brave because the strong connection between the film and Joachim Fest, who was condescending about Kershaw and, when interviewed, left little doubt that he found his own Hitler biography quite superior, could have affected Kershaw's judgement. But Kershaw was impressed by *Downfall*. In a perceptive review that left Fest's book about the bunker unmentioned while giving credit to the works of Trevor-Roper and Joachimsthaler, the movie was highly praised:

'... watching Eichinger's superb reconstruction, I could not imagine how a film of Hitler's last days could possibly be better done. [....] this portrayal by Ganz is Hitler much as I envisaged him when writing the final chapter of my biography.'[108]

But Kershaw also mixed his praise with reservations:

'Does it help us to understand Hitler any better? My own feeling is that, brilliant though the portrayal is, it does not. [...] I left the cinema gripped by the film. As a production, it is a triumph – a marvellous historical drama. As I made my way home, ready to congratulate Eichinger on his brilliant achievement, it crossed my mind that the success of *Der Untergang* might prompt a new type of Hitler-Welle (Hitler wave), this time in feature films. I hope not. [...] I am, of course, not suggesting that there should be a veto or censorship on the making of such films – Germany is a mature and stable enough democracy to put up with them. But are they needed? Will they bring new insights? Will it become any clearer why the people of a highly advanced, politically pluralistic, economically advanced, modern society thought, three quarters of a century ago, they had found national salvation in Hitler? Does Germany need this type of reminder of its past in order not to forget it?'[109]

It is interesting that Kershaw's enthusiasm for *Downfall* as an historical film should go hand in hand with questioning the 'need' for such a film, in other words, the relevance of *Downfall*. Historians such as Kershaw try to go beyond reconstructing historical events and attempt to explain why events happened the way they did; his publications on the Third Reich are probably better examples of this than his Hitler biography.[110] *Downfall* had no such ambition and is therefore questioned. But is the lack of explanation really such a bad thing? And if so, how exactly should Eichinger have introduced such explanatory models into his script? Is it necessary, or for that matter even feasible, for historical films to have the ambition of visualising literally the complex processes that have led a culturally developed nation to the horrors of Nazism? Is it intellectually appropriate to demand such a task of a medium that, when striving to reach a broad audience, must play by the rules of mainstream cinema? Also, are historical films by definition, to paraphrase Kershaw, made as 'reminders of the past in order not to forget'?

As I hope to have demonstrated by explaining why Germany had not produced such a film before, there is more to historical films than explanations of history. True, Germany does not need a film like this in order not to forget its past.

What it does need, however, as every country does that has dark pages in its history, is to come to terms with that past. The relevance of historical films may therefore not lie in their questionable ability to explain historical events but in their unquestionable power to launch or revive public debate. It has been mentioned already that in the long and continuing process of the German *Vergangenheitsbewältigung* (which was marked in 2006 by the Günter Grass controversy)[111] the television series *Holocaust* (1978) played an important role. In retrospect, the simple fact that this series reached far larger audiences than historical studies and thereby made public debate simply unavoidable far outweighed the mediocrity of *Holocaust*'s actual narrative. *Downfall*, which in spite of its shortcomings offers a well-thought-out historical reconstruction that through the character of Traudl Junge offers closure without being apologetic, is a textbook example of the further contribution historical films can offer to such processes.

Notes

1 Some of the ideas expressed here were outlined first in Vande Winkel, R. (21 January 2005) Mein Krampf, pp. 28-29 in *De Standaard*. International reviews of the film were obtained through Jay Weissberg and Vinzenz Hediger or consulted at the German Film Museum (Berlin), the Belgian Royal Film Archive (Brussels), Zeitgeschichte Online [http://www.zeitgeschichte-online.de/] and various other websites. Some clippings did not carry complete bibliographical data, which explains why some of the references below are incomplete. I am indebted to David Welch, Leen Engelen and my colleagues of the Working Group Film & TV Studies for comments on earlier drafts.

2 In the German language, the capitulation (May 1945) is still referred to as *Die Stunde Null* (zero hour).

3 Broadcast on 19 and 20 October 2005 in prime time (8.15-9.45 pm) by *Das Erste*, the national television channel of public broadcaster ARD. The first episode reached 7.2 million viewers, 3.46 million of which were aged 14-19. ARD press release of 20 October 2005. [http://presseportal.de.] The second episode attracted 6.9 million viewers. Meza, E. (23 October 2005) Hitler pic draws big auds for ARD, in *Variety*.

4 86.866.724 USD according to Box Office Mojo, consulted on 15 December 2005. [http://www.boxofficemojo.com].

5 In Germany and other 'region 2' countries where the cinematic release had been very successful, the film was released in a regular and a premium edition (with extra disc). In autumn 2005, immediately following the above-mentioned German broadcast, the extended televised edition was released in a new box, with two extra discs. It is not known whether this will also happen in 'region 1', where for the moment only the regular version is available.

6 Kirschbaum, E. (26 September 2004) Hitler causes stir: good reviews for a bad, bad man, in *Variety*. The journalist wrote about Germany, but elsewhere too, the film caused commotion. The French newspaper *Libération* was for instance 'alerted' by the 'abundance' of letters and e-mails it received after the film was released in France. Lefort, G. (24 January 2004) 'La Chute' rebondit en France - 'L'émotion était palpable', in *Libération*.

7 Compare the enthusiastic review by Hitler biographer Ian Kershaw to the far more negative evaluation of Peter Longerich and Eichmann biographer David Cesarani. Both reviews are discussed further in this chapter.

8 Hansen, E. (16 September 2004) Downfall, in *The Hollywood Reporter*.

9 Kohler, M. (2004) Der Untergang, p. 27 in *Film-dienst*, 57 (19).

10 Mejias, J. (16 September 2004) So muß es gewesen sein, in *Frankfurter Allgemeine Zeitung*.

11 Wenders, W. (21 October 2004) Tja, dann wollen wir mal. Warum darf man Hitler in "Der Untergang" nicht sterben sehen? Kritische Anmerkungen zu einem Film ohne Haltung, in *Die Zeit*.

12 Winkler, M. M. (ed.) (2004) *Gladiator: Film and History*. Malden, MA - Oxford: Blackwell. On pp. 31-44 the film's historical advisor, Kathleen M. Coleman, expresses her frustration with the final result.

13 An attempt was made by Bischof, W. (ed.) (2005) *Filmri::ss. Studien über den Film 'Der Untergang'*. Münster: UNRAST-Verlag. Only four of the eight essays included really deal with the film.

14 *Kolberg* 'demonstrated' that the united effort of 'front' and 'home' (the military and civilians) could defeat any enemy. Many myths surround this film, for instance the 'fact' that 187,000 soldiers were in 1943-1944 kept from the front to serve as extras for director Veit Harlan. For a deconstruction of such often-repeated implausibilities, see Paret, P. (1994) 'Kolberg' (1945) as historical film and historical document, pp. 433-448 in *Historical Journal of Film, Radio and Television* 14 (4).

15 Almost every book on Nazi film propaganda includes this speech. (Some authors state that Goebbels and his staff previously attended a private screening of the film together.) The citation and translation used here, was taken from Welch, D. (2001 rev.) *Propaganda and the German cinema 1933-1945*. Oxford: Clarendon Press, p. 197.

16 Bulgakowa, O. (1995) Der Mann mit der Pfeife oder das Leben ist ein Traum. Studien zum Stalinbild im Film, pp. 210-231 in Loiperdinger, M., R. Herz et al. (eds) *Führerbilder. Hitler, Mussolini, Roosevelt, Stalin in Fotografie und Film*. München - Zurich: Piper.

17 *Fall of Berlin* consisted initially of two feature-length films, the second focused on the battle of Berlin. Mitchell, C. P. (2002) *The Hitler Filmography*. Jefferson: McFarland & Company Inc., p. 58-62. The film is analysed in Taylor, R. (1998 rev.) *Film propaganda. Soviet Russia and Nazi Germany*. London-New York: I.B. Tauris Publishers, pp. 99-122.

18 Norddeutscher Rundfunk (Germany), Westdeutscher Rundfunk (Germany), Degeto Film (Germany), Österreichischer Rundfunk (Austria), EOS Entertainment (Italy) and Rai Cinemafiction (Italy).

19 For a short, very interesting characterisation of Eichinger, see Elsaesser, T. (2005) *European Cinema Face to Face with Hollywood*. Amsterdam: Amsterdam University Press, pp. 314-316.

20 Ernst Nolte's similarly titled essay, published in 1986, sparked off the *Historikerstreit* (historians' dispute), which is analysed in Kershaw, I. (2000 rev.) *The Nazi dictatorship: problems & perspectives of interpretation*. London: Hodder Arnold.

21 Also released as *Our Hitler*.

22 Interview with Bernd Eichinger, published on the movie's official website [http://www.der-untergang.de].

23 Fest, J. (2002) *Der Untergang: Hitler und das Ende des Dritten Reiches. Eine Historische Skizze.* Berlin: Alexander Fest Verlag. Translated as Fest, J. (2004) *Inside Hitler's Bunker: the last days of the Third Reich*. London: Pan Books. In Germany, it was reprinted in one volume in 2004 together with a transcript of the movie dialogue (cinema version - without the additional scenes shown on television). Fest, J. & B. Eichinger (2004) *Der Untergang. Das Filmbuch*. Reinbek bei Hamburg: Rowohlt Taschenbug Verlag.

24 Interview.... [http://www.der-untergang.de].

25 In the following paragraphs, information on previous 'Hitler films' is, unless otherwise noted, taken from Mitchell, C. P. (2002). An interesting appraisal of such films and their reception in Germany can be found in Töteberg, M. (2004) Hitler - eine Filmkarriere, pp. 405-434 in Fest, J. & B. Eichinger.

26 Christoph Schlingensief's *100 Jahre Adolf Hitler - Die letzte Stunde im Führerbunker* (*100 years Adolf Hitler - The last hour in the Führer bunker*, 1989) is not listed here because of its experimental character and relative short length (60 minutes, to reconstruct Hitler's final hour). Likewise eccentric productions such as *The Death of Adolf Hitler* (1972) are also to be disregarded in this context. For more information on such films, see Mitchell, C. P. (2002).

27 Musmanno, M. A. (1950) *Ten Days to Die*. Garden City: Doubleday & Co.

28 Trevor-Roper, H. (1947) *The Last Days of Hitler*. New York: Macmillan.

29 O'Donnell, J. P. (1978) *The bunker: The history of the Reich Chancellery group*. Boston: Houghton Mifflin.

30 Fest, J. (2002), p. 201. See also Lukacs, J. (1997) *The Hitler of history*. New York: Alfred A. Knopf, pp. 8-9.

31 Joachimsthaler, A. (1995) *Hitlers Ende. Legenden und Dokumente*. München: Herbig. In 2004, coinciding with the release of *Downfall*, the book was reprinted.

32 Probably the first in-depth study was Kuby, E. (1965) *Die Russen in Berlin 1945*. München: Scherz. The most famous recent example is Beevor, A., *The Fall of Berlin 1945*, New York, 2002, Viking. Probably thanks to Eichinger's film, the book was in 2004 also published under the altered title *Berlin: the Downfall 1945*.

33 The term 'sketch' is not intended pejoratively: the original German subtitle describes the book as 'an historical sketch', see Fest, J. (2002). Regarding the correction of outdated details: Speer could for instance lean on new forensic evidence regarding Hitler's right-hand man, Martin Bormann. It was not until 1999, when DNA testing was carried out on remains that had been found during roadworks in 1972, that Bormann's death on 2 May 1945 was irrefutably confirmed. Until then, although a positive dental records identification had been carried out in 1972, Bormann (who had been sentenced to death in absentia at the Nuremberg trials) was rumoured to have escaped justice.

34 This is not to argue that *Downfall* approached the subject in a manner identical to its predecessors. A detailed comparison of the various Führer bunker films would certainly be useful, and will probably be made by future scholars, but cannot be accomplished within the scope of this contribution. A first attempt can be made by comparing the entries of the respective titles in Mitchell, C. P. (2002).

35 Fest, J. (1973) *Hitler - Eine Biographie*. Frankfurt - Berlin: Ullstein.

36 In 1977, Fest wrote the script for a documentary he co-directed with Christian Herrendoerfer. *Adolf Hitler, eine Karriere* (*Adolf Hitler: A Career*) was based on his own biography.

37 See for instance Fest's praise for Eichinger in their joint publication. Fest, J. & B. Eichinger (2004), p. 463.

38 Joachim Fest [Obituary] (13 September 2006), in *The Times*.

39 A 52 p. educational booklet, explaining to teachers how to use *Downfall* for various subjects and educational aims (history, German language teaching, religion and ethics, sociology and arts) was, coinciding with the film's release, distributed through various channels, including the official website. [http://www.der-untergang.de].

40 The 'new' name was not a pseudonym: Traudl was a nickname for Gertraude and Junge was the name of her husband, a member of the SS-Leibstandarte Adolf Hitler she met while working for Hitler. (He died during the war.) To avoid confusion I will often just refer to 'Traudl'.

41 Junge, T. & M. Müller (2002) *Bis zur letzten Stunde. Hitlers Sekretärin erzählt ihr Leben*. München: Claassen Verlag, p. 257.

42 Müller, M. (1998) *Das Mädchen Anne Frank: Die Biographie*. München: Claassen Verlag.

43 Junge, T. & M. Müller (2002). Translated as Junge, T. & M. Müller (2003) *Until the Final Hour: Hitler's Last Secretary*. London: Weidenfeld and Nicolson,

44   Business data for *Untergang, Der* (2004) [http://www.imdb.com]

45   Berghahn, D. (2005) *Hollywood behind the wall. The cinema of East Germany*. Manchester - New York: Manchester University Press, p. 64.

46   Remarque, who lost his German citizenship in 1938, was the author of *Im Westen nichts neues* (1929), on which Lewis Milestone based his classic film *All Quiet on the Western Front* (1930). The novel and the film infuriated the Nazis; in the 1950s Remarque was also considered a traitor by many older Germans. Placke, H. (1998) Die politischen Diskussionen in den fünfziger Jahren um die Remarque-Filme. Teil I: Der letzte Akt (Österreich, 1955), pp. 215-252 in Schneider, T. F. (ed.) *Das Auge ist ein starker Verführer. Erich Maria Remarque und der Film*. Osnabrück: Universitätsverlag Rasch.

47   *Süddeutsche Zeitung*, cited by Töteberg, M. (2004), p. 417.

48   Dillmann, C. & R. Loewy (2004) *2 x 20. Juli. Die Doppelverfilmung von 1955*. Frankfurt am Main: Deutsches Filminstitut - Deutsches Filmmuseum.

49   Berghahn, D. (2005), pp. 55-97, includes an overview of these West German developments in her analysis of East German anti-fascist films.

50   Kershaw, I. (2000 rev.), p. 255.

51   Paraphrase of Edgar Reitz, who intentionally excluded the Jewish genocide almost entirely from his historical narrative *Heimat* (1979-1984), a series intended as an answer to *Holocaust*. Kaes, A. (1992) *From Hitler to Heimat: The Return of History as Film*. Cambridge: Harvard University Press, pp. 184-187.

52   Saul Friedländer, cited in Kershaw, I. (2000 rev.), p. 241.

53   The Goldhagen debate (sparked off by Daniel Jonah Goldhagen's controversial 1996 publication *Hitler's Willing Executioners*) and the Wehrmacht Exhibition are discussed in Kershaw, I. (2000 rev.), pp. 251-262.

54   The Wehrmacht Exhibition was partially discredited when, although its concept was historically correct, some of the pictures on display turned out to be fakes.

55   Friedrich, J. (2003) *Der Brand. Deutschland im Bombenkrieg 1940-1945*. München: Propyläen Verlag. A separate volume contains photographs: Friedrich, J. (2003) *Brandstätten - Anblick des Bombenkriegs*. München: Propyläen Verlag.

56   Taylor, F. (2004) *Dresden*. London: Bloomsbury.

57   Some highly respected scholars remain sceptical about such trends and about the possibility that 'the belligerent self-pity fostered by Downfall' would become 'a new form of German nationalism'. Cesarani, D. & P. Longerich (7 April 2005) The Massaging of History, in *The Guardian*.

58   German sales executive Andreas Rothbauer has pointed out that 'in the light of its success people have forgotten that buyers were initially very cautious' about *Downfall*. The enthusiastic reactions of the Toronto audience reportedly convinced initially reticent markets such as Israel (Shani Films) and the USA (Newmarket) to buy the film. Goodfellow, M. (11 September 2005) Continental firms rate Canuck fest as top spot for buying, selling pix, in *Variety*.

59   Fest, J. & B. Eichinger (2004), pp. 236-401.

60   Eichinger presumably intended to direct the movie himself. Financers probably decided to attract someone else after the last production Eichinger directed (*Der Grosse Bagarozy - The Devil and Ms. D.*, 1999) disappointed at the box office. Heidböhmer, C. (7 September 2004), Die letzten Tage des "Tausendjährigen Reich", in *Stern*.

61   Elley, D. (20 September 2004) Downfall, in *Variety*; Bradshaw, P. (4 August 2005) Bunker Mentality, in *Guardian Weekly*.

62   In a conversation with Melisa Müller, Junge described this moment as the starting point of her personal *Verarbeitungsgeschichte*. Junge, T. & M. Müller (2002), p. 261.

63   Joachimsthaler, A. (1995), p. 200. 'Whether he was told the details - how Mussolini was hanged upside down in a square in Milan, together with his mistress Clara Petacci, and stoned by a mob - is uncertain. If he did learn the full gory tale, it could have done no more than to confirm his anxiety, to take his own life before it was too late, and to prevent his body from being seized by his enemies.' Kershaw, I. (2000), *Hitler 1936-1945: Nemesis*. Middlesex: Penguin Group, p. 826.

64   Joachimsthaler, A. (1995), p. 144. Kershaw, I. (2000), p. 798.

65   Ernst Grawitz, vice-president of the German Red Cross. As hinted at in a short scene between Grawitz and Hitler, the doctor had good reasons to be afraid of falling into enemy hands. As the most important doctor in the SS he was responsible for overseeing many of the 'medical experiments' carried out in concentration camps. Grawitz also played an active role in the choice of gas to murder Jews.

66   Fest, J. (2002), p. 140 and 162.

67   Rosenstone, R. (2001) The Historical Film: Looking at the Past in a Postliterate Age, pp. 50-66 in Landy, M. (ed.) *The HistoricalFilm: history and memory in media*. New Brunswick, New Jersey: Rutgers University Press.

68   Junge, T. & M. Müller (2002), pp. 38-44.

69   Fest, J. (2002), pp. 66-69.

70 Hermann Fegelein was indeed executed after Hitler learned of Himmler's betrayal. ('For Hitler, it was the closest he could come to revenge on the Reichsführer-SS himself' - Kershaw, I. (2000), p. 819). But, unlike what the movie shows us, Fegelein had been arrested (for having disappeared from the bunker without notice - 'desertion') shortly before the news about Himmler had reached Hitler. Kershaw, I. (2000), p. 816.

71 Hitler telling a representative (Walter Hewel) 'Politics? I am done with politics. When I am dead, you'll have plenty of political decisions to make' is moved from its original setting (the Führer bunker at night) to the day-time reception at the Chancellery. Fest, J. (2002), p. 55. Several other examples could be given.

72 Fest, J. (2002), p. 86.

73 The German word *Geschichte* can be translated as 'history', but also as 'tale' or 'story'.

74 Westphal, A. (24 August 2004) Einfühlung in den Führer, in *Berliner Zeitung*. Wengierek, R. (25 August 2004) Bruno Ganz gibt Hitler ein Gesicht, in *Die Welt*. Eichinger and Hirschbiegel made these statement at a press screening organised on 22 August 2004 to launch a press campaign preceding the official premiere (9 September) and release (16 September).

75 Kniebe, T. (15 September 2004), Mit den kleinsten gemeinsamen Nenner, in *Süddeutsche Zeitung*.

76 Wildt, M. (2005) 'Der Untergang': Ein Film inszeniert sich als Quelle, pp. in *Zeithistorische Forschungen / Studies in Contemporary History (Online ausgabe)*, 2 (1). [http://www.zeithistorische-forschungen.de]; Knörerer, E. (22 September 2004) Riecht wie Führerbunker, in *Perlentaucher* [http://perlentaucher.del].

77 See also Ruoff, A. (2005) Die Renaissance des Historismus in der Populärkultur. Über den Kinofilm 'Der Untergang', pp. 69-78 in Bischof, W. (2005).

78 Silberman, M. (1995) *German cinema: Texts in context*. Detroit, Michigan: Wayne State University Press, p. x.

79 Silberman M. (1995), p. x.

80 Schenck, E.-G. (1970) *Ich sah Berlin sterben. Als Ärzt in der Reichskanzlei*. Hertford: Nicolaische.

81 Moss, S. (1 April 2005) Stormtrooper superstars, in *The Guardian*.

82 Reinecke, S. (15 September 2004) Der Arzt von Berlin, in *Tageszeitung*; Kraüter, H. (20 September 2004) Der gute Mensch in Hitlers Bunker?, in *Frankfurter Allgemeine Zeitung*; Cesarani, D. & P. Longerich (7 April 2005).

83 Cesarani, D. & P. Longerich (7 April 2005). I should point out, as this chapter will show, that my overall evaluation of the movie is less negative than Cesarani's and Longerich's.

84 Neumann, K. (2005) Downfall: almost the same old story, in *Rouge*, (6). [http://www.rouge.com.au/]; Wildt, M. (2005).

85 Fest, J. (1999) *Speer. Eine Biographie*. Berlin: Alexander Fest Verlag. Recently Speer

86 Fest, J. (2005) *Die unbeantwortbaren Fragen. Gespräche mit Albert Speer*. Reinbek: Rowohlt.

87 Speer, A. (1969) *Erinnerungen*. Berlin: Ullstein.

88 Fest, J. (2002), pp. 199-200.

89 Reuth, R. G. (1990) *Goebbels*. München: Piper, p. 614.

90 Wenders accused the film producers of having carried out Hitler's orders that his body not be seen by the (Soviet) victors: 'Why not show that the swine is finally dead?' Wenders, W. (21 October 2004). Wildt, M. (2005) also accused the producers of having turned Hitler's body into a 'sacrilege object' by not showing the Führer's corpse. See also Meyer, M. (22 September 2004) Gleichschritt in den Operntod, in *Neue Zürcher Zeitung*.

91 Fest, J. (2002), pp. 139-140.

92 Fest, J. (2002), pp. 161-163. This was the composer Matvey J. Blanter whom Stalin had commissioned to write a symphony about the fall of Berlin. He had been ordered to hide in the armoire because, as a civilian, he had no uniform and could therefore not be seen (by Krebs) sitting side by side with Soviet generals.

93 In Mel Brooks' comedy, *The Producers* (1968), Broadway producers try to swindle their investors by making the worst play imaginable: *Springtime for Hitler* a musical celebrating the life and times of the Führer. Mitchell, C. P. (2002), pp. 181-183.

94 Junge, T. & M. Müller (2002), pp. 45-46.

95 Junge, T. & M. Müller (2002), p. 195.

96 Junge, T. & M. Müller (2002), p. 183.

97 Junge, T. & M. Müller (2002), p. 197.

98 Junge, T. & M. Müller (2002), pp. 191-193.

99 Junge, T. & M. Müller (2002), p. 196.

100 As mentioned above, this is followed by the biographies of most protagonists as well as a short excerpt of the aged Traudl, talking about her own coming to terms with the past.

101 Schultz, S. M. (2005) Die harmonische Leinwand. Filmische Stereotypen bei der Darstellung von Nationalsozialismus und Holocaust in aktuellen deutschen Produktionen, pp. 87-88 in Schenk, R., E. Richter, et al. (eds) *apropos: Film 2005. Das Jahrbuch der DEFA-Stiftung*. Berlin: DEFA-Stiftung - Bertz+Fischer.

102 Junge, T. & M. Müller (2002), p. 234.

103 Junge, T. & M. Müller (2002), p. 235.

104 Schirrmacher, F. (15 September 2004) Die zweite Erfindung des Adolf Hitlers, in *Frankfurter Allgemeine Zeitung*.

105 Schleider, T. (24 August 2004) Ganz wie in echt, in *Stuttgarter Zeitung*.

106 Kershaw, I. (1998) *Hitler 1889-1936: Hubris*. Middlesex: Penguin Group; Kershaw, I. (2000).

107 Kershaw's review of the film was reprinted in many international newspapers.

108 Kershaw, I. (17 September 2004) The Human Hitler, in *The Guardian*. [http://www.guardian.co.uk]

109 Kershaw, I. (17 September 2004).

110 Kershaw, I. (2000 rev.); Kershaw, I. (2001 rev.) *The 'Hitler myth': Image and Reality in the Third Reich*. Oxford: Oxford University Press.

111 In August 2006, novelist Günter Grass belatedly disclosed his Waffen-SS membership during the later stages of World War Two. As the leftist writer had for many decades criticised Germany's treatment of its Nazi past as too slow and too hesitatant, his statement caused a great stir. In the last weeks of his life, Joachim Fest was among Grass's critics.

Ivan Lapshin (left), a high-ranking officer with a background in the Cheka, and Khanin (right), a Jew and a writer, are both likely to be repressed during the Stalinist Terror. © Lenfilm Studio

The Time Which Is Yet To Come: Understanding *My Friend Ivan Lapshin* (1983-1985)

Jasmijn Van Gorp

Among historians and film scholars, the representational nature of both history and film has led to to debates and theoretical reflections on how films construct history.[1] This question is of special interest for films made in a society where 'history' was determined from above, dictated from primarily ideological motives. Indeed, in Soviet society, history and particularly the sensitive periods of Stalinism, the Second World War and the Russian Civil War[2] were to be treated in a certain mythological way.[3] It was only during glasnost that writers, historians, journalists, educators and filmmakers could turn their attention to the historical past without the mythologizing restraints. In cinema, the investigation of the hitherto unknown details of the Stalinist Terror started with Alexei German's *Moi Drug Ivan Lapshin* (My Friend Ivan Lapshin, 1983/1985), even before the winds of reform had begun to blow new life through Soviet society. In this chapter I try to understand *My Friend Ivan Lapshin* by confronting its intended reading with its public and critical reception.

Stalinism and Soviet 'history'

History in the Soviet Union had always been something of a mythological experiment for the simple reason that historiography was always subject to Communist Party control and manipulation.[4] History was constantly being revised and updated to serve the interests of the current leadership.[5] It is not surprising, therefore, to find that the historiography of the Stalinist period was subject to the Party's falsification.

Stalinism as a system was consolidated in the course of the late 1920s and 1930s. From 1929 to 1953 it made an imprint on Soviet society and aspired to totalitarian control of all aspects of life, leaving little private space for its citizens. One feature of the Stalin years was the Terror: the violence inflicted on the Soviet population by the government, especially through imprisonment, the gulags, executions, famine linked to collectivisation, and deportations.[6] The most notorious aspect of the Stalinist era was the Great Terror of 1937-1938. The number of victims, many of them prominent officials, was extremely high.[7] Politically, Stalinism came to an end in 1953 with the death of the dictator. In February 1956, Khrushchev launched his campaign of destalinisation at the twentieth Communist Party Congress. The effect of the thaw on historians began almost immediately, and continued for ten years. In the course of the twenty years dominated by Brezhnev and his successors, Andropov and Chernenko, unofficial discussion of the past was gradually silenced. The KGB imprisoned the most outspoken and persistent dissidents, permitting only a limited number of others to emigrate.[8]

In the course of 1987 and 1988, Soviet citizens began to study their country's past, and the Stalinist past in particular, as a consequence of Gorbachev's policy of glasnost. In many publications, members of the intelligentsia – writers, historians, journalists, educators, filmmakers – started to call the tragedy of the recent past by its real name, exposing the glorified exploits and phoney values of the Soviet past as empty myths.[9] Soviet cinema played an important role in opening up this debate.[10] The first filmmaker to demythologise the Stalinist past was Alexei German with *My Friend Ivan Lapshin*.

The ordeal of the film's production

Alexei German, born in St Petersburg (formerly Leningrad) in 1938, is widely recognised as one of the most ambitious and original directors of Russian cinema.[11] German graduated from the *Leningrad State Institute of Theatre, Music and Cinema* in 1960 as a theatre director. In 1964 he switched over to cinema when he joined *Lenfilm*, the film studios in St Petersburg, to co-direct *Sedmoi sputnik* (*The Seventh Companion*). In the next twenty years, he made only three films: *Proverka na dorogakh* (*Trial on the Road*, 1971), *Dvadtsat dnei bez voiny* (*Twenty Days Without War*, 1976) and *My Friend Ivan Lapshin*. In 1998 he made his last film, *Khrustalev, mashinu!* (*Khrustalev, my car!*).[12] Each of his films focuses on moments in which history and myth have become entangled. German describes his films as '*antipotochnye*', 'against the current': questioning certainties and undermining 'truths'.[13]

His Soviet films were all beset by delays and censorship or simply shelved. A similar fate befell My *Friend Ivan Lapshin*. The film is based on a novel written by his father Yuri German (1910-1967). It was the elder German who asked his son in 1961 to make a film of his story *One year*.[14] The novel was written strictly according to the tenets of Socialist Realism, a doctrine he firmly believed in. According to the rules laid down in 1934, Socialist Realism 'demands of the artist the truthful and historically concrete representation of reality in its revolutionary development.'[15] Socialist Realism was a highly allegorical form of narrative in which reality was tailored to celebrate the achievements of the state and the goals of the Party. The doctrine required the artist to show how all conflicts could be resolved with the aid of the Party, and that the future was being built in accordance with its correct policies. Socialist Realism ruled Soviet art from the 1930s through the 1950s and has steadily withered away in the decades since.

The filming of My *Friend Ivan Lapshin* finally began in 1979 and ended in 1982. Immediately after the first screening, the film was attacked from within *Lenfilm* itself. An article in the studio's newspaper called it a 'disgusting film'. Then, Goskino, the State Committee for Cinematography, told German to re-shoot half of the film, which German refused to do.[16] After a two-year skirmish with Goskino, the film was released in 1985 at the very beginning of Gorbachev's glasnost. Before analysing the film and its reception, it is important to discuss what the concept of historical film implies.

Framework of analysis

My *Friend Ivan Lapshin* is an historical film, explicitly representing the Stalinist past and implicitly the Terror. The very word 'represent' is a bit ambiguous. Historical films do not so much represent history as produce or construct it according to their own rules.[17] Following Pearson,[18] I can say that historical films indicate a complex circuit made up of aspects of historical 'reality', cinematic representations, creators and perceivers, in which the conventions of representation must be shared by creators and perceivers alike for communication to take place. This circuit offers a useful tool for the analysis of *My Friend Ivan Lapshin*.

The creator of the film, Alexei German, plays a vital role in my analysis. In fact, I will analyse the film in terms of what the director tries to say with his film. It was not the director's intention to make a historically accurate film about how life 'really' was in the 1930s: 'When people tell me "you recreated that time", it is of course pleasant to hear, but who knows, maybe it wasn't quite that way at all.'[19] German shares with us the postmodern vision[20] that what happened in the past cannot be known: it is impossible to know the truth about the past and speak about History with a capital H.[21] In postmodernist historical films the concept of 'culture as chaos'[22] is projected on the image of history, often using memory to try to make sense of the past. As my analysis will show, this is exactly what German does. It is this feature that explains why *My Friend Ivan Lapshin* belongs to the postmodernist art genre.

Apart from the creator, the perceivers are another important element in my analysis. German created *My Friend Ivan Lapshin* for a Soviet audience from which he expected an active role: German's film gets its meaning through interaction with the viewer. The Soviet audience had a shared image of the 1930s, partly based on their collective memory of socialist realist films about this period.[23] As I will demonstrate, German wanted to shatter this image by undermining Socialist Realism in all its aspects and deconstructing history. He expects the viewers to share with him both the conventions of Socialist Realism as well as the genre conventions of postmodernist art films.

Using Hayward's distinction between seamless realism and aesthetically motivated realism, the term 'realism' can be related to both socialist realist films and postmodernist art films.[24] Socialist realism is a typical example of seamless realism whose ideological function is to convey the illusion of realism. Conversely, postmodernist art film makes use of the realist aesthetic, recognising the existence of a multiplicity of realisms. What is accepted as realistic is vulnerable to change since it depends on conventions of representation.[25] By scrutinising the intended or original reading of the film, I will now see how

German constructed and deconstructed history.[26] I will start with the narrative structure of the film and briefly mention its style. My attention will be largely dedicated to the content of the film. In a closing discussion, I will confront this original reading with the actual reception of the film.

Snatches of memories

The film's frame is set in 1983 and consists of a prologue and epilogue. This frame determines the narration's point of view as Alexander tries to remember the events set in his childhood in the years 1935-1936 at the onset of the Stalinist Terror. The boy Alexander lives with his father, Zanadvorov, police officer Ivan Lapshin, policeman Vasili Okoshkin and housekeeper Patrikeevna in a communal apartment in the provincial town Unchansk. Lapshin and his team are trying to track down a criminal, Soloviev, so far unsuccessfully. Meanwhile, Lapshin's best friend, the writer Khanin, arrives in Unchansk. He is upset because his wife has suddenly died of diphtheria. Lapshin invites him to stay in the communal apartment. The next day, Khanin attempts suicide, but fails. Lapshin helps him to pull himself together by taking him along while tracking down Soloviev. Meanwhile, a company of actors arrives in Unchansk to perform an agitprop theatre piece. One of them, Natasha Adashova, gets help from Lapshin in finding a real prostitute to give a better performance of her role as a prostitute in the play. Adashova, Lapshin and Khanin become friends and start hanging around together. Lapshin falls in love with Adashova, but she, in turn, falls in love with Khanin. Since Khanin has only recently lost his wife, he does not reciprocate Adashova's feelings. Some months later, Lapshin finds Soloviev. The criminal begs for mercy. At first, Lapshin agrees, but then kills Soloviev anyway. Khanin leaves town and Adashova and Lapshin go their separate ways. In short, the film is a detective story and a love triangle that falls apart, or so it seems at first viewing.

In My Friend Ivan Lapshin German sets aside conventional narrative structures. Instead, the viewer is confronted with Alexander's incoherent snatches of memory. German created the memories by ignoring conventional techniques. The long travelling shots and the subjective camera are tended to disorient the viewer, especially given the lack of classic establishing shots and shot-reverse shots. The film is also characterised by postmodernist montage: it frequently jumps from one

Ivan Lapshin, about to kill the criminal Soloviev despite a promise of mercy. © Lenfilm Studio

scene to another without indicating how the two scenes are related temporally and spatially. For example, in one scene Lapshin is walking down the corridor in the police headquarters, he then turns a corner to arrive in the corridor of his own apartment.

By using this postmodernist memory mode, the filmmaker approaches history as the personal memory of one individual. In this respect Beumers wrote that 'history is not an amalgam of stories that constitutes a myth, but a phenomenon that is remembered differently and for different things by different people at different times.'[27] German shows that history is constructed by human consciousness and, consequently, that it is not objective.

Unfulfilled genre expectations

The problem of disorientated viewers could be solved by a voice-over that provides some guidance. The presence of a voice-over encourages the expectation of a socialist realist film in which the narrator seems to be in possession of the truth. He controls and/or filters all information for the viewers, interpreting events in accordance with their revolutionary significance. Alexander does indeed supply commentary in a socialist realist style, but on several occasions his words do not correspond to the images. Consequently, it is difficult for the viewer to determine the value of the events and situations depicted.

The narrator tries to establish Lapshin as a socialist realist hero by using a more impressive voice. Alexander announces that Ivan Lapshin is his personal hero, again encouraging the expectation of the stereotype of the positive socialist realist hero. In the course of the narrative, however, it becomes clear that Lapshin is far from a positive hero in the socialist realist sense. Lapshin is a pathetic character, haunted by doubts and nightmares. In one scene Lapshin delivers firewood to the theatre, an illegal action, hardly acceptable behaviour for a positive hero. In another scene, when Alexander explains that Lapshin has caught the notorious Soloviev and his gang, his statement casts the affair in the light of a heroic and dramatic adventure befitting a socialist realist hero. But in fact, the film depicts these events as not heroic at all. Lapshin and his comrades are shown victimising the citizens living in Soloviev's neighbourhood and Lapshin brutally shoots Soloviev after promising him mercy.

The viewer expecting to see a socialist realist film is again and again confronted with contradictory images. Thus the socialist realist doctrine is undermined by unfulfilled genre expectations. My Friend Ivan Lapshin must be understood as 'the film-maker's attempt to confront the false history presented in socialist realist films by bringing up the genre conventions of Socialist Realism only to smash them down'.[28] This mechanism an sich also subverts Socialist Realism. It is obvious that this reading requires a prior knowledge and active response from the viewer. In socialist realist films, to the contrary, there is no room for interpretation, not to mention interaction.

A small, real history?

In My Friend Ivan Lapshin there is no explicit mention of the historical background except for a (physical) portrait of Kirov at the beginning and of Stalin at the end of the film.[29] Instead, German evokes the atmosphere of provincial life in 1935/1936 on both the figurative level by using a documentary style and on the narrative level through the focus on ordinary life. This everyday life of the people is portrayed as harsh and sometimes brutal. While Lapshin removes two frozen corpses from a bunker, a woman screams desperately at a man she blames for wasting fuel. There is the same reaction when Patrikeevna discovers that Okoshkin has used up all the sugar. Another example of the brutality of life appears in the scene in which Lapshin and his troops burst into a bunker trying to find Soloviev: the bunker is filled with poor families, including many wailing women and children. A hiccupping old lady and a woman struggling with her disobedient dog are other indications of ordinary life.

In My Friend Ivan Lapshin history is made up of many small things; German does not give us the conventional broad view of politics and historical events. The film depicts the intrusion of history into the lives of average people in a small town. Rifkin writes: 'German takes Lapshin out of the distorting spotlight of "Big History" and makes the story of Lapshin more typical and thus more valuable.'[30] By ignoring the official view of history, German tries to demystify the 'realism' of Socialist Realism.

German also evokes the atmosphere of the 1930s by his style of filmmaking. He shot the body of the film in black and white with a succession of filters and uses poor lighting and sound recording. Most of the time, the characters are unaware of the camera, but sometimes they stop and look directly at the camera with all the naïveté of the candid images in documentaries and newsreels of that time. The dialogue is frequently drowned out by senseless chatter and the view of important characters is often blocked by figures crossing the screen. These details enhance the documentary effect of the film, characteristic of aesthetic realism. This manner of representation is more reliable than the 'official' style with its bright colours, foreground dialogues and actors in the centre of the picture.

Socialist illusions

German pushed the demystification of the official doctrine a step further in the film's content. He uses a play-within-the-film to show that the people in the 1930s lived in a world of illusion. In a Socialist Realist play, Adashova has to play the part of a reformed prostitute. Some days before, Adashova comes to Lapshin's police station to rehearse a scene with the real prostitute Katka Napoleon. Katka understands perfectly well that the ideal world Lapshin and Adashova are striving for is one big illusion. She tries to make them understand this by doing something unexpected. Adashova is reading some lines when the prostitute grabs her for fun and tries to push her over just as Lapshin enters the room. Adashova and Lapshin are furious, but Katka insists it was only a joke. Nevertheless, Katka is tried and sentenced for assault. Ironically, the real prostitute is sentenced for her acting or game, while the actress fails to act Socialist 'realistically'. The play turns out to be a flop: a wheel comes off one of the carts and Adashova's acting is terrible. The fiction of the play is undermined and becomes real, while the value of Katka's joke in the rehearsal scene is misunderstood by Party members Lapshin and Adashova. The illusion of Socialist 'realism' and of 'Socialist life' is shattered by this complex interweaving of fact and fiction.

Together with Katka, Zanadvorov realises that Soviet life is an illusion. In Socialist Realist texts unorthodoxy was forbidden. So it comes as no surprise that the male protagonists in *My Friend Ivan Lapshin* have a different understanding of politics. This is explained in the scene in which Lapshin

My Friend Ivan Lapshin's ironic final scene: a live band playing optimistic marching music to inspire hope for a glorious future. © Lenfilm Studio

daydreams about clearing the land, planting an orchard and strolling in that orchard one day before he dies. Zanadvorov doubts that Lapshin's dream will come true. Zanadvorov understands perfectly well what is going on, but angers Lapshin by saying so, and yet Lapshin does seem to understand what is happening. He cannot sleep and bursts into tears on several occasions. Unlike them Khanin understands nothing. In one scene he flatly denies the rumours about the suicide of his hero, the poet Mayakovsky, despite the fact that he himself recently attempted to commit suicide. Khanin continues to live in an illusionary Socialist world.

It is at this point that German makes a statement about the present time. There is nothing in the frame story that suggests that life in 1983 is glorious. In 1983 the city of Unchansk has spread over to the other side of the river and has new asphalt roads, but in fact little has changed. Buttafava stated that: 'At the end of the film, after the catharsis and the catastrophe, the 'return to the future' from the Stalin-period town […] to the same city fifty years later, is not the return to a more liveable, more comfortable, more judicious contemporaneity.'[31] The frame set offers a dim view of modern Soviet life. The world depicted in 1935 is in many ways clearer than that of the 1980s. It is a statement that the present is swallowed by the past. German shows that the consequences of Stalinism were pervasive in 1983 society. Opening up the past to the present is a familiar aesthetic strategy of postmodernism.[32]

And what will happen next?

According to Socialist Realism 'the artist was to see the germs of a Communist future in the present.'[33] German shattered this illusion not only in the frame story, but also in the actual story set in 1935/1936. At first sight, there is no explicit mention of the Terror in My Friend Ivan Lapshin. The year 1935, after Kirov was assassinated, was the last moment before the outbreak of the Great Terror, a moment when it was still possible to nurture the illusion of a perfectly shaped future world. Yet, by means of omens and an Aesopian language, the director looks to the future by helping the viewer to imagine the dark fate of the story's characters after the film ends.

There are clear premonitions of a dark future when a mirror is shattered and Zanadvorov says: 'This is a bad omen. And by the way, for all of us.' When in Lapshin's birthday scene Okoshkin mentions how his love for a salesgirl torments him, a guest tells him: 'Shoot her and then shoot yourself.' History proved that similar words would become only too painfully true after the end of the film. When Lapshin near the end of the film is about to leave town for a 'refresher course' he seems to have no idea of the dark fate that awaits him. The 'refresher course' he faces functions as another omen. These various omens are overshadowed by the detective story and the love triangle and unambiguously inform the viewer that many of the film's characters will soon become victims of the Great Terror.[34] Lapshin, a high-ranking officer with a background in the Cheka (the secret police), is a likely target for repression. Adashova, an actress, and Khanin, a Jew and a writer, are both almost certain to be repressed as members of the creative intelligentsia. Alexei German confirms the dark fate of the protagonists, especially Lapshin: 'I can't imagine a Lapshin who survived the year 1936.'[35]

Besides omens, German also uses Aesopian language to depict the fate of the film's characters and, consequently, to debunk the myth of a glorious future and thus imply what could not be said openly.[36] During the 1960s and 1970s, an era of increasing censorship, many dissident filmmakers, including Alexei German, used this Aesopian language to say what they wanted to say. One of the best examples of this coded language can be seen in the episode in which Lapshin meets Khanin in the foyer where a scientific experiment with a fox and a rooster sharing a pen is in progress. Khanin makes a play on words when saying: 'The sly old fox takes me to distant forests.' This comment may be understood as an allegorical reference to Stalin as the fox-like predator who takes people away to Siberian forests. The message is clear: many of the characters will soon become victims of the Terror.

Another example follows the fox-rooster scene. Adashova, Khanin and Lapshin are sitting at a table. Lapshin interrupts Adashova's statement about the unrealistic champagne quota in the years 1938 and 1942 by saying it would be millions of bottles and not thousands. Khanin replies: 'A thousand here, a million there – it's of no concern to this woman who is used to extravagance.' This is a clear allegorical allusion to the Stalinist way of thinking: innocent people had to be killed as an inevitable consequence of measures necessary to protect the state against saboteurs and spies.

German made it hard on himself by using omens and Aesopian language instead of simply shifting the events to a year later in time. That is, the novel of father Yuri German depicts events taking place in Leningrad one year later, from December 1936 through some months of the following year. German shifted the events to the geographically undefined city of Unchansk in 1935-1936. Rifkin sees this decision in the light of German's intention to depict small-scale history: 'He had to shift the temporal and spatial setting [...] to assure that the filmic Lapshin would be uncorrupted by the Terror which had already begun in Leningrad at this time.'[37] On the other hand, Graffy suggests that it was the era in which the film was made that forced German to depict the Terror indirectly.[38] Direct depictions of the Stalinist Terror were forbidden in 1983. All dissenting expressions were suppressed. Consequently, German could have shifted his film from 1936 to 1935 to evade the censor. Alas, to no avail: the film was banned for two years.

Discussion: confronting the audiences

My *Friend Ivan Lapshin* can be seen as a riddle composed by the director for the viewer to solve. With this film, Alexei German subverts the accepted tenets of Socialist Realism, as well as the official interpretation of history. At the same time, he crucially influences both the doctrine and the dogma by his stubborn search for truth and, paradoxically, his denial of certainty. German wants to show the viewer the impossibility of a total and true grasp of history. The director, therefore, deconstructs the Stalinist past and the consistency of history as an objective phenomenon. The core question now is: did German manage to convey this message to the audience?

My *Friend Ivan Lapshin* was banned for two years (partly because of its focus on ordinary life) and was released in 1985.[39] The Soviet critics thoroughly appreciated the film. In 1986 it won the Brothers Vasiliev State Award. In 1989, the film was selected as the best Soviet film of all time, garnering the votes of nine out of ten critics. Significant for my analysis, however, is the reception by the general audience. The film reached the Soviet audience only in 1986 when it was shown on television. The Russian newspaper *Izvestia* announced the film by giving the viewers some practical advice: 'Try not to eat while you are watching the film. Let nothing distract you. Do not make a phone call. Try to surrender yourself to this kind of art.'[40] This 'warning' was indeed timely. The film became the subject of heated debate among the home-screen viewers. At once exciting and disturbing, it offered a glimpse of a sensitive period in Soviet history, and yet it proved to be quite disturbing simply because it was too soon for the general public to take in what it was seeing. Most people just could not believe it. Soviet audiences were used to Socialist Realist films about the 1930s in the 'official style' which in their eyes was realistic – heroes and heroines striving for an ideal Socialist world.[41] The ambiguous narration, unconventional techniques, the focus on everyday life and the documentary style left the audience confused. Some wanted to burn the film in public and some would have liked to see German burn as well.[42]

According to Rifkin, this severe reaction demonstrates that the memories of the 1930s were still of spiritual importance to the audience.[43] German had committed a sacrilege. In terms of my framework: the Soviet audience did not share with the director the conventions of postmodernist art films. Nor did the audience grasp German's hidden message. What was German really saying about the Stalinist years, besides the fact that life was hard and drab in the provinces? German's message that Lapshin was doomed to perish became obvious only after glasnost had become widely accepted by 1988-1990.[44] German had created a film for an audience that did not yet exist. He was a pioneer who gave the green light for the exorcising of Stalin in the glasnost cinema.

In the West, the reaction was comparable to that of the Soviet critics. The film won the Bronze Leopard and FIPRESCI award at Locarno in 1986. The Western film festival audience, familiar with postmodernist art films, could appreciate the film's unconventionalities. Yet this was not universally true. The film also troubled some Western critics who thought they perceived a certain nostalgia for those Stalinist years. The negative view of the frame story especially was considered a sign that German longed for the old Stalinist regime.[45] They failed to grasp German's postmodernist vision about past and present.

Alexei German was not really enthusiastic about travelling with his film beyond the borders of the Soviet Union. He was convinced that Western people would never understand the film since they were unacquainted with the conventions of Russian culture. When German heard the rumour that his film had been shown abroad, he reacted irritably: 'When a foreigner is watching a film like *My Friend Ivan Lapshin*, I have the impression that it is the same thing as when an African is being explained why a wool cap is worn by Russians. And you have to explain why there is cold weather; otherwise he won't be able to understand.'[46] Film critic Yevgeni Soerkov expressed this opinion metaphorically: 'This kind of film is like an iceberg: in the West you only see the peak, but in Russia we also see the seven-eighths below the surface.'[47] Both German and Soerkov completely ignore the difference in awareness of genre conventions in the two audiences. Indeed, it is quite difficult for a Western viewer to understand or even notice all the omens and allegorical references. And they will certainly be free of any Socialist Realist genre expectations for the obvious reason that they are unfamiliar with the doctrine's strict conventions. But the same can be said about the Russian audience and postmodernist art film conventions. German's limited awareness of foreign audiences is paradoxical given that postmodernist films precisely propagate a multiplicity of interpretations, providing the viewer with room for a personal reading. German claims that there is no 'right' history, but the same can be said about the meaning of *My Friend Ivan Lapshin*. It seems that German himself, together with his target audience, may not have been quite ready for his own film.

Notes

1 O'Connor, J. E. (1988) *American History/American Film. Interpreting the Hollywood Image.* New York: Continuum; Rosenstone, R. A. (ed.) (1995a) *Revisioning History. Film and the Construction of a New Past.* New Jersey: Princeton University Press; Rosenstone, R. A. (1995b) *Visions of the Past: the Challenge of Film to our Idea of History.* Cambridge: Harvard University Press; Sorlin, P. (1980) *The Film in History. Restaging the Past.* Oxford: Basil Blackwell.

2 Soviet government historiography traditionally referred to the Russian Civil War (1917/1918-1922) as the "Civil War and Military Intervention of 1917-1922".

3 Graffy, J. (1993) Unshelving Stalin: after the Period of Stagnation, pp. 212-267 in Taylor, R. and D. Spring (eds) *Stalinism and Soviet Cinema.* London and New York: Routledge, p. 216.

4 Boym, S. (1993) Stalin is With Us: Soviet Documentary Mythologies of the 1980s, pp. 201-211 in Taylor and Spring (1993), p. 201.

5 Gillespie, D. (2003) *The Russian Cinema.* London: Longmann Group, p. 60.

6 According to Evan Mawdsley the term 'Terror' is the central concept because 'it communicates the extreme cruelty involved. [...] The word 'repression' is too vague. [...] Westerners often talk of the 'purges', but the removal and execution of officials was only a part, in time and scale, of the criminal violence of the regime.' Mawdsley, E. (1998) *The Stalin years. The Soviet Union, 1929-1953.* Manchester: Manchester University Press, p. 97.

7 There is no agreement on the number of victims of the 'Great Terror'. Mawdsley (1998) mentions 680.000 executions in 1937-38. Conquest (1990) estimates about one million executed and two million deaths in camps. Conquest, R. (1990) *The Great Terror: a Reassessment.* Oxford: Oxford University Press.

8 Davies, R. W. (1989) *Soviet History in the Gorbachev Revolution.* Houndmills: Macmillan, pp. 1-6.

9 Davies (1989) analyses how this intelligentsia constructed the past.

10 Spring, D. (1993) Stalinism - the Historical Debate, pp. 1-14 in R. Taylor & D. Spring (eds) *Stalinism and Soviet Cinema.* London & New York: Routledge, p. 3.

11 Graffy, J. (2000) German, Alexei Y., pp. 83-84 in R. Taylor, N. Wood, J. Graffy and D. Iordanova (eds) *The BFI Companion to Eastern European and Russian Cinema.* London: BFI.

12 He is now working on his fifth film *Trudno byt bogom* (*It's Hard to be a God*), scheduled for release in 2007.

13 Interview in Fomin, V. (1996) *Kino i vlast, Sovjetskoe kino: 1965-85 gody.* Moscow: Materik, p. 200.

14 *One year* is a rewriting of Yuri German's novels *Lapshin* (1938) and *Zhmakin* (1938).

15 Kenez, P. (2001) *Cinema and Soviet Society. From the Revolution to the Death of Stalin.* London and New York: I.B. Tauris, p. 123.

16 Wood, T. (2001) Time Unfrozen. The Films of Aleksei German, pp. 99-107 in *New Left Review*, 7, p. 102.

17 Sobchack, V. (2003) What Is Film History?, or, the Riddle of the Sphinxes, pp. 300-314 in C. Gledhill and Williams, L. (eds). *Reinventing Film Studies.* London: Arnold, p. 311.

18 Pearson, R. (2001) Representation, pp. 386-387 in R.E. Pearson and P. Simpson (eds) *Critical Dictionary of Film and Television Theory.* London and New York: Routledge.

19 Rifkin, B. (1992) The Reinterpretation of History in German's Film *My Friend Ivan Lapshin*, pp. 431-447 in *Slavic Review*, 21 (3), p. 446. Rifkin's translation of a quote in German, A. (1986) Kino prozeastaet iz poezii: beseda s T. Iensen,' *Voprozy literatury*, 12, p. 150.

20 For an interesting account of Russian postmodernism and history, see Lipovetsky, M. (1999) *Russian Postmodernist Fiction: Dialogue with Chaos.* New York: M. E. Sharpe.

21 Rosenstone, R. (1996) The Future of the Past. Film and the Beginnings of Postmodern History, pp. 201-218 in V. Sobchack (ed.). *Persistence of History. Cinema, Television, and the Modern Event.* New York: Routledge.

22 This term is borrowed from Lipovetsky (1999), p. 155.

23 A good example of a Socialist Realist film set in the 1930s is *Volga, Volga* (1938) by Grigori Alexandrov.

24 Hayward, S. (2000) *Cinema Studies: the Key Concepts.* London: Routledge, pp. 311-313.

25 Hill, J. (2000) Narrative and Realism, pp. 206-213 in J. Hollows, P. Hutchings and M. Jancovich (eds) *The Film Studies Reader.* London: Arnold Publishers.

26 For this reading, I partly relied on the excellent analyses of Benjamin Rifkin (1992) and Herbert Eagle (1989), which I compared with other analyses and my own interpretation. Eagle, H. (1989) Soviet Cinema Today: On the Semantic Potential of a Discredited Canon, pp. 743-760 in *Michigan Quarterly Review,* 28 (4).

27   Beumers, B. (2000) Myth-making and Myth-taking: Lost Ideals and the War in Contemporary Russian Cinema. *Canadian Slavonic Papers*, 42 (1-2), p. 172.

28   Eagle (1989), p. 745.

29   Sergei Kirov, a rising star in the Communist Party of the 1930s, opposed Stalin and was assassinated, possibly on Stalin's orders. Stalin nevertheless used Kirov's death for his own ends and had many of his adversaries (as well as their families) executed for their alleged implication in Kirov's murder.

30   Rifkin (1992), p. 442.

31   Buttafava, G. (1992). Alexei German, or the Form of Courage, pp. 275-282 in A. Lawton (ed.) *The Red Screen: Politics, Society, Art in Soviet Cinema*. London and New York: Routledge, p. 282.

32   Lipovetsky (1999), p. 155.

33   Kenez, P. (2001) *Cinema and Soviet Society. From the Revolution to the Death of Stalin*. London and New York: I.B. Tauris, p. 23.

34   As noted by Rifkin (1992), p. 442

35   Rifkin, B. (1994) *Semiotics and Narration in Film and Prose Fiction: Case Studies of Scarecrow and My Friend Ivan Lapshin*. New York: Peter Lang, p. 189.

36   Johnson, V. (1996) Russia after the Thaw, pp. 640-651 in Nowell-Smith, G. (ed.) *The Oxford History of World Cinema*. New York: Oxford University Press, p. 645.

37   Rifkin (1994), p. 184.

38   Graffy (1993), p. 225.

39   Lawton (1992), p. 146.

40   Roodnat, J. (January 23, 1987) De heilige jaren '30 in *NRC Handelsblad*.

41   Roodnat (January 23, 1987).

42   Dérobert, E. (October 1986) Mythes fondateurs et fondements réels d'une société de La Vérification à Mon Ami Ivan Lapshine, pp. 35-38 in *Le Cinématographe*.

43   Rifkin (1992) comes to the same conclusion, p. 446.

44   Lawton (1992), p. 148 states 'later'. In an e-mail (October 8, 2004), director Yevgeni Tsymbal confirms my interpretation of this vague term as 1988-1990.

45   Lawton (1992), pp. 148-149.

46   Holloway, R. (1988) A Stubborn Quest for Historical Truth. Alexei German Interviewed in *Kinoeye*, 4 (4), [http://kinoeye.org/04/04/holloway04.php]

47   Van der Kaap, H. and M.-P. Meyer (1987) De ijsberg onder de Russische film, gesprek met E. Soerkov, pp. 4-9 in *Skrien*, p. 153. Yevgeni Surkov was editor of *Isskustvo Kino* for more than sixteen years.

Imelda Staunton as Vera Drake. © Ingenious Film Partners

Vera Drake (2004):
The comfort of strangers,
the discomforts of strangeness

Amy Sargeant

Vera Drake (2004) marked something of a departure for its director, Mike Leigh. The Cannes Festival, which had previously rewarded his *Naked* (1993) and *Secrets and Lies* (1996), nominating *All or Nothing* for the Golden Palm in 2002, rejected the film. It subsequently received the Golden Lion at the Venice Film Festival.[1] His earlier costume romp *Topsy-Turvy* (1999) had commented upon the modernity of the past, with W. S. Gilbert struggling to come to terms with the new-fangled telephone installed in his house, fulminating over newspaper reviews of his *Princess Ida* and enthusing over the spectacular Japanese exhibition at Humphries Hall, while *Vera Drake* reconstructed a past which, one can but hope, is firmly behind us.

Although lower-key and more understated than his other work, Leigh employed a similar set of character types, a stalwart company of actors accustomed to his working methods and a theme (the life of an abortionist in post-war London) familiar in its 'miserabilism'. 'You're born, you die and that's it…we're all gonna die one day…born alone die alone…nothing you can do about it', concludes Phil Bassett in *All or Nothing* – before deciding that life might, just, be worth living after all.[2] *Vera Drake* both adopts and conspicuously declines many of the established conventions of 'retro' British cinema. Its critical success, and that of Imelda Staunton (the eponymous Vera) who secured a best actress award at Venice and at the British Academy of Film and Television Arts, and an Oscar nomination for her leading role, re-opened the perennial debate over the vagaries and inadequacies of British film funding. The film received £1.25 Million of lottery funding administered through the UK Film Council; many other similarly funded projects have failed to secure distribution, let alone gain critical or commercial success.[3]

Here, I should like to discuss *Vera Drake* in the context of Leigh's other films and television dramas (especially its characterisations and performances) and alongside other recent reconstructions of the past of living memory.

Vera comforts strangers

At the outset, Vera is presented as a caring, sympathetic figure: she visits an elderly wheelchair-bound neighbour, George and his sick wife, Ivy, and invites bachelor Reg around for tea as a relief from his lonely diet of bread and drippings. She uncomplainingly cares for her bed-ridden, ungrateful mother ('she can't help it') and there is fond banter amongst herself, husband Stan and son Sid, a tailor. Ethel, her shy, even simple daughter who works in a light bulb factory, enjoys from a distance even if she rarely participates. There is much here of the 'matrilocality' reported by Michael Young and Peter Willmott in their seminal 1957 survey, *Family and Kinship in East London* and Imelda Staunton has spoken of her own memories of people 'helping one another out' in the white working-class neighbourhood of her upbringing.[4] Vera, Stan, Reg and Sid reminisce over shared wartime memories (the Blitz) and post-war experiences of National Service in Palestine, Germany and Burma.

This working-class conviviality is set against the cold upper-middle-class decorum of Mrs Wells, her barely-seen husband (a high-ranking civil servant in the Ministry of Defence) and daughter Susan, for whom Vera works as a char. While Mrs Wells seems to resent Susan's very existence and is content to leave her daughter for an evening in the company of David while she and Mr Wells attend a society function, Vera and Stan welcome Reg into their home and successfully arrange a match between Reg and Ethel. The homely, cramped comforts of Vera's Islington tenement household are also set against the upwardly mobile aspirations of Joyce, wife to Frank, Stan's younger brother, for whom Stan works in a garage: Frank and Joyce have moved to a semi in the suburbs and Joyce uses her pregnancy to bribe Frank into buying her a washing machine. As Philip French noted, 'she wants to have a baby, a washing machine and a television set, but not necessarily in that order'.[5]

Mrs Wells already has a television set with an ornamental sculpture posed on top of it. On Friday afternoons, unbeknown to her family, Vera performs another 'caring' role, as an abortionist for a hardened working-class woman with too many children to feed already; for a 'knowing' girl who may have been through it before; a girl whose boyfriend encounters Vera on the doorstep, only to have the door slammed in his face, perhaps not approving the girl's choice, or simply unaware; a married woman hysterical with guilt and fear who has had an affair while her husband was away in the army in Korea; for a Jamaican girl, presumably newly arrived in London (and who should return whence she came, says Lily) and entirely alone in a strange city. Vera's friend Lily, a female equivalent of the ubiquitous post-war small-time spiv, 'ingenious, pettily self-centred', receives payment in cash (two guineas) and in kind as an agent for Vera's services while Vera receives nothing, innocently dispensing charity, 'helping young girls out'.[6]

'She's a heart of gold…she's a diamond', insists Stan, 'she never did a dishonest thing in her life…whatever she's done, it's out of the kindness of her heart'. Vera is finally discovered by her family and the law when she performs an abortion on the daughter of a woman who recognises her from the time they worked together in a laundry in 1931: Pamela Barnes is taken to hospital, feverish and close to death, and the doctor dutifully reports the case. Stan continues to assert his solidarity with Vera. When the police come to his door and ask for her, he replies 'this is my wife', even though he later tells Sid that he would have 'put a stop to it' had he but known. Finally, Vera is differentiated from the tough 'professionals' who know the consequences of their crime from previous experience.

To the old rhetorical question 'Does Mike Leigh really love to hate people?' the answer merits modification: Mike Leigh has always disliked some people more than others.[7] Shirley and Cyril and Cyril's mother, Mrs Bender in *High Hopes* (1988) are handled more kindly than Mrs Bender's middle-class neighbours, the Boothe-Brains and her son-in-law, Martin, and, especially her childless daughter, Valerie, who keeps an Afghan hound as a substitute. Derek Malcolm duly noted that *Vera* 'showed a sympathy for its characters which Leigh has not always shown'. The judge and the police are shown to be resignedly performing their duty, rather than deriving any satisfaction from Vera's apprehension and committal: looking at the press gallery, the judge speaks of the custodial sentence as a 'deterrent'. The film carries a dedication to Leigh's parents – a doctor and a midwife. But Leigh again pitches women against one another in the matter of childbearing. Joyce celebrates her pregnancy and Ethel her engagement (and there is gentle joshing at the prospect of children to come), at a family gathering during which Vera is charged with preventing the birth of an unwanted child. While Vera is out on bail, the family comes together to mark Christmas (a collective celebration of birth). For Maurice and Monica Purley in *Secrets and Lies*, their want of a child is exacerbated by the reunion of Maurice's sister, Cynthia-Rose, with the child she gave away for adoption many years before. In *Topsy-Turvy*, Lucy Gilbert resorts to allegory to describe her angst-ridden, frustrated childlessness to her husband (who obtusely misses the point) while Sullivan's American mistress, Fanny, tells him that she will make her own arrangements to deal with her pregnancy (not her first): 'after all, it is 1885'.

Vera Drake as bio-pic

In the 1990s, bio-pics of artists of the recent past found favour, either entirely invented, as in *Life and Death on Long Island* (Richard Kwietniowski, 1996) or with varying degrees of factual accuracy. Isaac Julien addressed the life of writer Frantz Fanon (in *Black Skin White Mask*, 1996), while Julien Temple covered punk band The Sex Pistols in *The Filth and the Fury* (2000). *Backbeat* (Ian Softley, 1993, concerning the fifth Beatle), *Hilary And Jackie* (Anand Tucker, 1998, a much contested account of the life and loves of the cellist, Jacqueline du Pré), *Love is the Devil* (John Maybury, 1998, about the painter Francis Bacon), *Sylvia* (Christine Jeffs, 2003, concerning the lives of the poets Ted Hughes and Sylvia Plath) and Stephen Hopkins' 2004 *The Life and Death of Peter Sellers* provide further evidence of this trend.

Significantly, these films portray both characters and settings, 'known' commodities, familiar to much of their audience, who may be thought best capable of appreciating and evaluating their historical verisimilitude. They may, therefore, be thought to appeal to a broader public than histories set in a remoter past, the recognisable accuracy of which may be deemed to be the preserve of specialists: authenticity still counts generally, but arguably counts for more in certain instances. *Vera Drake* may be regarded, then, as another in this series of retro dramas. In that *Vera Drake* is partly concerned with legal process, it may more readily be compared with Mike Newell's 1984 *Dance with a Stranger* (about the life and loves of Ruth Ellis, the last woman to be hanged in Britain) and Peter Medak's 1991 *Let Him Have It* (the 1953 hanging of teenager Derek Bentley, who was exonerated in July 1998). Leigh, Newell and Medak present conscientious reconstructions of the past which are readily recognisable but which are far from fond or nostalgic in their depiction of the law as it then was. These films place the recent past at a distance, intimating progress in the present. In contrast to the celebrated cases of Ellis and Bentley, the fictitious Vera stands in for any number of anonymous, ordinary women who found themselves in her position. *Vera Drake* provides an antidote to the current glut of wartime memorabilia and a reminder that rationing continued well after World War Two had ended. It may also, perhaps, be compared to Atom Egoyan's 1999 *Felicia's Journey* and Peter Mullen's 2002 *The Magdalene Sisters* (set in the 1960s and also based on documentary evidence) which tangentially present a different, Catholic attitude towards unmarried pregnancy and abortion in Northern Ireland and the Irish Republic. Felicia, it transpires, is only one of a number of friendless girls whom a lonely man in Birmingham has 'helped'; unable to overcome the unhappiness of his own 1950s childhood he seems intent on preventing the birth of children he thinks will be born into poverty. In *Vera Drake*, Leigh reconstructs a period when contraception and abortion were not openly discussed, constructing his scenario around secrecy, illegality and various forms of inequity.

Design

Vera's design (overseen by Eve Stewart, from *All or Nothing* and *Topsy-Turvy*) and cinematography (directed by Dick Pope, also from *Life is Sweet*, *Naked*, *Secrets and Lies*, *All or Nothing* and *Topsy-Turvy*) serve a definite purpose in accurately evoking a particular period and atmosphere.[8] Unusually, for a costume film, the backing track is subdued: a broken nursery lullaby, plucked on a harp, underscores the title sequence (reappearing later with a mournful cello accompaniment) and there is a distant choral strain underlying the aftermath of Vera's arrest. It ends in dull silence, with Vera's family seated at the same table in her absence. Of music specific to the period there is little, partly as a consequence of Leigh's limited budget for copyright clearance. A jazz band, on set, provides music for the dance hall sequence; Ethel listens to the factory radio while she works. Vera and Stan, and Reg and Ethel, take trips to the cinema but we are not shown what they see.

Locations are dressed and props and costuming selected to support the film's setting. Eventually, we are informed by the dialogue that the action culminates in 1950-51 – there is no customary introductory subtitle, as, for instance in *Topsy-Turvy*. Knitted tea cosies, floral pinnies, bicycles, and vintage cars augment the 'austerity' of the Drakes' lives. Sid in his role as tailor is given the opportunity to comment upon the current style in double-breasted suiting; a customer is modelling himself on George Raft (but is prepared to forego the spats). More importantly, a certain limited palette of colour extends from the understated, slate-backed title sequence to the interiors of Essex Buildings (velour and moquette furnishings, veneers and wallpaper patterns merge into a drab mustardy ochre). Filming on location, Leigh's crew shared the closeness of the space: a table is unfolded for family meals then put away again; a single frame can be split between the living room (where George sits, oblivious) and the room in which Vera tends to his depressed, beleaguered wife: 'they don't understand nothing, men – bastards', Ivy concludes. Mrs Wells' apartment is spacious, high-ceilinged and airy with white upholstery and Constance Spry floral arrangements on pedestals, the brass fender to the marble fireplace shining (thanks to Vera's efforts).

The point here is not just that the film uses 'correct' material (such as a specific style of tomato ketchup bottle) but that props and settings tell us what Leigh intends for the audience to infer about the characters' social status. Joyce, a less shrill version of Abigail in *Abigail's Party* (1977) and Valerie in *High Hopes* (1987) – whose affectations in dress and noisy domestic décor proclaimed Leigh's disapproval – has a bedroom dressing table which heaves with pots of potions, perfumes and powder, reinforcing her as glamorous (but vain, artificial and materialistic) alongside her sister-in-law. Immaculately coiffed and manicured, Joyce, embodying 'the spirit of the coming decade', has a coat lined with a leopard-skin print where Vera wears frugal hand-knits and frumpy tweeds.[9] Her single piece of jewellery is the gold wedding ring which she has worn for 27 years and is painfully obliged to remove after her arrest, promptly clutching her finger as she senses its sudden bareness – a wound. The critic Anthony Quinn noted the film's attention 'to the way people used to look and dress twenty years older than they actually are'.[10] Joyce urges Frank (who seems less keen) into bed for sex; Stan and Vera in bed are companionable and try to keep each other warm; Joyce is the first to condemn Vera as 'selfish' and to label her a 'silly cow' while Frank reminds her that, after his own mother's death, Vera and his brother took care of him and paid for his apprenticeship. In other words, for all Leigh's vaunted improvisatory techniques in developing character, Joyce is a familiar type in Leigh's work.

The biscuit tin with its thatched riverside cottage lid, in which Vera keeps what the police refer to as 'her equipment' (at last, painstakingly inventoried and incongruously exhibited in court) seems to epitomise Vera's whole attitude to the procedure just as domestic and commonplace as the cups of tea she offers everywhere and to everyone. In practice, none of Leigh's actors, other than Staunton, knew what was in the cloth bag at the top of the wardrobe before the arrest.[11] Leigh, as ever, exerts ultimate control and exploits a privileged, monitoring, directorial position. As Paul Macdonald comments of *Secrets and Lies*, '[it] is served well by Leigh's working method because the whole drama is predicated on the gradual revelation of major secrets hidden between members of a family, with scenes dealing with the immediate responses of individuals to those revelations'.[12] Furthermore, often with Mike Leigh dressing props can suddenly assume particular significance if a performer suddenly decides in rehearsal to open a particular drawer or cupboard and use an object in action (as in his 1985 Northern Ireland BBC television drama, *Four Days in July*, featuring a Protestant and a Roman Catholic couple, either side of the sectarian divide, literally inhabiting the houses in which much of the action was shot). For the designer and art director, then, all dressing props are potential action props.

Language

Although Mike Leigh is credited as screenwriter as often as he is director, he does not produce scripts in the accepted sense. *Topsy-Turvy*, indeed, joyously celebrates the rehearsal process (and the demands of the cast) in the production of an historic, even 'classic', text, score and staging – the D'Oyly Carte Company's *Mikado*. He has said that he had been contemplating the idea for *Vera Drake* (the dramatic content) for a long time, planning the scenario and researching actual events, before the actors researched their own individual characters and improvised together.[13] Richard Titmuss, in his 1963 *Essays on 'the Welfare State'*, already notes the declining birth-rate in working-class London families over the previous decade and assumes that married women, with or without the consent of their husbands, have intervened to prevent unwanted births, either by contraception or abortion. 'Fifty years ago there was no birth control', says one of the interviewees in the Young and Willmott survey, 'but even then there were ways and means not to have children if you didn't want to have them'.[14]

In order to extract 'genuine' and spontaneous responses in performance, information was withheld from the actors. For instance, Staunton was not forewarned of the knock on the door which interrupts the cosy family party on November 17, 1950.[15] However, for all the research and preparation, Leigh has been criticised by retired midwives, active in the 1950s, for irresponsible factual errors. While the film was readily enlisted in Britain in response to the renewal of the abortion debate in the American Presidential Election (long-time campaigner and journalist Polly Toynbee declared it 'a much-needed antidote to "pro-life" propaganda') Jennifer Worth, a former midwife, thought the story 'implausible' and observed that Vera's method of procuring an abortion by flushing out the uterus with soap and water was invariably lethal and the film a 'dangerous fantasy'.[16] Others, assuming that the film was *about* abortion complained that it fudged the issues.[17] But abortion is not the primary subject. Rather, the film is concerned with Leigh's preoccupation with class and how it influences the availability of safe abortion and penalties for terminating pregnancies. Little is said about the conflicting rights of the mother and the unborn child, let alone of the father, unless perhaps by inference. Nothing is said of the age at which the foetus might be thought to acquire such rights, either legally or by religious conviction. The worldly-wise girls, mocking Vera's mumsy bonhomie, calmly sip gin, an older method of abortion which also steels the nerves.

The naming of Vera's actions is crucial to her own understanding as distinct from professional (legal and medical) nomenclature. For the most part, Vera talks in euphemisms, matching the ritualised banter of the Drake tea table. The police are the first to use the term 'abortion,' thereby precisely identifying the crime. She tells them that she simply helps girls 'when they can't manage'. 'You mean when they're pregnant,' gently prompts Detective Inspector Webster (Peter Wight). 'I help them to start bleeding again', she confirms evasively. 'You get rid of the baby – you perform abortions', he continues. 'That's not what I do, that's what you call it – I help them out', concludes a distraught Vera. The

Detective Inspector seems on the point of telling her that Pamela will not be able to have children, but then thinks better of it. Pamela's doctor distinguishes between a natural miscarriage and what he recognises as a 'termination'. When pressed by her clients, Vera admits, slightly nervously amidst her brisk buoyancy, that 'tomorrow, or the day after, you'll have a pain down below …it will come away…', but she seems unsure that the black girl understands her meaning and the girl, scared, is desperate for her to stay to keep her company. Eventually we are given to understand by her reactions to police questioning rather than her actual speech that Vera as a girl herself underwent a similar illegal operation. Would she, as a 'fallen' woman, ever have married Stan and enjoyed the happy family life we are shown if she had had that child? What Vera whispers to Stan is left unheard, kept between them.

A different verbal and hard currency is exchanged by Susan, the society friend to whom she turns for help (she works in a bank – a man's world). Over bone china, cake stands and silver plate, Susan refers to her situation in the third person, but the friend implicitly understands: 'you clot'. Advised that a note from a psychiatrist is required to smooth over legal niceties, she concocts a history of familial mental illness (a great aunt committed suicide) and meets no objection: 'I can't have it – I'd rather kill myself'. Asked by the doctor what the father thinks, Susan naively understands him to mean her own father rather than David. She returns home from the private clinic quietly triumphant, having for once taken control over her own life, as if this stark rite of passage allows her to score a point against her overbearing mother, who only raises her eyes to look at her as a prelude to unkind and outspoken opprobrium.

Inequities

The film's first half cuts between the Wells and the Drake scenarios. Vera, it should be noted, enters the Wells' townhouse by the tradesmen's basement entrance. However, in spite of her exemplary service, Vera fails to obtain a character reference from Mrs Wells when it is needed. Perhaps, like Sid, she thinks abortion 'dirty' and lives in blissful ignorance of her own daughter's 'clean' abortion. Susan's trauma at her rape and consequent pregnancy is not to be dismissed, but her innocence, her social status and her disposable income (she has just over £100 in savings for the delicate matter of a fee; the doctor settles on 100 guineas cash in advance) allow her to purchase the comforts of nurses and a prettily appointed bedroom which are not available to Vera's charitable cases. Reg speaks sympathetically (and knowingly – 'six of us in two rooms'): 'It's all right for the rich if you've got six kids, but if you can't feed them, you can't love them'.

Apart from this class inequity, there is also an unfairness between men and women: 'men don't understand', says the mother of seven, desperate at the prospect of another child to bear and rear. Lily says that the father 'can't control himself, if you ask me'. When one of the husbands interviewed by Young and Willmott between 1953 and 1955 told them that '"We wanted a baby", his wife retorted, "*You* may have done; I know *I* didn't..."'.[18] Sid and his friends barter cigarettes and tea for nylons in the pub, relatively cheap commodities with which to buy possibly costly favours from girls at a dance hall. Various critics drew a comparison between *Vera Drake* and Lewis Gilbert's 1966 *Alfie*, made prior to David Steel's 1967 Abortion Act which decisively reformed the legislation (with the exclusion of Northern Ireland).[19] A woman, the wife of a colleague at Alfie's chest clinic (whom Alfie has seduced for the hell of it) undergoes a sordid abortion at the clumsy hands of a corrupt professional. 'I know it don't look very nice', comments Alfie (Michael Caine), sardonically, 'but what does when you get up close to it?' Of course, in this version Alfie's bravura proves to be misplaced. Charles Shyer's 2004 American remake balked at the unpleasantness, with Alfie's conquest determining to have the child and the friend generously raising it as his own.

Historically, it seems to me, there was also something shocking in the antiquity of the law under which Vera is convicted. The 1861 Offences Against the Person Act sought to consolidate English and Irish criminal law by outlawing abortion. It allowed for the punishment of some instances of murder (inadequately defined, it was argued, in the earlier Parliamentary debates) by a custodial sentence rather than by the death penalty: even the provisions of the Act cast Vera's sentence as harsh (as the judge says, deliberately so). Vera is tried for the use of an instrument to procure Pamela Barnes' miscarriage rather than for some twenty years of 'helping girls out' which she tearfully acknowledges under police questioning.

But an impression is nevertheless conveyed of the law as an anachronism and iniquitous. Susan benefits from subsequent legal procedures; as a result of campaigns led by the Abortion Law Reform Association, in England and Wales the 1929 Infant Life (Preservation) Act permitted the termination of a pregnancy to save the mother's life. A judgement of 1939 extended the definition, justifying termination if the pregnancy threatened to leave the mother 'a physical or mental wreck': hence her friend's recommendation that she invent 'a fearful fib about some potty aunt or other'.[20] The psychiatrist's response, 'well, I don't think we can allow that to happen – can we?', when Susan mentions suicide, suggests a caring practitioner's concern for social, professional and legal propriety.

Vera's defence counsel presents a perfunctory case. Pamela and the other girls (and complicitly Vera) are effectively denied justice by their want of money and position. Vera, equally caring but acting outside the law, is apparently ignorant of and overwhelmed by the legal procedures which might offer her an expedient argument. Vera, employing more makeshift methods, ingenuously risks the life of the mother while relieving her of her unwanted child. There were seven attempts to change the law between 1952 and the introduction of Steel's Private Member's Bill in 1966, heralded as symptomatic of a new permissiveness, along with the legalisation of homosexuality and the abolition of the Lord Chamberlain's Office: 'The year 1967', concludes the historian Arthur Marwick, 'was something of an *annus mirabilis* as far as liberal legislation in the sphere of sexual mores was concerned', marking 'a retreat from the social controls imposed in the Victorian era by evangelicalism and non-conformity'.[21] Reform was partly prompted by experience elsewhere in Europe and partly by the thalidomide 'disaster' of 1961. However, the passage of the bill was far from straightforward or uncontentious, with its supporters receiving hate-mail from opponents. Contraception did not become freely available through the National Health Service, to married and unmarried women alike, until April 1974.

Vera Drake, then, while set in the recent past, tacitly reminds us of social progress in the intervening years and perhaps reminds us of what could yet be lost.

Notes

1   *Naked* and *Secrets and Lies* also reaped rewards for, respectively, David Thewliss and Brenda Blethyn.

2   Anonymous (15 May 2005) The British are coming, p. 3 in *The Observer*. Re 'miserabilist' drama.

3   Leigh, M. (6 March 2005) And not even the goody bag goes to…, p. 8 in *The Observer*; Cohen, N. 15 May 2005 Lights, cameras, turkeys, p. 29 in *The Observer*; Alberge, D. (20 October 2004), British film backers must take greater risks, says star, p. 22 in *The Times*.

4   Young, M. and P. Willmott (1957) *Family and Kinship in East London*. London: Penguin, pp. 44-64. Conducting their research in 1953-5, Young and Willmott contrasted the conviviality of East End terraces with the lack of community spirit in new housing estates in the suburbs, to which many former East Enders moved after the War. The 1986 edition of the book found them still railing against tower blocks and the architects and planners deemed responsible for them.

5   French, P. (9 January 2005) Tea and sympathy, p. 10 in *The Observer*.

6   Hughes, D. (1963), The Spivs in Sissons, pp. 83-100 in M. and P. French (eds), *Age of Austerity*. London: Hodder and Staunton; Sargeant, A. (2005) *British Cinema: a Critical History*. London: BFI, pp. 189-191.

7   *The Face* (December 1983), p. 18. Re *Naked*'s misogyny, see Monk, C. (2000) Men in the 90s in Murphy, R. (ed.) *British Cinema of the 90s*. London: BFI, pp. 163-4 and Malcolm, D. (6 January 2005) in *Evening Standard*. Reviews without a title or page number are taken from the BFI *Vera Drake* microfiche file.

8   For a further discussion, see Sargeant, A. (2002), The content and the form: invoking "pastness" in three recent retro films, pp. 199-216 in Monk, C. and A. Sargeant (eds) *British Historical Cinema*. London: Routledge.

9   Romney, J. (9 January 2005) Vera Drake, pp. 16-17 in *The Independent on Sunday*.

10 Quinn, A. *The Independent*. (BFI *Vera Drake* microfiche file)

11 O'Hagan, S. (5 December 2004) Interview with Mike Leigh, p. 3 in *The Observer* Review.

12 Macdonald, P. (1999) Secrets and Lies: Acting for Mike Leigh, pp. 144-145 in Lovell, A. and P. Krämer (eds) *Screen Acting*. London: Routledge. See also Clements, P. (1993) Four Days in July, pp. 162-177 in Brandt, G. (ed.), *British Television Drama in the 1980s*. Cambridge: Cambridge University Press and Clements, P. (1984) *The Improvised Play/The Work of Mike Leigh*. London: Methuen. In *Four Days*, the wives in both couples go into hospital to have their first baby and find themselves in adjacent beds. At time of writing, 'A New Play by Mike Leigh' (his first for twelve years) at the National Theatre, sold-out for its entire run, has been advertised without acquiring a name until a few days before its opening - here information was withheld from the audience, rather than from selected members of the cast. *Two Thousand Years*, with Allan Corduner, features two sisters, one who has stayed at home, one who has been successful in business: see Anonymous (18 September 2005), p. 11 in *The Observer Review* and *Saturday Review*, broadcast by BBC Radio 4 on 17 September 2005.

13 Alberge, D. (26 January 2005) Stage is set for a nailbiting finale, p. 8 in *The Times* and *Time Out* interview with Leigh and Staunton, BFI *Vera Drake* microfiche file

14 E.g. the 1958 essay 'The Position of Women' in Titmuss, R. (1963) *Essays on 'the Welfare State'*. London: Unwin University Books, pp. 90-92.
    'Until the passage of the Abortion Act 1967 most abortions in Britain were surreptitious and expensive or illegal and dangerous. Each year thousands of women risked death or mutilation by seeking abortion from back-street abortionists. Each year thirty or so died, and at least thirty thousand suffered the pain and shame of having to be patched up afterwards in hospital'. Hindell, K. and M. Simms (1971) *Abortion Law Reformed*. London: Peter Owen, p. 13.

15 Staunton (May 2005) interviewed in *Desert Island Discs* (BBC Radio 4).

16 Wood, G. (3 July 2005) Liberals ready to abandon US right to abortion, p. 20 in *The Observer*; Worth, J. (6 January 2005) A deadly trade, pp. 8-9 in *The Guardian*; Toynbee, P. (7 January 2005) Vera's timely reminder', p. 23 in *The Guardian*. The broader parameters of the debate are sketched in Cohen, M., Nagel, T. et. al. (eds) (1974), *The Rights and Wrongs of Abortion*. Princeton: Princeton University Press.

17 Lott, T. (16 December 2004), Will Mike Leigh's new film change anyone's mind about the rights and wrongs of abortion?, pp. 25-26 in *Evening Standard*.

18 Titmuss (1963).

19 O'Sullivan, C. (8 October 2004) Facing the facts of life in *Independent Arts and Books Review*; see also Phillips, A. and J. Rakusen (1988) *Our Bodies Ourselves*. London: Penguin, pp. 294-5. Debates over the length of a pregnancy at which it can be terminated and the rights of the woman and the unborn child continue.

20 *Parliamentary Debates CLIX* (1860). London: HMSO, pp. 270-280; *Parliamentary Debates CLXIII* (1861). London: HMSO, pp. 932-3. See also Abbott, M. (2003) *Family Affairs*. London: Routledge, p. 47. Section 58 of this Act makes it a felony punishable with life imprisonment for anyone, including the woman herself, unlawfully to procure an abortion. Section 59 makes it a misdemeanour punishable with imprisonment for three years to supply any instrument, poison or 'noxious thing' for an abortion. Hindell and Simms (1971), pp. 13-14, claim that 'As medical knowledge and techniques progressed rapidly in the latter half of the nineteenth century it became the accepted practice to perform the operation if it was thought necessary to save a woman's life. The techniques of abortion were fully explained and illustrated in the midwifery textbooks, but the practice was not protected by statute until 1929. The Infant Life (Preservation) Act made it legal to terminate a viable foetus (that is, one of twenty-eight weeks or more) in order to save the woman's life. But this hardly changed the legal situation at all until ... the Bourne case of 1938, according [to which] it was lawful to terminate, not only to save life but also to safeguard the woman's health and prevent her being ... a "physical or mental wreck". The only proviso was that the doctor must sincerely believe that the termination was for the purpose of preserving the life or health of the woman'.

21 Marwick, A. (1996) *British Society Since 1945*.Harmondsworth: Penguin, p. 141 and 147 and 141. Marwick, too, notes the pertinence of *Alfie*. See also David Steel's introduction to Hindell and Simms (1971), dedicated 'To the thalidomide mothers for whom reform came too late'. See also Hordern, A. (1971) *Legal Abortion: the English Experience*. Oxford: Pergamon, pp. 1-12, reporting an estimate that in Britain in 1967 'between 100.000 and 200.000 women had abortions performed, the vast majority of which were criminal' [p. 1]. BBC Radio 4's *The Reunion* 7 August 2005 invited Steel to talk about the Act - using excerpts from *Vera Drake* and from an interview with Mike Leigh.

Epilogue:
The Promise of History on Film

Robert A. Rosenstone

The promise of film to make us witnesses to history is no doubt older than the medium itself. Surely one of the impulses behind the invention of the cinematograph by Louis and Auguste Lumière was the notion that, as writing allows human beings to fix and contemplate the contents of their minds, a device to record moving images would allow them to fix and contemplate the world we see. If it seems unremarkable that as early as 1898 writers could express the idea that to record actuality on film – political and social struggles, strikes, wars, revolutions, political campaigns, famines – was to create a visual library that would let current and future generations literally see the past, it is more surprising to learn how early some visionaries saw this new medium as a way of not just recording but actually recreating the past.

In 1908, a French drama critic described the aspirations of film as not only the ability to reproduce the contemporary world, but also 'to reconstruct the great events of History through the performance of the actor and the evocation of atmosphere and milieu'.[1] D.W. Griffith, director of one of the first major historical films, *Birth of a Nation* (1915), was a virtual missionary on the topic. Claiming in 1915 that the greatest contribution of motion pictures had been 'the treating of historical subjects', he quoted unnamed 'educators' who had told him (or so he said) that a film 'can impress upon a people as much of the truth of history in an evening as many months of study will accomplish'.[2]

Just four years after the Lumières held their first public screening of actuality films in the basement of a Paris café in December 1896, their countryman Georges Méliès was consciously staging historical, if recent, scenes such as *L'Affaire Dreyfus* (*The Dreyfus Affair*, 1899) for the camera. The distinction between the documentary and the dramatic was not clearly demarcated in the early days of film. Often moments presented on screen as contemporary 'fact' were acted or shot with models: events such as the coronation of Edward VIII, or Teddy Roosevelt's charge up San Juan Hill. Soon films set in the past – often lost works we know today mostly by their titles, such as *L'Assassinat du Duc de Guise* (*The Assassination of the Duke of Guise*, 1908) from France, *Gli ultimi Giorni di Pompei* (*The Last Days of Pompeii*, 1908) and *La Presa di Roma* (*The Capture of Rome*, 1905) from Italy, and *Uncle Tom's Cabin* (1903) from the United States – were being distributed around the world. In countries as diverse in culture and history as Japan, Russia, Britain and Denmark, some of the earliest dramatic films (often based upon stage plays) involved the depiction of historical events and characters. Long before cinema reached its twentieth birthday in the mid teens of the twentieth century, the 'historical' was a regular part of screen fare.

Quarrels over this new sort of visual history arose almost immediately. But the issue of whether or not the cinema was a suitable medium for recounting the past was soon made irrelevant by the growing popularity of such films. The more enduring debates, the ones which have lasted until the present day, erupted over historical 'accuracy', or the 'interpretation' of particular events or individuals, or the 'fictionalizing' that was inherently part of this dramatic form. Among the earliest and most bitter of controversies was the one in the United States over *Birth of a Nation* (1915), with its overtly racist portraits of Black Americans during and after the Civil War. Yet this was more than a debate about film. The portrait of the defeated South as suffering under the depredations of ex-slaves during Reconstruction, its exaltation of members of the Ku Klux Klan as heroes, and its vicious stereotypes of African Americans as barbaric, uneducated, and uncultured were reflections of some scholarly interpretations of the day. Woodrow Wilson, whose historical works are one of the film's sources, was in the White House when the film was released. A Southerner by birth, Wilson was deeply moved by the work, and his response to it – quoted second hand but accepted by historians as more or less authentic – suggests something about the prevailing historical wisdom and proved to be prophetic for the future role of the historical film: 'It is like writing history with Lightning. And my only regret is that it is all so terribly true'.[3]

In publicly commenting on film (as well as in getting elected President), Wilson proved to be a rare historian. For most of the twentieth century, those in the historical profession ignored historical films. This was easy because professionals in the field saw their own work as a thoroughly empirical undertaking, a human science that properly made certain kinds of truth claims about the past, claims that could hardly be matched by the costume dramas, swashbucklers, and romances regularly turned out by studios around the world. So rarely did academics comment on the topic that Robert Novick's book, *That Noble Dream* (1988), a lengthy survey of American historical practice in the twentieth century, contains only a single reference to motion pictures. In a 1935 letter that is highly revealing about professional attitudes, Louis Gottschalk of the University of Chicago wrote the president of Metro-Goldwyn-Mayer: 'If the cinema art is going to draw its subjects so generously from history, it owes to its patrons and its own higher ideals to achieve greater accuracy. No picture of a historical nature ought to be offered to the public until a reputable historian has had a chance to criticise and revise it'.[4]

Factors other than the quality of films kept academics from considering motion pictures a serious way of recounting the past. The visual media fell on the wrong side of the once enormous wall that separated high culture from low (or mass) culture, which meant that films could not be taken seriously until that wall collapsed, as it began to do in the 1960s. More importantly, for at least the first half of the century academics were secure in the belief that their kind of knowledge of past politics, and economic, social and cultural life, was 'true' knowledge, and they were certain that the culture was willing to accept the truths about the past that they could provide. But after mid-century, as the claims of traditional history and its Euro-centred meta-narratives began increasingly to be called into question from a variety of disciplines and sources – by feminists, ethnic minorities, post-colonial theorists, anthropologists, narratologists, philosophers of history, deconstructionists, and postmodernists – a climate developed that allowed academics to take popular culture more seriously and to begin looking more closely at the historical film.

Not until the late 1960s did the number of historians interested in film reach a large enough mass to begin to create the meetings, essays, journals, and books that indicate a topic is on the scholarly map. The first conferences, held at such places as University College, London, and at the Imperial War Museum; the Universities of Utrecht and Göttingen; the Centre for Interdisciplinary Research at Bielefeld, were attended mostly by scholars from the continent (France, Germany, Denmark, the Netherlands, Belgium) and Great Britain, with a couple of visitors from the United States. These gatherings focused largely on the production, reception, and value of the actuality film rather than the fictional film and out of them grew the International Association for Media and History, which since 1981 has published the *Historical Journal of Film, Radio and Television*.

The scholarship that emerged from these early meetings and entered collections such as Paul Smith's *The Historian and Film* (1976) or Karsten Fledelius' *History and the Audio-Visual Media* (1979) dealt for the most part with the use of actuality film in historical research and as a teaching tool in the classroom. The first volume of essays to deal with dramatic works, K.R.M. Short's *Feature Films as History* (1981), mostly considered the question of how clusters of films made in certain periods could serve as windows onto an exploration of particular ideologies or climates of opinion – say, anti-Semitism in Europe, the Popular Front of the 1930s, or national consciousness in Germany and France in the 1920s. But a single essay in the volume edged in a radical new direction. In analysing Sergei Eisenstein's classic, *Bronenosets Potyomkin* (*Battleship Potemkin*, 1925), D.J. Wenden of Oxford considered the question of how a film, even though its content is highly fictionalised, might yet illuminate a historical event. After comparing the film's account of the ship's mutiny with written histories on the same topic, Wenden suggests that rather than creating a literal reality, Eisenstein makes 'brilliant use of the ship's revolt as a symbol for the whole revolutionary effort of the Russian people in 1905'.[5] This is the first instance (at least the first in print known to me) in which a historian makes a move towards suggesting that film might have its own specific way of telling the past, that the very nature of the medium and its practices of necessity create a particular kind of history that is different from what we normally expect to find upon the page.

Two historians in France during the 1970s also took steps towards investigating the notion of film as history: Marc Ferro and Pierre Sorlin. In the path-breaking essays that comprise *Cinéma et histoire* (1977), the former focuses most of his effort on the investigation of film as a cultural artefact, but in the final chapter he confronts the more problematic (and interesting) issue: 'Does a filmic writing of history exist?' Ferro's initial response is 'No'. Filmmakers, he argues, have nothing original to offer, and do no more than create 'a vision of history which has been conceived by others'. But, almost as an afterthought, Ferro admits that there are exceptions to this rule. Directors such as Andrei Tarkovsky, Ousmane Sembene, Hans-Jürgen Syberberg, and Luchino Visconti, transcend the ideological forces and traditions of their countries, create independent interpretations of history, and thereby make 'an original contribution to the understanding of past phenomena and their relation to the present'.[6]

Sorlin does not venture as far as Ferro. In his work, *The Film in History*, Sorlin expresses concern that films are ultimately 'all fictional'. Even those based on historical evidence tend to 'reconstruct in a purely imaginary way the greater part of what they show'. Still, such fictional history has some value. With regard to topics such as the French Revolution, the Italian *Risorgimento*, or the American Civil War, Sorlin suggests that groups of films do relate to the larger discourse of history generated by professionals in the field. In an argument too often ignored, he suggests that, exactly like written works of history, films must be judged not against our current knowledge or interpretations of a topic but with regard to historical understanding at the time they were made. His detailed chapter on Sergei Eisenstein's *Oktyabr* (*October*, 1927) mirrors the difficulties all historians have in dealing with works about the past in a medium that can seem so elusive. Initially Sorlin dismisses *October* as no more than Bolshevik 'propaganda', but a long analysis leads him to contradict himself and in the final paragraphs he can term it a view of the Russian Revolution that is independent of Bolshevik ideology – a judgement which suggests Ferro's 'filmic writing of history'.

In the quarter century since publication of *The Film in History*, an increasing number of historians around the world have begun to confront the challenge of the visual media in conferences devoted specifically to the topic (I have personally attended some of them in the the United States, Italy, Spain, Germany, Great Britain, Argentina, Brasil and Australia) and the volumes that grew out of them, on panels at annual meetings, and in reviews and essays in academic journals, many of which now regularly review films. The first major foray into the topic in the United States was a Forum entirely devoted to film in the December 1988 issue of *The American Historical Review*, that most conservative and traditional of historical journals. Here, my own opening essay, 'History in Images / History in Words: Reflections on the Possibility of Really Putting History onto Film', which argued in favour of beginning to take film seriously as a way of thinking about the past, was answered by four historians, three of whom agreed to a greater or lesser extent (though not without some criticisms). A highlight of the Forum came in the essay by Hayden White, who took the opportunity to coin an important and useful term, 'historiophoty'- defined as 'the representation of history and our thought about it in visual images and filmic discourse'.[7] For those who care about communicating the past, about telling what happened and trying to explain why, an exploration of the possibilities and parameters of historiophoty has to be a central concern.

Such a concern is largely missing from the writing of two other groups who have a stake in the relationship between history and film: the filmmakers and film scholars. No doubt it is unfair to ask for a theoretical approach from anyone who writes or directs the films which create the past. Yet some filmmakers have taken an interest in the theory underlying their productions. Sergei Eisenstein, for example, does occasionally invoke the Marxist dialectic in reference to his depictions of history, if only in passing. Clearly more interested in notions of montage or what he called 'intellectual' cinema, the Russian never offers any sustained explication of the relationship between his historical works and the past events they evoke or describe. Roberto Rossellini, whose more than a dozen films about the past may be the most sustained historical oeuvre of any director, provides contradictory ideas about his portrayal of history without ever bothering to resolve them. On the one hand, he invokes notions of the didactic film, one which can objectively describe the past and create a direct, unmediated vision; on the other, he insists that his works are based upon a moral vision, without admitting that such a moral vision inevitably creates a point of view which cannot be objective. More recent directors have overtly admitted history's subjective and fictional components. Rainer Werner Fassbinder, director of several works on the Third Reich and its legacy, did not hesitate to explain, 'We make a particular film about a particular time from our point of view'. Oliver Stone, who in half a dozen films has charted aspects of American society from the Vietnam war into the 1980s, initially claimed to be creating history, but then under attacks from the press, particularly about *JFK* (1991) and *Nixon* (1998), he retreated to an extreme subjectivist position, asking: 'What is history? Some people say it's a bunch of gossip made up by soldiers who passed it around a campfire'.

Scholars in Cinema Studies, who in recent years created a very active subfield having to do with historical films, don't have the Hollywood director's luxury of brushing off the topic so easily. Nor do they have the same dual intellectual worries that plague the practicing historian: first, about the many inventions that mix with the factual basis of what is put on screen, and second, about how particular interpretations relate to the larger discourse of history. From the historian's point of view (which is mine) even excellent and perceptive studies such as Anton Kaes, *From Hitler to Heimat: The Return of History as Film* (1989), Leger Grindon, *Shadows on the Past: Studies in the Historical Fiction Film* (1994), or Robert Burgoyne, *Film Nation: Hollywood Looks at U.S. History* (1997), works which are invaluable in telling us about the production, reception, and broad thematics of particular groups of historical films, neither answer nor ask the questions about historical discourse that ultimately matter to historians.

The problem arises, no doubt, from the incompatibility of academic discourses, the way each ultimately has its own particular stake in the world, its own aims that show up in the questions it asks and the language it uses to describe reality. For this historian, the central issue of the historical film revolves around the concept of historiophoty, and the issue of just what possibilities, codes and conventions there are for representing history and our thoughts about the past in visual images and filmic discourse.

Such an approach begins with a series of questions about works that may well contain a good deal of invented material. How do historical films add to or detract from our knowledge of the past? How can we trust what they tell us? Do they count as 'historical thinking' or contribute to something we might call 'historical understanding'? Can we properly label them History with a capital H? How do they relate to or engage the larger discourse on historical topics? If the historical film creates its own rules of engagement with the past (as I have argued elsewhere that it does)[8], how are we to understand the import and meaning of the histories it tells? How are we to annex that meaning to the history we already (think we) know? How are we to evaluate the history they convey?

Without mentioning the notion of historiophoty, and without directly asking the questions I have posed above, the essays in *Perspectives on European Film and History* seem (to some extent) either to engage with, or be shadowed by that term and those questions. Several of them suggest ways in which dramatic films work to establish a connection with the world of the past, demonstrating how image, word and sound help us to understand certain historical moments. Others present such works using specifically filmic techniques to comment upon and critique various received or researched historical notions. Collectively, these essays locate, excavate and analyse a group of European historical films, suggesting in what ways and to what extent some of them render serious versions of the past, and how these versions relate to the larger discourse. The topics and the approaches are diverse, and ultimately have one thing in common: they deal with films that focus on moments and events in European history. Interesting to me is the fact that when I first read the essays, I thought they were all produced by historians, only to learn that the mostly young scholars who wrote them came from various disciplines: history, communications, and cinema studies. The rare coming together of disciplines by this group of authors makes for an admirable collective undertaking, one which shows how this branch of academic study clearly benefits from the overlapping approaches of different fields.

Early in the twenty-first century, we are well aware that there are many pasts and diverse histories – the traditional oral and textual; more recently, the visual, and now, the electronic. Emanating from different geographical locations and created under radically different conditions, in the Third World as well as the First, on the periphery and margins as well as in the centre (and we know very well that one person's centre is another's periphery), these diverse approaches to the past escape the realm of professional History. Such awareness is, in fact, clearly part of that condition we label, for want of a better term, post-modern. The larger question for the historian and I should hope for other fields as well, is how all these histories and pasts relate to each other? Can they ever be put together in one overarching narrative again; can we tell the story of a nation, a region, a continent, or of humankind? And if not, how can we create stories of the past, on the page or on film, that work towards understanding, that bring us together in our common humanity rather than rendering us into separate nations, regions, cultures, traditions, continents, and ethnicities that so often stand in opposition to each other?

No set of diverse essays in any academic field can resolve such a broad question. But they can shed light on aspects of the issue. This volume consists of a series of forays into the contested terrain of film and history. Each approaches a particular text with a fine combination of theory and practice. Taken together, they represent a high order of scholarship, intelligence and insight – as well as a sense that even in this kind of micro-study, something much larger is at stake: how we can collectively understand our past in this visual and electronic age? Since film and its younger sibling, television, are now the major ways in which people across the globe confront the past and learn history, these case studies help to take us further along on the road to understanding the practice and possibilities of historiophoty, or to put it another way, the role that the visual media play in helping us to confront and understand our individual and collective past.

Notes

1   Quoted in Tredell, N. (ed.) (2002) *Cinemas of the mind.* Cambridge: Icon Books, p. 15.

2   Quoted in Silva, F. (ed.) (1971) *Focus on Birth of a Nation.* Englewood Cliffs. N.J.: Prentice Hall, pp. 59, 98.

3   Quoted in Schickel, R. (1984) *D. W. Griffith: An American life.* New York: Simon and Schuster, p. 270.

4   Quoted in Novick, P. (1988) *That noble dream: The 'objectivity question' and the American historical profession.* Cambridge: Cambridge University Press, p. 194.

5   Wenden, D. J. (1981) Battleship Potemkin - Film and reality, pp. 37-61 in Short, K. R. M. (ed.) *Feature films as history.* Knoxville: University of Tennessee Press, p. 40.

6   Ferro, M. (1977) *Cinéma et histoire.* Paris: Editions Denoël. Quotation from English translation by Naomi Green (1988) *Cinema and history.* Detroit: Wayne State University Press, pp. 158-164.

7   White, H. (1988) Historiography and historiophoty, pp. 1193-1199 in *The American historical review,* vol 93 (5), p. 1193.

8   Rosenstone, R. (1995) *Visions of the past.* Cambridge: Harvard University Press.

Notes on the Contributors

Brett Bowles is Assistant Professor of French Studies at the State University of New York, Albany, and book review editor for the *Historical Journal of Film, Radio and Television*. He has published widely on French cinema of the 1930s and 40s, particularly the fiction films of Marcel Pagnol and French-language newsreels made during World War Two. His book on Pagnol is forthcoming from Manchester University Press.

James Chapman is Professor of Film at the University of Leicester. He has wide-ranging research interests in British film and cultural history and his books include *The British at War: Cinema, State and Propaganda, 1939-1945* (1998), *Licence To Thrill: A Cultural History of the James Bond Films* (1999), *Saints and Avengers: British Adventure Series of the 1960s* (2002) and *Past and Present: National Identity and the British Historical Film* (2005). He is a Council member of IAMHIST and review editor of the *Journal of British Cinema and Television*.

Liesbet Depauw graduated as a master in Communication Sciences at the Ghent University in 2002. The next year, she started working as a researcher for the same university, mapping the history of the Belgian Film Classification. The project was funded by the Belgian *Research Foundation – Flanders* and had Prof. Daniel Biltereyst as its supervisor. Recently, she obtained a Ph.D. grant by the Scientific Research Council, Flanders, and is now preparing a doctoral thesis concerning the Belgian discourse on violence in the media.

Bruno De Wever is associate professor at the Department of Contemporary History of Ghent University and fellow at the Netherlands Institute for Advanced Study (2001-2002). His teaching includes history of the twentieth century and the representation of history in film. He published books and articles about nationalism and World War Two in Belgium. He was co-editor of the *Encyclopaedia of the Flemish Movement*, a major reference work on the subject of nationalism in Belgium.

Leen Engelen is assistant professor at the Department of Media Studies of the University of Amsterdam. She studied Communication Sciences at the Catholic University of Leuven and at the University of Ulster (Northern Ireland). In her PhD research she looked at the representation of World War One in Belgian fiction films from the interwar period. Her current research project deals with the representation of Belgium's colonial past in fiction films from the 1950s. She is secretary general of the International Association for Media and History (www.iamhist.org).

Willem Hesling is associate professor at the Centre for Media Culture and Communication Technology of the University of Leuven. His research focuses on the theory of audiovisual communication, historical film and the history of film.

Uli Jung is film historian and researcher at the English Department at the University of Trier, Germany. He is general editor of the book series *Filmgeschichte international* (Cinémathèque Municipale de Luxembourg). His academic publications include the following *Filmkultur zur Zeit der Weimarer Republik* (1992, co-ed.), *Der deutsche Film: Aspekte seiner Geschichte von den Anfängen bis zur Gegenwart* (1993, ed.), *Robert Wiene – Der Caligari-Regisseur* (1995, co-author, Engl. ed. 1999); *Dracula: Filmanalytische Studien zu einem Motiv der spätviktorianischen Populärliteratur* (1997), *Schrift und Bild im Film* (2002, co-ed.), *René Deltgen – eine Schauspielerkarriere* (2002, co-author), *Geschichte des dokumentarischen Films in Deutschland*, vol 1: *Kaiserreich* (2006, co-editor).

Robert A. Rosenstone has published works of history, biography, and criticism, along with a memoir entitled *The Man Who Swam into History* (2002), and a novel, *King of Odessa* (2003). A longtime professor of history at the California Institute of Technology, Rosenstone is author of *Crusade of the Left* (1970); *Romantic Revolutionary: A Biography of John Reed* (1975) *Mirror in the Shrine* (1988), *Visions of the Past* (1995), and *History on Film / Film on History* (2006). He has served as historical consultant on several feature films and documentaries, including the Academy Award winning *Reds* (1982). In 1989 he created a film section for the *American Historical Review*, which he edited for seven years. Rosenstone has lectured on film and history at universities on six continents and has given courses on the topic at the University of Barcelona, the European University Institute, Oxford University, and the University of Tolima, in Colombia.

Amy Sargeant is Reader in Film at the University of Warwick. For 2005-2006 she was Senior Research Fellow at the Paul Mellon Centre for the Study of British Art and Architecture. Formerly a production designer herself, she has written extensively on design in film and television and is the author of *British Cinema: a Critical History* (BFI, 2005) and co-editor, with Claire Monk, of *British Historical Film* (Routledge, 2002).

Pascal Vandelanoitte obtained his Master's degree in Communication Studies at the Catholic University of Leuven. His doctoral research deals with the possibilities and boundaries of historical cinema as a form of historical knowledge, with an emphasis on auteur cinema, treating movies by Andrei Tarkovsky, Werner Herzog, Luchino Visconti and Miklós Janscó.

Roel Vande Winkel is Postdoctoral Fellow at the Belgian *Research Foundation – Flanders*, member of the Working Group Film & TV Studies (Ghent University) and Visiting Professor at the Sint Lukas Hogeschool Brussel. His research deals with with various topics relating to Belgian and German film and media history. He is the European book review editor for the *Historical Journal of Film, Radio and Television* and has published in various national and international film historical journals and reference works. With David Welch, he edited *Cinema and the Swastika* (Palgrave, 2007), the very first publication to bring together comparative research on the international expansion of the Third Reich cinema.

Jasmijn Van Gorp is a PhD student and assistant at the Communication Studies Department of the University of Antwerp. She obtained her Master's degree in Communication Studies at the Catholic University of Leuven in 2002. Her main research interests are related to the field of film and media studies. Her PhD project focuses on the construction of national identities in post-Soviet Russian cinema.

INDEX